I AM YOUR FATHER

A masterpiece of excellent scholarship, heart-moving storytelling and compelling vision. It is so comprehensive, clear and compassion~~~ ~ ~~~ ! with my heart, reaffirmed my relationship with A'' ` to reach out to the fatherless.

Ed Piorek, Pastor En ⟨barcode D0808705⟩ ⟩na Niguel, California, ww

Mark's new book took me on a ⟨...⟩ ,ny Father's heart and captured the very essence of the ⟨...⟩ ..rRs unique perspective on spiritual adoption creates a road map that will lead you into the arms of the Father.

Barry Adams, Father Heart Communications, www.fathersloveletter.com

Step under the umbrella of the Father's love and be changed forever through the pages of this book. Encounter God as your Father and join the vital shift needed for the transformation of society. This book will change your life and our world!

Ché Ahn, Senior Pastor, HRock Church, President, Harvest International Ministry

I see it in every culture: serious social problems that are rooted in fatherlessness. Mark cites many examples of how this tragedy can poison our ability to relate well to others and to God. Read this much-needed book carefully, and discover how kind and caring our God really is!

John Arnott, President of Catch the Fire Ministries and Partners in Harvest

Mark writes that "fatherless children are 33 times more likely to be seriously abused". If we ignore the issue of fatherlessness, what sort of message to the future are we sending? The world's children are waiting for our freedom, even as they are longing for their own.

Ben Cooley, Founder and Leader of Hope for Justice, www.hopeforjustice.org.uk

Mark zeroes in on the bull's eye of pain in our culture, and helps us see the potential for healing and hope. I pray that as you read, you are awakened to know who your Father really is!

Brian Doerksen, Christian singer, songwriter, and author, www.briandoerksen.com

In the eloquent, systematic and theologically sound way that is uniquely his own, Mark Stibbe addresses the 'orphan heart condition', takes us to the loving arms of the Father, and encourages us to cry from our hearts, 'Abba Father'. It is one of the most valuable and practical handbooks on the healing of the heart that I have come across.

    Lois Gott, senior co-pastor of Bethshan Church, Newcastle

For many years our communities have lived under the spectre of fatherlessness. As a pastor of a multi cultural church I am constantly addressing this issue with the only viable solution: the gospel of Jesus Christ. I invite every person who has ever longed for a father's love, or who is longing for freedom from the orphan heart, to read this book.

    Troy Goode, Senior Pastor, New Dimension Church, Providence, Rhode Island, USA, www.newdimensionchurch.org

With striking stories, uncommon insight, and deeply scriptural answers, this astonishing landmark book is destined to become a classic. Here's help for a broken nation. It's a 'bombshell' of a book, offering hope and healing for thousands of lives. Here's the proof that our Father God can fix everything.

    Greg Haslam, Senior Pastor, Westminster Chapel, London

The message of the Father's love has burned in Mark Stibbe's heart for years. This is one of the most important and profound messages of our day, and is sure to be a central part of what God uses to bring healing to the body of Christ.

    Bill Johnson, Senior Pastor, Bethel Church, Redding, California, USA, www.ibethel.org

Mark is a loved and respected brother. His latest book contains major areas of revelation that every Christian needs to be grounded in. I recommend Mark as a major player in the prophetic teaching of the Father today and this book to all of the Body of Christ. A must read.

    M. James Jordan, Father Heart Ministries, Taupo, New Zealand, www.fatherheart.net

Stunningly engaging, honest, and beautifully written. Mark unpacks the issues and symptoms surrounding the pandemic of fatherlessness. This book is a treasure. I am certain the Father Himself will meet you in its pages and lead you into the wonder and utter freedom of life lived as children of God.

    Kathryn Scott, (worship leader and writer of songs such as 'Child of God', and 'Hungry'.) www.hungryworshipper.com

I AM
YOUR
FATHER

What Every Heart Needs to Know

Mark Stibbe

MONARCH
BOOKS
Oxford, UK & Grand Rapids, Michigan, USA

First published in the UK in 2010 by Monarch Books
(a publishing imprint of Lion Hudson plc)
Wilkinson House, Jordan Hill Road, Oxford OX2 8DR, England
Tel: +44 (0)1865 302750 Fax: +44 (0)1865 302757
Email: monarch@lionhudson.com
www.lionhudson.com

Reprinted 2011.

ISBN 978 1 85424 937 1

Distributed by:
UK: Marston Book Services, PO Box 269, Abingdon, Oxon, OX14 4YN
USA: Kregel Publications, PO Box 2607, Grand Rapids, Michigan 49501

The text paper used in this book has been made from wood independently certified as having come from sustainable forests.

British Library Cataloguing Data
A catalogue record for this book is available from the British Library.

Printed and bound in the UK by MPG Books.

Dedication

*To Oli Griffiths, with deep
gratitude for helping me to get
the Father's House started.*

Acknowledgments

I want to convey my heartfelt thanks to a number of people who have helped me with this book.

First of all, I want to thank my family for their constant support. Being married to a writer is not easy. Being the children of a writer is a challenge too. I couldn't have completed this literary assignment without the understanding and love of my nearest and dearest. This is a long book – nearly 100,000 words! – so I owe a big debt of gratitude.

I also want to pay tribute to my team at the Father's House Trust – to Catriona Reid (my reader and researcher), to Juliette Ratcliffe (who has been invaluable on issues related to psychology), Oliver Griffiths (design and media), Helen Clark and her team of intercessors, and especially Vicky Akrill, my director of operations at the Father's House. Vicky's input has been wide ranging, insightful and invaluable.

I would thirdly like to thank the many influential Christians who wrote such effusive endorsements of this book. In all my years of writing I have never received such glowing accolades prior to a book's publication. It has given me a weighty sense of the book's potential significance and some realistic grounds for hoping that the Father will use it to bring healing to millions of people, both inside and outside of the church.

Finally, I want to express my gratitude to Tony Collins and the team at Monarch who have been right behind this project from the start. To have a publisher who really believes in the message and the messenger is a great asset and I can't thank Tony and his staff enough. As always, it has been a joy working with the good people of Monarch.

About the Father's House Trust

Dr Mark Stibbe is the founder and leader of the Father's House Trust, a charity dedicated to taking the message of the love of the Father all over the world, and to bringing an end to fatherlessness on the earth.

The Father's House Trust seeks to fulfil this vision through five main objectives.

First, the Trust runs schools for leaders that major on the message of the Father's love and the healing of wounded hearts. These are home-based schools in Watford, where the Father's House is located. These schools focus on an encounter with the transformative power of God's love.

Second, the Trust runs the same kinds of schools but away from its home-base in Watford, and in churches with which the Trust feels a particular partnership. These partner churches are developing all over the world and have a city-changing impact.

Thirdly, the Trust is involved in running annual conferences that serve its vision. These are again based in our own town of Watford. In addition, Mark Stibbe and his team contribute to strategic conferences in the UK and abroad.

Fourthly, the Trust seeks to engage actively with contemporary culture, and specifically to put fatherhood and fatherlessness on the map in realms like government, education, the media, the arts, and family life. The Trust seeks to influence the influencers in these realms.

Fifthly, the Trust is passionate about ministering to the poor and fighting for the cause of the orphan and the widow, in accordance with the biblical mandate to look after those without fathers and those who have lost their husbands (James 1:27).

To know more about the Trust, please consult the website at www.fathershousetrust.com

CONTENTS

FOREWORD

Rarely does an author come along who writes from such personal experience that their writings actually give hope to the reader that they are not alone in their journey. Mark Stibbe is such an author.

My first introduction to Mark was in a "Father Loves You" Conference that my husband Jack Frost and I attended in Toronto, Canada, in November 2003. Jack and I used to be main speakers at this conference each year. When we were not invited to do this one year, we decided that we would attend anyway because we heard that Mark was going to be ministering and we wanted to hear him speak. Jack had recently read one of Mark's books on the Father's love – *From Orphans to Heirs* – and was deeply touched by his ability to communicate from such a personal level that you could immediately place yourself and your own experience in the middle of Mark's life story.

Mark's new book *I Am Your Father* again shows the humility of this man. His character leaps off the pages and convinces you that his revelation is real. It captivates you to a point where you can hardly put the book aside for normal daily activities. You have to read on and find out how you can have the same kind of profound and intimate relationship with a loving Father. In showing the way, Mark never gives you a list. His style is more like Jesus': he tells you stories and provides applications that take the reader to a point of decision and change.

Mark is an author who knows personally how it feels to be without value to an earthly father or mother. Having been placed in an orphanage in 1960, he was adopted into a loving father's home and his situation changed dramatically from that time on. In spite of this transformation in circumstances, the seed of rejection was already sown in the heart of the little child. Subsequently, through his personal quest to have a relationship with his Heavenly Father, Mark found his heart's true home and was enabled to share with others how to find healing in the embrace of *Abba*, Father.

We are living in an era of fatherlessness. Fathers have shirked their own obligations and responsibilities because they too have been hurt, abused or neglected by their own fathers, and this has produced a pandemic of fatherlessness (to use Mark's phrase) throughout the world.

The command to honour your father and mother has become a joke to many people today. How do you honour the person who has abused you, made you the source of their pain when you did not ask to be born, or simply abandoned you because your existence was an intrusion into their plan for their lives?

Many ministries today have been called to help fulfil the prophecy in Malachi 4:5–6: "See, I will send you the prophet Elijah before that great and dreadful day of the Lord comes. He will turn the hearts of the fathers to their children, and the hearts of the children to their fathers; or else I will come and strike the land with a curse." I know of none that communicates this better than Mark's ministry, the Father's House Trust.

It is the desire of the Father's House Trust to change our world, to eradicate fatherlessness and to prevent future generations from becoming fatherless too. This book will help any reader to begin the journey of embracing the truth: that we are loved by a kind Father who will not leave or forsake you, no matter what your circumstances.

I can only imagine the countless hours of research that have been spent in writing this book and in providing a description of the love that alone fills the hole in the soul. Nothing fills the deep needs of our heart like the Father's love. In underlining this point, Mark has demonstrated how many others have found their freedom in this divine love. Through exciting tales of his own personal experience with orphan issues, the experiences of his adoptive father and through illustrations from many real-life stories, Mark has been able to motivate us into a realization that we all need a more personal journey with God as our Father.

I believe this book will end up generating literally thousands of testimonies of changed lives. Indeed, it would be no surprise to me if *I Am Your Father* joined the bestseller list for books that bring healing to the hearts of families. Nor would it surprise me to learn that it had become a source of revelation for many who are seeking a closer relationship with their Heavenly Father.

If you take the time to read it and apply it to your situation, it will change your life too.

Trisha Frost, Co-Founder/President, Shiloh Place Ministries

PART 1

THE
WOUND

Chapter 1

A FATHERLESS WORLD

It is a compelling photograph. The scene is an airport arrivals hall. As you look at it you see two smiling faces. The taller figure is the father, who has just arrived from Africa. He is a Kenyan man dressed in an immaculate dark suit with a tie tied to perfection. He is wearing black spectacles and he is smiling, not at the person taking the photograph, but at someone to his left, invisible to us.

The smaller of the two figures is his son, a slightly chubby boy, aged ten, who has folded his arms tightly over the hand of his father, a hand that's reached out across the boy's shoulder and is draping limply over his son's bright white shirt. The boy is clutching his father and has a look of joy on his face. The photograph seems to be portraying a picture of family bliss.

But the photograph is deceptive, and the camera lies. The boy – known to his father as Barry – has not seen his father for eight years. In fact, the last time Barry saw his dad was when he was two years old. His father had left his mother and returned to Africa. Now, for a few weeks, he will be reunited to his father in America. But then his father will disappear one more time, and this time the boy will never see him again. Not in real life, anyway. He will meet him in a dream later on in life – a dream in which Barry will find his father under lock and key in a prison cell, cutting a forlorn and tragic figure. He will tell his father that he loves him and wake up later with his pillow soaked with the tears he has shed while asleep.

Who is this boy so overjoyed by an encounter with his dad? Who is this son who will not let go of his father's embrace? The

boy was known to his father as Barry, but to us he is known as Barack Obama, the forty-fourth President of the United States. Barack Obama is the ten-year-old boy in the photograph. His story is told in one of the bestselling biographies of recent times, *Dreams from My Father* – an elegantly and honestly written account of Barack Obama's search for his father. It is a story about a grown man's attempt to arrive at a more informed sense of his own history and identity, through learning about the father who abandoned him, the father he never really knew. It is a book justly praised by all who have read it. And it is a book that reveals so much about the world in which we live today.[1]

A Father's Day confession

On Father's Day 2008, Barack Obama was invited to speak at a church in the south side of Chicago. He decided to use the opportunity to make a plea to the men of his own community – the African American community – to make fatherhood a top priority. You can catch the full speech on YouTube, but here are a few telling sentences:

If we are honest with ourselves, we'll admit that what too many fathers are is missing – missing from too many lives and too many homes. They have abandoned their responsibilities, acting like boys instead of men. And the foundations of our families are weaker because of it... We know the statistics – that children who grow up without a father are five times more likely to live in poverty and commit crime; nine times more likely to drop out of schools and twenty times more likely to end up in prison. They are more likely to have behavioural problems, or run away from home, or become teenage parents themselves. And the foundations of our community are weaker because of it.[2]

In this eloquent and memorable address Obama launched an appeal to African American men to stop abdicating their paternal responsibilities and stop deserting their children. He called on men, before anything else, to be present to their children as fathers. Obama has two children of his own. He has made fatherhood a primary goal in his life. Indeed, he has openly stated that before being a good President, his greatest ambition is to be a good father. In Barack Obama America has a President who understands fatherlessness from his own painful experience, but who also prioritizes fatherhood in his own private life. Whatever one's political allegiances, this fact alone should give cause for hope in the fight against the curse of fatherlessness.

Obama's call to the men of his community was and is a vital one. Much of my public speaking in the United States is done in churches from the African American constituency. Every time I speak about the unconditional love of God the Father, men and women of all ages start weeping. There is a visceral sense of father loss in the African American community. Friends of mine who are their bishops and pastors have told me that the African American community is into its third generation of fatherlessness. They also add that when you include in the mix the appalling history of slavery, you can understand why the message of God the Father's unconditional love has such a deep impact.[3] Many within these churches are bound by chains that derive from a deep sense of abandonment. Many are slaves to performance or pleasure, desperately trying to find value and love through making it to the top, or through toxic relationships. It is a tragic situation.

What is more tragic is the fact that fatherlessness isn't just confined to one part of American life; it is now widespread throughout every segment of US society. Every part of the United States is now affected by the pandemic of fatherlessness, so much so that the country has recently been referred to as 'Fatherless America'.[4] And the social consequences have been dire. The research compiled over the last twenty years has demonstrated conclusively the following depressing statistics. Fatherless children in the USA are:

- 8 times more likely to go to prison
- 5 times more likely to commit suicide
- 20 times more likely to have behavioural problems
- 20 times more likely to become rapists
- 32 times more likely to run away
- 10 times more likely to abuse chemical substances
- 9 times more likely to drop out of high school
- 33 times more likely to be seriously abused
- 73 times more likely to be fatally abused
- one-tenth as likely to get A's in school
- on average have a 44 per cent higher mortality rate
- on average have a 72 per cent lower standard of living.[5]

US society is now reaping a whirlwind from decades of growing fatherlessness. And the saddest fact of all is that this same country is one of the most Christian nations on the face of the globe. How does that compute? If the Gospel is indeed the hope for a nation, then how have we arrived at a point where a country with more churches than just about any other has such a seriously sick and fatherless society? How come a nation so steeped in a rich history of Christian faith can be in a situation where nearly 50 per cent of its children no longer have any meaningful contact with their own fathers? What is going on?

Perhaps here we need to understand the deep significance not only of the time but also the place in which Barack Obama chose to give his rousing call to fathers. Yes, it is of course significant that he chose Father's Day, the day in every year when fathers are honoured. But it is even more important that the President-to-be chose a church building to deliver this rallying cry. Christians are supposed to be salt and light in society. By delivering his speech in a Christian congregation, Obama was sending a clear signal to every church from every denomination in his country that they are not to be fatherless communities. Put in another and perhaps more dramatic way, Obama was rightly saying that the churches are called to be a part of the solution to fatherlessness, not a part of the problem. That is a call that stretches beyond the shores of the United States to every country in the world, including my own nation, the United Kingdom.

Fatherless Britain

In 2008 I was called up for jury service for the first time. For many years I had managed to get away with avoiding the call because I was a pastor. But then the law was changed and I found myself invited to a crown court not far from where I lived. I remember going rather reluctantly because of the inconvenience to my schedule. I came back after two weeks very glad that I'd been.

My abiding memory of the two cases was this. Both of the accused were young males from a local town. Both had been charged with extreme violence. Both had mums in court. But neither of them had dads anywhere in evidence. In the end, both were convicted and, as it turned out, our "guilty" verdicts were vindicated by a long list of antecedents (previous cases of criminal behaviour). Indeed, there was a certain amount of gloating in both juries. People were saying, "We got it right." But I was left asking the question, "Where are all the dads?"

A few months later I found myself in the town where the two boys lived. I was at an afternoon tea party in support of a local inter-church outreach initiative. A lady came to sit next to me who turned out to be the Mayor. We started talking and she asked what I was doing. I replied that I was about to move to her area to begin a charity dedicated to reversing the pandemic of fatherlessness – a charity called The Father's House. I told her about my jury service and the two fatherless boys from her town. She was immediately engaged and told me that she had been speaking to her male police officers and they had very recently told her that they now feel that in their dealings with troubled youngsters on the streets they are performing a role that traditionally belonged to the father of the family. In the great vacuum of fatherlessness, policemen are now often providing both the authority and affection that dads should be showing. But the dads are no longer around. Britain is now fatherless.

Not long ago a UK prison chaplain decided to offer the 500 male prisoners in his prison the opportunity to say thank you to their mums. Mothering Sunday was approaching and the chaplain thought it would be good to give each prisoner the option of a free Mother's Day card to sign and send, free of charge, to their mothers. The offer was accepted by every single one of the prisoners.

The chaplaincy team was so encouraged by the response that they started planning for Father's Day. In May they offered the same 500 prisoners the same option – this time a free card to sign and send to their fathers, saying thank you. Not one of the prisoners accepted the offer. Not one card was sent.

This poignant story vividly illustrates the point that no one can now run away from. Fatherlessness is now rampant in British culture. For about a century – certainly since the time of the First World War – there has been a demonic assault against fatherhood in the UK and worldwide. This has created a social disease that has infected most nations in the world. Fathers are becoming an endangered species. Soon there is a danger that they may even be extinct, and the consequences are already devastating.

When fathers are absent

Further evidence for this is the acknowledgment of what is now dubbed "Broken Britain". Some sectors of society are beginning to wake up to the catastrophic consequences that fatherlessness has caused in the UK. At the forefront of the campaign to highlight these issues is a non-party political organization known as the Centre for Social Justice (CSJ). This has provided the statistical evidence that backs up what many of us have known experientially and anecdotally for many years: that the breakdown of the family – and in particular the absence of fathers – has produced dire social consequences.

CSJ has underlined the fact that Britain's record on family breakdown is now the worst in Europe. The absence of fathers has become an issue of special (though not exclusive) concern to CSJ. Three quarters of the households on social housing estates in the UK are now headed by lone parents, usually mothers. Only 15 per cent of social-renting households are headed by a couple with children. Nationwide, 15 per cent of babies are currently born without a resident biological father and approximately 7 per cent are born with no registered father on their birth certificate.[6]

The consequences for children are toxic. CSJ has collated the evidence and now conclusively demonstrated that children who grow up without fathers, in a lone-parent environment, are 75 per cent more likely to fail at school, 70 per cent more likely to be drug addicts, 50 per cent more likely to develop an alcohol problem, 40 per cent more likely to have serious problems with debt, and 35 per cent more likely to experience unemployment and a need for social welfare.[7] Fatherlessness is now reaping a whirlwind of destruction in UK society. We should not be surprised to hear that there has in recent years been a tripling of children murdering children, that 70 per cent of young offenders come from fatherless homes, that in 2008 11,000 children were treated for addiction to drugs and alcohol, that the UK has the highest rate of teenage pregnancy in Western Europe, and that it is also witnessing an unprecedented surge in street-gang membership in its inner cities. UNICEF's 2007 report on childhood development found that, out of all the industrialized nations, Britain is the worst country for a child to grow up in (it came 21st out of 21) – far worse than all the other countries in terms of poverty, happiness, relationships and risk.[8]

Today, the Centre for Social Justice is swimming against the tide of political correctness and declaring that we cannot go on tolerating everything and anything. They are reminding us that "healthy marriages build healthy families, and healthy families build healthy society".[9] Where marriage is undermined and fathers are absent, society slips towards lawlessness and violence as children resort to gangs as an alternative to family (as a place where they can belong and find value and identity). Broken Britain is a very dark landscape indeed.

The Orphan Maker

How is this situation ever going to be reversed? Nothing is going to change until we understand that this is a spiritual issue. I write from a Christian world-view. In other words, I look at what's happening in the world through biblical spectacles. I interpret what is happening in the world through what I know from reading the Bible. What I learn from the Bible is that the world is at war and has been at war since the very dawn of time. Reading history with a Bible-informed mind means that I see beyond the physical realities of life to the invisible spiritual dimension of existence. That perspective opens up a far bigger landscape than the merely temporal and tangible view of life. It reveals a cosmic battle between a loving God and the powers of darkness.

Beyond what is visible to the naked eye there is a great battle taking place between light and darkness, good and evil. The Bible shows that this battle began right at the start of human history. At some point in the life of heaven, there was a catastrophic rebellion in which an angel originally known as Lucifer – meaning "Light Bringer" – attempted to usurp God's authority. Very little about this primeval story is told in the pages of the Bible, but a glimpse is given in the words of Isaiah 14:13–14, which many Bible scholars believe depicts – at least in part – the motivation of this ancient insurrectionist:

Nothing is going to change until we understand that this is a spiritual issue.

> *You said in your heart,*
> *"I will ascend to heaven;*
> *I will raise my throne*
> *above the stars of God;*
> *I will sit enthroned on the mount of assembly,*
> *on the utmost heights of the sacred mountain.*
> *I will ascend above the tops of the clouds;*
> *I will make myself like the Most High."*

Here the five statements beginning "I will" point to the choice that Lucifer made – as an angelic being endowed with free will – to become like God and even to dethrone God. This rebellion failed, which is why the prophet precedes these verses with this remark in Isaiah 14:12:

How you have fallen from heaven,
O morning star, son of the dawn!
You have been cast down to the earth,
you who once laid low the nations!

It is also why the same writer follows verses 13–14 with this reminder of Lucifer's fate:

But you are brought down to the grave,
to the depths of the pit.

There is a lot that we could say about this moment but two things need emphasizing. The first is that Lucifer chose to embrace what I call "the orphan condition". In other words, instead of living and serving in heaven before the throne of the Father, Lucifer rebelled against the Father and fell from heaven to earth, indeed to a place lower than the earth. Lucifer chose an eternity of self-imposed isolation and abandonment when he could have lived for ever in the presence of the Father's love, which is the very atmosphere of heaven. Most tragic of all, the Bible tells us that he took a great number of the angels of heaven with him. He did not fall alone but he influenced many other celestial beings to enter the orphan state with him (Revelation 12:7–9). The Bible teaches that these "fallen angels" morphed into what we would now call "demons" or "unclean spirits". With the devil they work to oppose the Father's will on the earth.

This brings me to the second point. When Lucifer fell from heaven, he did not become inactive in history. Far from it, he became Satan, a name that means "adversary". He became the enemy of God and his first act was to retaliate against God. He wasn't powerful enough to oppose God directly, so he decided to seek vengeance by destroying what God had made.

In the guise of a serpent he wends his way into the Garden

of Eden and tempts God's first human children with the same ambition that he had once had in heaven – to become like God. Tragically, Adam and Eve yield to this temptation and lose their childlike innocence. They become aware of their nakedness and feel shame. They try to hide from God in the garden but they are discovered and they, along with the serpent, are punished. For Adam and Eve this means banishment from the Garden of Eden and a loss of intimate communion with the Father. The final words of Genesis 3 graphically portray the moment when Adam and Eve become exiled from the Father's love:

So the Lord God banished him from the Garden of Eden to work the ground from which he had been taken. After he drove the man out, he placed on the east side of the Garden of Eden cherubim and a flaming sword flashing back and forth to guard the way to the tree of life.

From all of this we learn two vital truths. First, that there is an arch-enemy of God. His name was Lucifer but is now Satan. He was a glorious angel in heaven but he is now a dark shadow. In choosing to rebel and to become independent, Satan chose of his own free will to become the Ultimate Orphan. He no longer lives in the presence of the Father but has opted for an eternal, orphan state.

Secondly, Satan is not just the Ultimate Orphan. He is supremely the Orphan Maker. In the Garden of Eden, he enacted his plan of revenge against the Father in the only way he knew how. He attacked God's children and succeeded in tempting them to choose the orphan state. They too became separated from the Father's love. They too became spiritual orphans and indeed, every human being since Adam has been a spiritual orphan as a result. Ever since Eden, human beings have been separated from the Father's love and presence, at least until a decisive moment in history – the moment when Jesus was born.

The Father's only Son

The birth of Jesus is the most significant event in human history. The Bible teaches that Jesus is the one and only Son of God by nature and that the Father sent him into this world to be born as a human being. The reason for this is given in a majestic passage in the writings of the Apostle Paul, in Galatians 4:4–6:

> *When the time had fully come, God sent his Son, born of a woman, born under law, to redeem those under law, that we might receive the full rights of sons. Because you are sons, God sent the Spirit of his Son into our hearts, the Spirit who calls out, "Abba, Father."*

What Paul is saying in these timeless sentences is that Jesus came to rescue human beings from their orphan state. Jesus of Nazareth knew God personally and intimately as *Abba*, Father. *Abba* is the Aramaic word for "Daddy". It is a relational, not a remote, form of address. Jesus knew God as *Abba* in heaven before he was born on earth. He knew God as *Abba* on earth in his short life as a human being. He now lives forever in heaven at the Father's right hand, worshipping God Almighty as his *Abba*, as his Daddy.

The Good News told in the Big Story of the Bible is this: Jesus came into the world while we were still far away from the Father, living in the legacy of the rebellious independence of the first Adam. He came to die on the Cross so that we who were far away could be brought near, having intimate access to *Abba*, Father through the work of the Cross and through the power of the Holy Spirit. Thanks to what Jesus did, all human beings can now be reconciled to the Father. If we choose to say yes to his loving invitation, we can be rescued from our spiritual orphan state and can become sons and daughters of God by adoption, speaking to God in the same way that Jesus does. In other words, we can call God *Abba* too! If we make the decision to do this, we will no longer be under Satan's rule, we will be under *Abba*, Father's rule.

So, thanks to Jesus we are no longer orphans. Jesus has dealt Satan a decisive blow in his crucifixion and resurrection. The enemy has been defeated, though he fights on. The final victory is only a matter of time but the war between light and darkness will be concluded. In the time-frame between Jesus' life and death two thousand years ago and his return at the very end of history, those who have become the adopted children of God have many battles to fight. Satan is still at work trying to create orphans and widows. He seeks to wreak havoc on the earth by creating fatherless children wherever

> Thanks to what Jesus did, all human beings can now be reconciled to the Father.

he can. But the church is Dad's Army and we are on the winning side! We know how the book ends. At the conclusion of history, the Bible shows the devil and all his fallen angels being condemned to an eternity of torment, while those who have chosen to embrace the Father's love on this earth get to spend eternity in the Father's house. As the Apostle John puts it in the final chapter of the Bible (Revelation 21):

> *Then I saw a new heaven and a new earth, for the first heaven and the first earth had passed away, and there was no longer any sea. I saw the Holy City, the new Jerusalem, coming down out of heaven from God, prepared as a bride beautifully dressed for her husband. And I heard a loud voice from the throne saying, "Now the dwelling of God is with men, and he will live with them. They will be his people, and God himself will be with them and be their God. He will wipe every tear from their eyes. There will be no more death or mourning or crying or pain, for the old order of things has passed away."*

A world at war

To some readers this may all seem too much like a mythical universe rather than the real world – more like Middle Earth than Planet Earth. But that would be a mistake. The world-view of the Bible is a warfare world-view. Before a person becomes a Christian, they are by and large blind to supernatural realities. They more often than not buy into a materialistic world-view that says, "If you can't see it, touch it and measure it, then it can't be real." But when a person becomes a Christian, the lights come on and everything changes. True enlightenment fills the soul. The eyes of our hearts are illuminated by divine wisdom, by a heavenly perspective on earthly realities. Suddenly the person who formerly mocked the idea of angels and demons becomes very aware of their existence and understands that there is an intense and ferocious battle going on between light and darkness.

The Apostle Paul was a man well aware of the forces of evil that warred against him. He knew that he was in a spiritual battle. In Ephesians 6:12 he wrote:

> *Our struggle is not against flesh and blood, but against the rulers, against the authorities, against the powers of this dark world and against the spiritual forces of evil in the heavenly realms.*

This is a key statement in Paul's letters. He knew from personal experience that the powers that opposed him were real and toxic. These powers are not described in any detail here or anywhere else in Paul's writings. They are merely mentioned in passing. The important thing for Paul is not the powers themselves. Rather, his interest is first of all in the fact that Jesus has been raised and exalted far above these powers. In his death, resurrection and ascension, Jesus is high and lifted up far above all the powers of darkness in the universe, whether visible or invisible. So, in the same letter to the Ephesians (1:20–21), Paul describes how God's power:

raised him [Jesus] from the dead and seated him at his
right hand in the heavenly realms, far above all rule
and authority, power and dominion, and every title
that can be given, not only in the present age but also
in the one to come.

Paul's interest is not in the nature or the structure of the demonic powers. His point is that Jesus is Lord; that he rules over everything and everyone, whatever their title or name.

The second thing Paul is interested in is the fact that those who have chosen to follow Christ are "in Christ". If Christians are "in Christ", and if Christ reigns above all the demonic powers at work in the world, then we are reigning with Christ in the heavenly places and we have nothing to fear. This is exactly what Paul believes and preaches. In Ephesians 2:6 he says: "God raised us up with Christ and seated us with him in the heavenly realms in Christ Jesus." This great declaration shows that we have been given an extraordinary position once we are "in Christ". We have a position of supreme authority over the powers of this world. This position belongs to us because it belongs to Christ. Once a person is in Christ, Christ's authority over the dark powers becomes their authority too!

But not only does Paul speak of *position*, he also speaks of *power*. We have a position of authority, which means that we are no longer cowering under the powers but reigning over the powers with Jesus, who is Lord. At the same time, God has not just granted us an amazing position; he has also given us matchless *power* to combat the devil's work. This divine strength is in fact the same power that God exerted to raise Jesus of Nazareth from death 2,000 years ago. It is the same power that God used to lift Jesus up into the heavenly realms, to be seated in great glory. This power God gives to us, if we are in Christ. That is why Paul prays that Christians would know the "incomparably great power" given to those who believe (Ephesians 1:19). A powerless church is no church at all. That is also why in Ephesians 6:10–11 Paul urges all those who follow Christ:

Be strong in the Lord and in his mighty power. Put on the full armour of God so that you can take your stand against the devil's schemes.

The church as Dad's Army

Paul's vision for the church is a truly inspirational one. The church is not a passive audience called to sit in dusty old buildings singing funereal hymns and listening to dreary preachers. It is an army of God-lovers who are called and armed to advance the reign of God and take ground that the enemy has previously occupied. The church is not supposed to be a static, worldly institution but a supernatural, advancing, conquering force in the world. While the world's armies conquer through the love of power, God's Army conquers through the power of love – the Father's love. The church is supremely an army, Dad's Army on the earth. And this army is on the winning side. As Jesus of Nazareth said 2,000 years ago in Matthew 16:18, "I will build my church and the gates of Hades will not overcome it."

It's for this reason that it was so important that President Barack Obama chose to address the issue of fatherlessness in a church congregation. The world is gripped by a demonic pandemic of fatherlessness that is ultimately the work of Satan, the Orphan Maker. The church is God's antidote to this disease. The church is not supposed to reflect the world; it is called to redeem the world. The church is not meant to be a community that mirrors the host culture which it serves; it is meant to be an alternative community, a counter-culture, in which the evil systems of this world are not just questioned but transformed. I don't know what your vision of the church is, but mine is of a family filled with the Father's love – a family called by Jesus, empowered by the Holy Spirit, and combating fatherlessness all over the world.

From 1996 to 2009 I was the senior leader of St Andrew's Church in Chorleywood, just outside North London. Our vision – cast early on under my watch – was to be so filled with the

> The church is not supposed to be a static, worldly institution but a supernatural, advancing, conquering force in the world.

Father's love that we couldn't resist giving that love away, especially to the lost. For the first half of my time at St Andrew's we built a spirituality of the Father's love, teaching on the Father heart of God and spiritual adoption. During that season I published my book *Orphans to Heirs* (which arose out of a teaching series in the church) and I started a *Father Loves You* course – a discipleship programme designed to help new believers to be healed from their father wounds and enter a lifelong, intimate communion with *Abba*, Father. In the second half of my time at St Andrew's we adopted a strategy for taking this love to our community and beyond. We developed mission-shaped communities (MSCs) of up to fifty adult members in each and we sent them out from our church centre.

What happened next is told in the book *Breakout*, written by Andrew Williams and myself. These MSCs went out and met in school halls, community centres, coffee shops, homeless shelters and the like. They invaded the world's space with the Father's love. By the time I left in 2009 there were thirty-two MSCs going in and out of the church centre every month, like lifeboats at a lifeboat station. They were completely mission focused. Their purpose was to go and rescue those in peril on the sea of life, which most did with extraordinary effectiveness. In the last two Alpha Courses we held at our church centre before Andrew and I left, there were over 100 non-Christian guests at each. There were tables with the learning disabled (from the MSC dedicated to serving that particular community). There were tables with homeless people, the deaf, troubled teens, and all sorts. It was not just a meal for the middle classes. It was a banquet for the broken – just like the meals the Messiah had with the marginalized in the Gospels. All of the guests became Christians in these two courses and they were then integrated into the MSCs that had brought them – into extended families where they could grow as the adopted sons and daughters of God. It was an exceptional and exciting season in which the church grew, through daring mission, to over 1,700 members. Truly, the church had left the building and the adventure had been restored to the Christian venture!

This is what I believe the church is called to be – not a self-absorbed aggregate of squabbling individuals but a family of adventurers who want to take their Dad's lavish love to the unloved. I can safely say that in my twelve years as leader of St Andrew's Chorleywood, while I made mistakes and we confronted many difficulties, it felt like the church was at last doing what it was always supposed to do. As the mission focus increased, so did the miracles. In particular, we saw a surge of healing miracles as we launched out to save the lost. Most moving of all, we also saw a dramatic increase in mercy as the Father's compassion gripped us in new ways and led to a radical outpouring of generosity towards the poor and a brand-new emphasis on justice. James 1:27 became especially important to us as a community:

> *Religion that God our Father accepts as pure and faultless is this: to look after orphans and widows in their distress and to keep oneself from being polluted by the world.*

This revelation changed us. Instead of building a huge mega-church for consumer Christians, we now set ourselves to restoring broken walls (Isaiah 58:12). Instead of building a cruise ship where believers could get more and more spiritually obese, we created a lifeboat station where everyone knew that our purpose in life was to do everything we could to save the lost. It was a time I'll never forget.

The hearts of the fathers

The truth is, we are in a war, and the war is getting fiercer. The enemy has been defeated already but he fights on and he fights with insidious and underhand tactics. One of his primary tactics in the last one hundred years or so has been to undermine fatherhood throughout the world. He has wreaked havoc in families on every continent and in the process eroded the foundations of society, creating an ever darkening urban landscape of lawlessness. This is what the Apostle Paul would have called one of Satan's chief "schemes" (2 Corinthians 2:11). His strategy is to create a fatherless world. His desire is to make orphans and widows wherever he can, depriving children of their fathers and wives of their husbands. Nothing brought this to light more clearly for me than a very recent TV programme called Inside 9/11, about the events leading up to the terrorist attacks on 11 September 2001. The first few seconds of the documentary showed a terrorist leader preaching hatred on camera. He was one of the most sinister and demonized people I have ever seen. These were his simple but disturbing words: "Blood must flow. There must be widows. There must be orphans." For me, that single remark graphically highlights the demonic plan that is at work in the world.

While the father of lies seeks to murder and destroy families, the true Father – the Dad whom Jesus came to reveal – is busy working in the opposite spirit. In the Bible he is constantly described as the Father to the fatherless and the defender of the widow. In the Old Testament, King David had this startling revelation of the character of God. You can find it in Psalm 68:

A father to the fatherless, a defender of widows,
is God in his holy dwelling.
God sets the lonely in families,
he leads forth the prisoners with singing.

God the Father's greatest passion is to care for orphans and widows. Time and again the Old Testament links these two groups of people – those without fathers and those without husbands. Time and again orphans and widows are singled out as the focus of the Father's special affection. We know he loves everyone, but he is especially fond of the fatherless and the widow. That is why we hear the prophet declaring these simple words in Isaiah 1:17:

> *Seek justice,*
> *encourage the oppressed.*
> *Defend the cause of the fatherless,*
> *plead the case of the widow.*

All this highlights the importance of what Barack Obama was doing on Father's Day in the Chicago church. In defending the cause of fatherhood in that particular church he was advocating the cause for every church. The church is a community of people who have been adopted by Jesus into a loving, worldwide family. This family is ignited by the fire of God, the Holy Spirit, to take the Father's love to the fatherless all over the world. It is a family at war – at war with the ultimate orphan who seeks to turn children into orphans and wives into widows. Until Jesus returns, this family of God is to take the Father's love to the fatherless and make every effort to reverse the curse of fatherlessness on the earth. In embracing this great task, the church is living in the end-times purposes of God. As the end of history draws nearer, Malachi prophesies that there will be a time when the hearts of the fathers will be turned towards their children, and the hearts of the children to their fathers (Malachi 4:5–6). These words close the Old Testament and they are full of prophetic significance for today.

Today, those who have decided to follow Jesus have the power of the Holy Spirit within them, the Spirit who enables us to know that we are God's children and cry out "*Abba*, Father!"

For the church to fulfil this task, those who are already members of God's family need to have their father wounds healed.

That is why I've written this book, to help those with hearts broken by their earthly fathers to find in their Heavenly Father the love of all loves. To understand why this is so important, I wanted in this first chapter to paint on a very large canvas. The Big Story or "meta-narrative" of the Bible has clearly shown us that there is an intense spiritual battle taking place. On the one hand, the ultimate orphan is at work, trying to create orphans and widows, and drive families apart. He has been doing this since the Garden of Eden. On the other hand, our Father in heaven has been warring against the Orphan Maker. He began his rescue plan by adopting the nation of Israel as his chosen people. He then sent his One and Only Son to this same nation to die upon the Cross. When Jesus shed his blood at Calvary, the devil's hold on the planet was loosened and a way was opened up to the Father by which all could choose to come home into his arms of love. Today, those who have decided to follow Jesus have the power of the Holy Spirit within them, the Spirit who enables us to know that we are God's children and cry out, "*Abba*, Father!"

Jesus promised in John 14:18, "I will not leave you as orphans." It's time to be set free from the orphan state. It's time to fall in love with the world's greatest Father. It is time to war against fatherlessness with the Father's love.

Chapter 2

SINS OF THE FATHERS

On 25 June 2009 Michael Jackson, one of the world's most revered pop icons, died of a massive heart attack, aged fifty.

Michael Jackson was one of the greatest innovators in pop music history. His record *Thriller* is still the best selling album of all time. His dance routines and stage shows are to this day regarded by many as unrivalled. Fans still refer to him, even after his death, as "the ultimate live performer". With the music video genre he raised the bar to a height rarely attained by anyone else. I remember the first time my family and I saw the video of Jackson's "Earth Song" (1995). It portrays a landscape of poverty, war, injustice, ruin and catastrophe. As Jackson's singing soars to a haunting lament for the healing of the earth, the wrongs recorded in the first half of the video begin to be reversed. As he stands between two trees crying for the earth (in cruciform position), a great and mighty wind begins to blow across the fractured planet in response to his song. A dead father comes back to life. Felled trees return to their roots. And a slaughtered elephant, brutally shot, has its tusks restored and then returns to its feet – regal, strong, and alive. I remember the sense of awe in my whole family as we listened and watched. We all agreed – it doesn't get any better than this. It was quite simply unforgettable. It was Jackson at his most majestic.

At the same time, while most would acknowledge Jackson's creative genius, many would also accept that he was a profoundly flawed man. Perhaps the most poignant revelation of this was his 1993 interview with Oprah Winfrey. Jackson rarely gave interviews but on this occasion he allowed Winfrey to come to his famous Neverland ranch and ask him questions live on air. During the interview, facts began to emerge about his childhood. He revealed how he had felt extremely lonely growing up in the family home. He shared how he had been terrified of his father, Joe Jackson – so scared that sometimes he would vomit when his father entered the family home. In 2003, Joe Jackson confirmed as much when he made this bizarre statement during an interview: "I whipped him with a switch and a belt. I never beat him. You beat someone with a stick."[10] During rehearsals, Joe Jackson would sit in a chair with a belt in his hands, ready to hit his son Michael if he didn't measure up. On one notorious occasion, Joe Jackson wanted to teach his children a lesson for leaving their bedroom windows open at night. He waited until his children were asleep and then entered Michael's room wearing a mask and screaming. For years afterwards Michael would suffer terrifying nightmares of being abducted from his bedroom at night. Perhaps the saddest moment in Michael's interview was when Oprah Winfrey asked him if he ever got angry with his father. Michael replied, "Sometimes I do get angry. I don't know him the way I'd like to know him. My mother's wonderful. To me she's perfection. I just wish I could understand my father."

A global pandemic

In some ways, Michael Jackson is a sign of the times. The truth is, we live in a world where fathers are more often than not absent or abusive. Joe Jackson may be the visible tip of the iceberg, but the iceberg is enormous and its reach goes very deep indeed. While not all fathers may go to the extremes that Joe Jackson went to, many are failing to provide the love that is essential to the development of the world's children. Today good fathers are becoming increasingly rare and fatherhood is in danger of becoming extinct. For over one hundred years, there has been a growing war against fatherhood, an aggressive and unrelenting demonic campaign to remove fathers from private life and public debate. In Western nations like the UK and the USA, we are now beginning to witness the awful effects of the ever-increasing rise in absent, abandoning and abusive dads. The absence of good, male, parenting role models has resulted in a society where young people are more and more vulnerable to teenage pregnancy, gang warfare and addiction to drugs. While there is a cluster of complex reasons for this, the number-one cause behind the pathology of most of our social ills – from sexual confusion and promiscuity to criminal behaviour – is fatherlessness. This may be politically incorrect right now to say, but Christians are not called to be politically correct. We are called to be prophetically direct. And we cannot afford to remain silent any longer.

> The absence of good, male, parenting role models has resulted in a society where young people are more and more vulnerable to teenage pregnancy, gang warfare and addiction to drugs.

Anyone who saw Michael Jackson's face during the Oprah Winfrey interview will have seen a loneliness, despair and melancholy also seen in the eyes of countless people today, especially the young. People today are growing up in the "Orphan Generation", a generation in which children do not receive the unconditional love of a father. The result of this is a great sadness which I call "the father wound" – the traumatic wound of being alienated from a father's tender love. It is a wound that affects almost everyone today, from the rich and famous to the poor and unknown. In fact fatherlessness, like death, is a great leveller. It is just as likely to be found in the wealthy mansions of the world's celebrities as it is in the council houses of the growing underclass. It is everywhere, and no mask or makeup can cover the desolation it causes.

Perhaps one of the most poignant remarks Jackson ever made was in a speech at the Oxford Union in 2003. He said, "If you enter this world knowing you are loved and you leave this world knowing the same, then everything that happens in between can be dealt with."[11] Tragically, Michael Jackson was never to experience the truth of this in his own life. Throughout his life he was denied the accepting, affectionate love of an affirming father. At his death his mother was there, but his father was not – a fact that speaks volumes. Michael Jackson tried to compensate for this great loss by creating Neverland, but even here he could not find the happy and innocent childhood he had been denied. Indeed, it was perhaps especially here that the greatest darkness intruded.

Seven kinds of bad dad

Michael Jackson was right – knowing that you are loved is all important, especially for children. The experience of being accepted and cherished for who we are is critical to our wholeness both individually and in our relationships with others. This gift is primarily given to us by our parents. In the earliest years (0–2), a mother's love is vital. The experience of being nurtured, fed, soothed and comforted by a mother is essential for healthy human development. From the age of three onwards (and especially between the ages of three and five), the father's role becomes vital. This is when the father's love is really needed in addition to a mother's love. That is in no way to minimize the role or the importance of a father in a child's life prior to three years of age. It is simply to say that from the age of three onwards the father's encouragement, playfulness, and mentoring become essential to the child's heart. This continues as the child becomes an adolescent and then a young adult. Throughout these years of development, the father's role is indispensible. As Dr George Rekers has commented:

A positive and continuous relationship to one's father has been found to be associated with a good self-concept, higher self-esteem, higher self-confidence in

I AM YOUR FATHER

personal and social interaction, higher moral maturity, reduced rates of unwed teen pregnancy, greater internal control and higher career aspirations. Fathers who are affectionate, nurturing and actively involved in child-rearing are more likely to have well-adjusted children.[12]

The experience of being accepted and cherished for who we are is critical to our wholeness both individually and in our relationship with others.

The problem, of course, is that dedicated fathers are increasingly rare. In fact, it is no exaggeration to say that inadequate fathering has become the norm. Today, we have far too many bad dads. In a sense, of course, all dads are bad dads. Two thousand years ago, Jesus of Nazareth said this about fathers to his disciples in Luke 11:11–13:

Which of you fathers, if your son asks for a fish, will give him a snake instead? Or if he asks for an egg, will give him a scorpion? If you then, though you are evil, know how to give good gifts to your children, how much more will your Father in heaven give the Holy Spirit to those who ask him!

Jesus compares earthly fathers to his Heavenly Father in this passage. He says that earthly fathers are "evil", yet they give good gifts to their children. How much more will God the Father, who is good, give the gift of the Holy Spirit to his children. The surprising word here is the word "evil". Earthly fathers who give the right things to their kids are described as "evil". Even fathers who do what they are supposed to do are therefore imperfect. All dads are sinners in need of forgiveness, whether they fulfil their responsibilities or not. There is only one perfect Father, the one whom Jesus called "*Abba*, Father".

Even the most committed fathers, deep down, will admit that this is true. I am the father of four children. I can safely say that being a dad has been the greatest challenge of my life, far greater than being a pastor, a speaker, an author or anything else, for that matter. While I love my daughter and three sons very dearly, I have not always shown them that love when they needed it or in the way they desired. There have been times in their lives when I have not been present as I should, either physically or emotionally. There have been times when I have said and done things that I should not have. There are regrets mingled with the joys. As one who greatly values fatherhood, I would say that it is a tough calling to be a father. Anyone can *become* a father. But it's a different matter altogether *being* a father. I totally empathize with the father who overheard his son praying at bedtime: "Dear God, make me the kind of man my Daddy is." Later that night, the father prayed, "Dear God, make me the kind of man my son wants me to be."[13] As Elizabeth Elliot once remarked:

> *if you take being a father seriously, you'll know that you're not big enough for the job, not by yourself... Being a father will put you on your knees if nothing else ever did.*[14]

Even the best fathers are imperfect and painfully conscious of falling short of what they could be. But the tragic fact is that there are an increasing number of really poor examples of fathering in the world today. This poor fathering covers a wide spectrum from extreme abuse to low-level neglect. As Dr Robert McGee rightly says:

There is only one perfect Father, the one whom Jesus called *Abba*, Father.

> *not everyone goes through the severe trauma of abuse, abandonment, or gross neglect. But many fathers may nibble around the edges of these faults, perhaps leaving tiny bite marks in the spirits of their children rather than gaping holes of emptiness.*[15]

Today there is a growing body of literature devoted to what I call "negative father types". As people become more and more aware of the problem of fatherlessness in society, so they are beginning to describe what bad dads look like. Dr Jane Myers Drew identifies four in her book, *Where Were You When I Needed You Dad?* She calls these Absent, Abusive, Judgmental, and Distant.[16] Dr Stephen Poulter identifies four damaging fathering styles in his book *The Father Factor*. He calls these the Superachieving Fathering Style, the Time-Bomb Fathering Style, the Passive Fathering Style, and the Absent Fathering Style.[17] Dr Robert McGee identifies six: the Abusive Father, the Absent Father, the Workaholic Father, the Passive Father, the Ill Father, the Manipulative or Perfectionist Father.[18] In my own work I have so far identified seven negative father types. If you have been poorly fathered, you may well identify with one or more of these. Not every negative father fits neatly into one category. There may be some overlap and there may be some positives mixed in with the negatives. But ask yourself, "Which one of these best describes my father? If I had to sum up my experience of being fathered, which one of these father types would cover that?"

The absent father

I define an absent father as a father who does not live with his child or is away from his child for much of the time.

There can be a number of reasons why a father is absent. The first can be because of distance. Maybe a father is away because his work takes him away. He may not want to be away from his children, but away he is. Fathers in the armed services often fit this bill. They may love their children but their job requires them to be away from home for significant periods of time. Dads who travel long distances because of their work can often fit this description too. They are absent more than present at home. At times the father may actively choose to put his career before his children. This kind of father may give generous presents out of guilt for not being there. But no financial or material gifts can compensate for the child's sense of father loss. It is the man, not the money, that the child longs for.

If the first cause of absence may be distance, the second could be death. This absence is particularly traumatic if the father's death is premature and occurs while the child is growing up. It is especially traumatic if the father commits suicide.

A third cause of absence is divorce. A father may be absent from his children because of legal restrictions imposed on his visiting rights or because he chooses not to have any meaningful involvement after being separated from the mother. As Robert McGee observes: "today's high percentage of divorce means that many children miss out on having a father present during their earliest years."[19]

A fourth kind of absence can be caused by disinterest. I have recently seen the most remarkable healing in a woman whose father chose never to be there for her. Her most painful memories concerned him not being at her graduation ceremony and her wedding. He wasn't there because he couldn't care. Disinterest can be a devastating cause of absence too.

A fifth cause of absence can be disease. This can come in all sorts of forms. If a father is hospitalized for long periods, a child will feel that the father is absent. If the father is home but bed-ridden or seriously depressed, the father still appears absent.

A final cause of absence may be desertion. When a father chooses to abandon his child or his children the wound is devastating. This is my story. Our biological father deserted my mother before my twin sister and I were born. It has taken decades to have that sense of abandonment healed.

The apathetic father

The apathetic father is the father who is emotionally distant from his children. The word "apathetic" comes from the Greek word *apatheia*. The word *pathos* means "emotion" and the prefix *a* means "without". Someone who is apathetic is, accordingly, without emotion. "Sympathy", on the other hand, comes from the Greek word *sympatheia*, with means "(together) with emotion". A true father is someone who is emotionally engaged with his children, rejoicing when they rejoice, weeping when they weep. A poor father is emotionally detached and does not feel what his children feel. He may be present physically but absent emotionally. Or, as the saying goes, "the lights are on but no one's at home".

Children require a lot of affirmation and affection from their fathers. When the father is apathetic he wounds his children by neglecting them emotionally. When the father is only ever interested in the newspaper or the TV, the child will be wounded by this repeated pattern of apathy. The child longs for a father who is completely attentive to them, who establishes and maintains eye contact with them when communicating, and who is not just sympathetic but empathetic – feeling for them in their troubles as well as in their triumphs. Children long for a kind and sympathetic dad.

Why do apathetic fathers behave in such a detached way? It may be for a number of reasons. If the father has a very demanding job in which his own emotional batteries are depleted, then he may want to engage but not have the resources to do so. This was my problem as a pastor. The church I led had well over a thousand members. The church house that we lived in was right on the car park where the church building was. I was literally on call twenty-four hours a day, seven days a week, and throughout the year. The job was profoundly rewarding but it was all consuming. While some of my four children were going through their teens I was not really engaged with them emotionally. I was permanently tired and, when at home, would fall exhausted on the sofa to watch sport on TV. This led to the unbearable contradiction of being a man who ministered to abandonment all over the world while in many ways abandoning some of my own children when they most needed me. That was something we had to put right before it was too late.

The father's apathy may have many causes. It could be the exhausting nature of the father's job. It could also be that the father was himself fathered in this way; that his own dad was apathetic and he has followed his father's example. Maybe his father was brought up in the "big boys don't cry" school and was incapable of demonstrating any emotion. The father's passivity in this instance is directly linked to the Stoicism of the father that he knew as a child.

Finally, it could be that the father has consciously rejected the child, perhaps because he feels the child is not his own, and has chosen to become detached and disinterested as a result.

Apathetic fathers are, accordingly, emotionally unavailable fathers. Their distance causes a deep wound. When a father ignores his child he transmits a message that injures a child's soul – it says in effect, "Your concerns are not as important as mine." This kind of neglect creates a toxic sense of worthlessness and loneliness. The child feels that he or she is not important and retreats into a world of hiding, of suffering in silence. Or they begin to misbehave wildly so as to capture their father's attention. Either way, the child brought up by the apathetic father will almost always believe the lie that you should be wary of intimacy. Longing to be loved, the children of apathetic fathers substitute work for relationships and hide behind busyness.

The addicted father

I define the addicted father as a father whose life is dominated by his dependency on a mood-altering substance or behaviour. This father becomes so attached to the object of his desire that he cannot be functionally attached to his children and is often a "rageoholic" – he often bursts into extreme fits of anger in the presence of his child.

One of the commonest examples of the addicted father is the alcoholic father. In the USA more than 28 million Americans are the children of alcoholic fathers. Nearly 11 million of these are under the age of eighteen.[20] The pattern of alcoholic fathering is often generational, with the sons of alcoholic fathers being at fourfold risk compared with the sons of non-alcoholic fathers. Families affected by alcoholic fathers are invariably disrupted. There are usually higher levels of conflict, emotional or physical violence, stress, financial worries and marital strain where the father is an alcoholic. Being brought up by an alcoholic father leaves a lasting legacy of emotional pain.

More disturbing even than the alcoholic father is the drug-addicted father. Recent research has demonstrated that being raised by a father who abuses drugs is even more harmful to children than being raised by a father who is an alcoholic. Such children exhibit higher levels of anxiety, depression and anti-social behaviour patterns than the children of alcoholic fathers. Children of drug-addicted fathers are exposed to even more violence, conflict and poor parenting than the children of alcoholic fathers. Being raised by addicted fathers is extremely harmful to children and leads to anxiety disorders, depression, low self-esteem, fear, lack of empathy for others, and dysfunctional behaviour (such as attention deficit disorder and defiant and antagonistic behaviour).

The addicted father is increasingly commonplace. The primary reason for this is because we live in a culture of addiction where there are countless substances and processes immediately available to people, which enable the addict to become comfortably numb. The problem with this is that the pain doesn't go away and the dependency almost always harms others, especially children. The old lie that says, "It doesn't matter what you do as long as it doesn't hurt someone else" is precisely that – a lie. Every addictive behaviour, however solitary, affects someone else adversely, sooner or later. Anyone who believes otherwise should visit the Red Light District of Amsterdam, as I did in 2009 with a group of Christian intercessors. Some of the girls we saw advertising their bodies in shop windows were not there by choice but because they had been abducted and drugged. More tragic still are the little children's shoes that hang outside some of the windows, indicating that sex with children (usually the victims of human trafficking) is available in those venues. Addiction is profoundly harmful, not just to the addict but to others.

Children of addicted fathers are at far greater risk of harm than children of non-addicted fathers. The consequences are often desperately sad. Recently I was visited by a young mother who needed counselling. She had been visited at home by another young mum and her little boy. Her friend's son went upstairs to play with her three-year-old daughter. At one point it went quiet so the mums went upstairs to see if all was well. When they opened the door to the daughter's bedroom they found both children naked and the five-year-old boy acting out scenes that he had witnessed in the hardcore pornographic DVDs belonging to his father. The mother of the daughter was utterly traumatized by this, even more so when the boy's parents descended into denial, anger and blame-shifting (so often symptoms of addictive behaviour).

The addictive father is a father who harms not only himself but his whole family, including his children. Children of addicted fathers start to believe that if they had been a better child, then the father would never have behaved in this way. A great, gaping father void opens up in the soul as a result. As one woman wrote:

> *Since I truly have not had my father in my life since I was five years old (most of that time was spent in and out of rehab centres), him not being here as I mature into a young woman seems almost like the norm to me. Yet, I know it is sad. A father is supposed to be*

49

*there for his daughter throughout her development and
into the rocky parts of her life, and mine isn't. No. He
chose the drugs over me, his own flesh and blood. The
drugs are the children he cuddles and loves more than
anything else. They are the centre of his universe, and
I, unfortunately, am being forced to fend for myself
and go it alone through the tough and scary times of
my development... without his hand to hold me or
his touch to show me it's alright. He hid his love from
me and now we are both paying for it in misery and
sadness.*[21]

The achievement-driven father

The achievement-driven father is the performance-oriented father
who drives his children to become what Dr Stephen Poulter calls
"super-achievers".[22] He expects high standards and makes you feel
that you have to do well in exams, sports, and your career if you
are to be valued and loved. This kind of father does not give you
permission to make mistakes; failure is not an option. He is a
perfectionist who demands the best. His children always have to
look good and they always have to win.

The achievement-driven father is precisely that, *driven*. He
is driven by the need to succeed, so he drives his children; in fact,
he sometimes drives them mad. Of course, it is not wrong as a
father to want your children to do well. With the right motivation
and in the right context, being a cheer-leader to your children
and encouraging them to achieve their goals is really healthy. But
when a father urges his children to succeed because he will not
show his love for them unless they do, that is wrong. When a
father causes his children to believe that they have to earn his love
through performance, this is also profoundly wrong and harmful.
When a father forces his children to achieve *his* goals rather than
their goals, this is unjust. A father's love should be unconditional

and it should respect the child's individuality. It should not be dependent on what a child does or doesn't achieve.

The problem with the achievement-driven father is that he obliterates his child's uniqueness. Almost always the father drives his children to succeed to compensate for his own sense of inadequacy. In causing the child to perform, he is often trying to create a "mini me", a miniature version of himself – or a miniature version of the person his own father wanted him to be, but which he failed to live up to. Fathers like this create a culture of striving which harms a child emotionally and also physically. I have personally prayed for children who have become sick because of the negative influence of their achievement-driven fathers. When they have dealt with the wounds that their fathers caused them emotionally, many times they have been healed physically too.

The achievement-driven father damages his child because the message he constantly transmits and reinforces is this: "Achieve or you're nothing." This results in a deep sense of insecurity; the child feels that their worth is dependent upon their attractiveness and achievements. Whatever they do is never quite good enough. They never measure up. If a book was written about their lives, it would have to have the title of one of Charles Dickens' novels: *Great Expectations*. From their childhood they have learned the lesson, "I Do, Therefore I Am." Children like this grow up to become anxious adults who can sometimes be very hard on themselves and often workaholics.

The authoritarian father

A good father manages to balance the two essential qualities of affection and authority. He loves his children and demonstrates that love in many different ways. One of these ways is the measured and appropriate use of authority, particularly when having to use discipline. No child who has been exposed to the loving and justified use of paternal discipline will resent this later on in life.

It will be regarded as the protective setting of boundaries for the child – boundaries which will help the child develop and grow into a responsible adult. The right use of authority is accordingly a vital and accepted part of functional fathering.

Having said that, it is one thing when a father uses authority lovingly, but it is quite another when he uses it harshly and unfairly. When this happens, authority becomes authoritarianism. The authoritarian father is the fifth negative father type in our list.

The authoritarian father is what I call the Drill Sergeant. He is extremely strict and rules the family with an iron rod. He exercises authority in order to manipulate, control, dominate and coerce his children, and in the process creates a culture of fear. Children in the home of an authoritarian father are constantly intimidated into being compliant to the father's rules. If the achievement-driven father suppresses a child, the authoritarian father *oppresses* a child.

Authoritarian fathers tend to be very judgmental, injuring their children by devastating judgments and the unjustly tough use of punitive discipline. They dictate in very narrow terms what the child is to do and how the child is to behave, limiting in the process the child's natural impulses to explore, experiment, play and develop. Later on in life the child of an authoritarian father may grow up not really knowing who they are, adopting a false self rather than knowing and celebrating their true self. Often the oppressed children of such fathers turn into approval addicts, striving to earn other people's acceptance and admiration because deep down they suffer from a profound sense of fear. Afraid of disapproval, they conform to other people's expectations and become man-pleasers. Alternatively, having spent so much of their upbringing being "goody-goody" conformists, they then go in entirely the opposite direction and become unable to submit to any kind of authority, even loving authority. Worse still, they may become rebellious, defiant rule-breakers. Having lacked periods of freedom in their childhood and adolescence – periods in which self-expression can happen – they turn into either approval addicts or anarchists. When they themselves become fathers, they in turn become either excessively permissive (in reaction against their fathers) or they repeat the sins of their own fathers and became dogmatic dictators themselves.

The abdicating father

German-born, American film star Marlene Dietrich once remarked that "a king, realizing his incompetence, can either abdicate or delegate his duties. A father can do neither."[23] Marlene Dietrich's life spanned almost the entirety of the twentieth century (1901–92). But this is the twenty-first century, and today there are many fathers who both abdicate and delegate their duties.

The abdicating father is the father who fails to be directly involved in a frequent and meaningful way in his children's lives. This failure of responsibility can take many forms. In reality there is a spectrum when it comes to the abdication and delegation of this duty of care. At one end there is the failure to deliver on promises made to a child. Many fathers promise to take their children on holiday, or out for a meal, or away for a day of fun, but fail to keep their word. They promise presents or money but don't do that either. If this becomes a regular pattern it can seriously injure a child's sense of security, significance and self-worth. If it happens at a particularly sensitive time it can cause major damage. I was praying for a woman recently whose father and mother divorced when she was very young. The father promised that he would come and take her out for her fifth birthday. She got ready and dressed up but he never kept his promise. There was no sound of the doorbell ringing – just a deafening silence. Decades later she was still hurting from the devastation of that disappointment. There was a deep and aching father-shaped cavity in her heart.

At the other end of the spectrum is the father's delegation of his responsibility to someone else. This can be to the mother of the family. "Leave it to Mum" is an attitude taken by some who father their children inadequately. Historically, especially in the more affluent sectors of society, fathers have delegated their role to non-family members – for example, to the nanny or the au pair. I was counselling a middle-aged man recently who saw nothing of his father in his childhood because he was brought up by his nanny. Even his mother was by and large absent from his life, nurturing and caring for his older siblings, but leaving him to the nanny figure in the house. The consequence of this was that the man invested his affection for both his father and his mother in his nanny and was traumatized when she eventually left the family.

Dr Jane Myers Drew highlights the hurtful impact of what I call the abdicating father. She observes:

> *sometimes a father encourages false expectations, regularly making plans with his child that he does not carry out. Repeated broken promises can leave a son or a daughter hurt, bitter and suspicious. The youngster grows up repressed, mistrusting others, and lacking good communication skills.*[24]

The abusive father

All the negative father types are damaging, but the most damaging of all is the abusive father. Here there may be a measure of overlap with other father types already mentioned, such as the authoritarian or the addictive father. But the abusive father needs to be singled out. I define the abusive father as one who intentionally shames his children through inflicting verbal, physical and sexual harm. The abusive father is essentially a domestic terrorist and he is for a child the ultimate nightmare. The one supposed to be your greatest shield and protector turns out to be the greatest threat to your safety.

There are different kinds of abuse. There is first of all verbal abuse. Words are extremely powerful; they can build a person up or they can tear a person down. Abusive fathers use words to shame their children. Michael Jackson, in the interview I mentioned earlier with Oprah Winfrey, told of how his father Joe Jackson repeatedly told him he was ugly when he became a teenager and developed acne. The consequences of this insult were there for everyone to see in Michael's desperate attempts as a middle-aged man to cover up every imperfection in his physical appearance and keep himself looking like a pre-teen. Verbal abuse by a father causes very long-lasting injury. The father is the one who is supposed to communicate honour. He is the one who is meant to affirm his sons in their masculinity and his daughters in their femininity. He is the one who is supposed to tell his sons they are warriors and his daughters they are princesses. When fathers tell their children that they are ugly, it makes them feel worthless. When fathers say they wish they had never had children, or that the child is a "loser" or a "failure", they experience emotional abuse. For the rest of their lives they will often believe the lies that were branded on their hearts by these words.

The sad fact is that fathers don't just use words to abuse. They also use physical violence. They use beatings, slaps, punches, throwing, and other forms of maltreatment. One of Michael Jackson's brothers told how, on one occasion, Joe Jackson held Michael upside down and literally pummelled him. Some fathers tragically resort to physical abuse. Even more tragically, some resort to sexual abuse, shaming their child through inappropriate touch, indecent use of sexual language, and many other ways. I have counselled and prayed for a number of adults whose entire lives were wrecked by a sexually abusive father. Until encountering the holy love of the perfect Father, they have worn a cloak of shame, living in the grey half-light of victimhood, unable to trust men and especially male authority figures.

The effects of the abusive father are often disastrous. As Robert McGee says, "the abused victim, in many cases, grows up to be an abuser of his or her own children... generation after generation will often suffer the tragedy of abuse."[25]

Effects on the sexes

Before concluding this rather dismal tour of the landscape of fatherlessness, I want to consider briefly the damaging effects that these negative father types have on male and female children. Dr Robert McGee says that "both males and females whose fathers have been weighed in the balance and found wanting to a significant degree will have problems at some point in their lives."[26] Positive fathers create a sense of womanliness in daughters. They also help to bring boys into true manhood. Where this kind of fathering is absent, girls can often grow up with an incomplete idea of femininity and boys with a distorted view of masculinity. While the effects of poor fathering on girls and boys are sometimes shared, some are distinctive. We will consider first the damaging effects for girls.

Girls who suffer from "dad deprivation" may grow up feeling very unsure about their femininity and self-worth. In the absence of a father's endorsement they may well doubt their attractiveness and value. This can cause them to try to become a super-achiever in sports or academic studies in order to attract attention and praise. Confused about their identity, it can lead them to becoming tomboys. Where fathers are absent, girls may try to fill the father-shaped void in inappropriate and harmful ways. Tragically, many teenage girls in the UK become pregnant as they turn to boys or men for the hug that they never had from their dads. Others may form attachments to older (sometimes family) men in order to compensate for what they lacked as daughters. In more extreme cases, they may turn to the dark underworld of prostitution. Strippers often act out in front of men in order to find the affection and affirmation they have lacked from their dads.

Girls who have been poorly fathered often grow up to

become suspicious of men, and even hate men. This is particularly true when a father abandons his family and a daughter lives alone with her mother. If the mother uses the daughter's anger against her father, the hatred of men can intensify. All this leads to a profound paradox. Women who have been poorly fathered yearn for intimacy with men and yet at the same time deeply mistrust them. As a result, many women embrace unrewarding relationships and then stay in them far too long. Others end up marrying men like their fathers. They find someone like their father in the desperate hope that their husbands or partners will provide what their fathers didn't. But this actually compounds the problem. When this man turns out to be toxic, the pain is doubled. Not only is there the pain of the original abandonment. There is now the new pain of the recent abandonment by the husband or partner. The tragedy is that so often this cycle begins again, and indeed is repeated again and again as girls seek in men for what they can only find in *Abba*, Father.

> The Father wound, however deep and terrible, can be healed effectively and permanently.

If the effects of poor fathering on girls are damaging, the effects on boys are equally toxic. Boys who lack good dads grow up without a good male role model. This leads to an underdeveloped sense of masculinity, of what it means to be a man, and also an unformed idea of how to relate as a man to a woman. Sometimes this can even lead to a great confusion not just about identity but even about gender, especially where an over-attachment to the mother develops. Some boys, convinced that they would have been better off as a girl, change their gender or act out a female role. Some men so despise their fathers for the way they have treated them that they vow never to be like them. In making this vow, they actually and unwittingly make a vow not to be male. Having rejected the father, they have rejected the masculine, so they end up embracing the feminine in the formation of their identity.

Like girls, boys also look for a father's honour and a father's hug in toxic places. They look for it in performance, achievement, work, money, position, sporting prowess, and fame. They also look for it in homosexual relationships, turning to other men for the embrace they never had as a boy. Sometimes boys will turn to violence and to gangs. Here the need for a father and a family is met (in a limited way) in the gang leader and in the sense of being part of a tribe that really looks out for each other. In other cases, boys will become involved in men-only institutions, covert or public, in order to compensate for their deep sense of father loss.

Both girls and boys experience lasting harm from the negative father types described in this chapter. They grow up with an aching void in their hearts over what they have missed from their fathers. Some end up feeling nothing. Choosing to protect their hearts, they develop "frozen feelings" as a survival mechanism. Others end up feeling too much, and then numbing the pain through whatever anaesthetizing substances (like alcohol, food or drugs) or behaviours (like sex, work or violence) lie to hand. These become "father substitutes", but of course nothing earthly can satisfy the father hunger in the human soul.

The legacy can be lasting and destructive. The saying is true: "like father, like son" – and in that I include, of course, daughters. The sins of the fathers reap a whirlwind in people's lives. All that is bad news, but the good news of this book is that the father wound, however deep and terrible, can be healed effectively and permanently. The good news is that the generational curse of poor fathering can be ended and indeed transformed into the generational blessing of good fathering. Healing can happen and does happen. We see it daily. But this healing begins with a choice – a choice to acknowledge our own pain. Not everyone has a bad dad, but far too many do today. As we conclude this chapter, I encourage you to look at your own life script, to consider carefully your own story, and to identify your own father wounds.

Father Wound Inventory

Put a X on the lines below. If your X lies nearer the wound end of these lines, then acknowledge that you have been unjustly denied a father's love in these areas. If your X lies nearer the blessing end of the spectrum, then give thanks for your father's gift to you in this area.

MY FATHER

Wound	Blessing
1. Absent in my life	Present in my life
2. Detached and disinterested	Emotionally engaged with me
3. Abandoned me	Stuck with me
4. Addicted/compulsive	Self-controlled/sober
5. A strict disciplinarian	Loving in the use of discipline
6. Critical/demanding of me	Accepting/affirming of me
7. Encouraged me to earn love	Loved me for who I was
8. Left it to others to look after me	Looked after me personally
9. Didn't keep his promises to me	Always kept his promises to me
10. Abusive/harsh with me	Kind to me
11. Shamed me	Honoured me
12. Left me a bad example as a legacy	Left me a good example as a legacy

Chapter 3

THE ORPHAN HEART

Not long ago I was invited to speak at a number of venues in Paris. After several days of hard work I had a morning off for relaxation, so my hosts asked me if there was anywhere I'd like to visit. I had never seen Notre Dame Cathedral before, so off we went to join hundreds of tourists in a slow march around what felt to us like a massive museum. I have to say I was unmoved by the place and disappointed by the lack of any real sense of the presence of God. My host clearly picked up on my frustration so asked me if there was anything else he could offer me by way of diversion. I told him that I love second-hand bookshops. His eyes immediately lit up. "There's one within walking distance of the cathedral. It's called Shakespeare and Company. Do you want to go?" There was no need to answer. He could tell by my reaction that I was more than keen, so off we went.

I can safely say that Shakespeare and Company was every second-hand bookshopper's dream. It was one of those places where there seemed to be more rooms than you anticipate. You know the kind of thing. You go up one set of stairs and enter a room full of bookcases, with books piled up everywhere you look. When you get to the last set of shelves, you find there's another room beyond, similarly overflowing with old volumes. Not only do there seem to be more rooms than you expect, there also seem to be more floors! You climb up one set of stairs, go through every room, then find that there's another set of stairs, and up you go. I could spend a whole day and possibly even a night in such a never-ending house of mystery.

I was clearly not alone in that because one of the strangest sights in the shop was the beds. In a number of the rooms there were single beds positioned next to walls where there were boards instead of bookshelves. We later learned that the owner of the shop was a man called George, noted for his hospitality. In fact, on one of the walls there was a sign with a verse from the Bible – Hebrews 13:2 – about entertaining strangers, for by so doing some people have entertained angels without knowing it. The owner's practice was to allow travellers to come and stay the night and have breakfast in return for a little help around the bookshop – two hours' work a day. And judging by all the thank-you letters all over the walls, the hospitality had really blessed those who had stayed. One letter caught my eye, written by a young man (probably a student) called Eddy. It said this:

> *I came to a bookshop and found more than ever what I was looking for. I sat on the beds. I saw the inscription: "BE NOT INHOSPITABLE TO STRANGERS LEST THEY BE ANGELS IN DISGUISE." I felt goose-pimples on my skin. I've found what I'm looking for and have never felt more welcome and at home anywhere in my life... this is one of the last true places remaining in the world.*

Other letters were more tragic. One older man wrote:

> *I came to this place as one would enter a chapel. I've spent the last hour trying to decide if I should end my life; my 21-year-old son was a victim of bipolar disease and committed suicide, by jumping off the Brooklyn Bridge. If he could have discovered your bookshop – this miracle – perhaps he would have survived.*

I was arrested by the words "chapel" and "miracle". Here, in a second-hand bookshop, I found everything that I had missed in my meandering tour of the historic cathedral. Here was the presence of God. Here was the sense of the Father's inviting love and inclusive compassion – not in the vast ecclesiastical building but in an old dusty bookshop, built on the foundations of a seventeenth-century monastery noted for its care of the poor. I was deeply moved by this place and by the vision of the enigmatic man who had nurtured its sacred ambience. And I was especially moved by the last letter we looked at, pinned to a board beside one of the beds. It simply read as follows:

Dear George, I am just a poor poet. All my life I've only known one father: you. I see you for a few weeks every couple of years. It's not much but it's all I've ever known in that department. You are everything I've ever known in that department. You are like everything I've ever heard about fathers.

I was rooted to the spot as I read this and I am not ashamed to say that my eyes filled with tears. Reading this last message was like hearing the cry of our fatherless world. It was like tuning in to the lament of our orphan generation. I don't think I have ever seen such a poignant expression of the primal wound at the very core of contemporary culture – the wound of fatherlessness.

A condition of the soul

In his book, *Fatherless America*, David Blankenhorn says:

fatherlessness is the most harmful demographic trend of this generation. It is the leading cause of declining child well-being in our society. It is also the engine driving our most urgent social problems, from crime to adolescent pregnancy to child sexual abuse to domestic violence against women.[27]

It is very hard to disagree with that conclusion. At the same time, it is not enough to point to the dire consequences of fatherlessness.

If there is to be any kind of redemption in our current situation we must understand the root as well as the fruit. What is the root of the social ills that we are witnessing all over the world, and especially in the Western world? What do we really mean by "fatherlessness"? Is it merely a social reality or something deeper than this – a condition of the soul?

I believe that the key to understanding fatherlessness is what I call "the orphan heart". I have been using this phrase for a number of years in workshops, lectures and conferences all over the world, and I haven't been in a context yet where there hasn't been at least some sense of recognition. Just a few weeks ago I was in Uganda, speaking on the subject of the orphan heart, and the audience uttered a collective sigh of relief. Many came up to me afterwards and told me that I had described not only the people that they were seeking to help on a daily basis, but also their own lives. It was as if the lights had suddenly come on. There was a palpable sense of discovery. And that was hopeful, because – as the saying goes – discovery is the route to recovery.

So what is "the orphan heart"? To understand this phrase we need to first look at the word "orphan" in the Bible. This word is used a lot, especially in the Old Testament. The Old Testament is for the most part written in Hebrew and the Hebrew word translated "orphan" is *yatam*. The word *yatam* is used forty-two times and the first of these is in Exodus 22:22. In the seventeenth-century King James Version this verse reads, "Ye shall not afflict any widow, or fatherless child". "Fatherless child" is a translation of the word *yatam*. This translation helps us to understand the meaning of the word "orphan". It refers to a son or a daughter who has lost their father. Several scholars have argued that the word "orphan" implies the loss of both parents (i.e. the mother as well), but this flies in the face of the scholarly consensus. Most scholars agree that *yatam* refers to a child who has lost his or her father, and they have added that it is very difficult to isolate even one instance in the Old Testament where the word *yatam* could refer to a child who has lost both parents. *Yatam* therefore means "fatherless", which is why we read in Psalm 109:9, "may his children be fatherless and his wife a widow". Here the word "fatherless" (*yatam*) clearly refers to the father alone. The word "orphan" accordingly means "fatherless".

So now we come to the second word in the phrase, "orphan heart". In the Bible, the word "heart" refers to more than our emotions and affections. The Bible comes out of a predominantly Hebrew culture and here the heart refers to the inner person, the centre of our personhood, the soul. The heart is the invisible core of our being while the body is the visible exterior to our lives. This means that the Bible understands the human heart in a deeper way than we tend to in the West. We tend to understand the heart in an emotional, sometimes sentimental way. But in the Bible the word "heart" refers to the deep centre from which our thoughts, motivations, feelings, words, decisions and actions derive. When I use the phrase "the orphan heart", I mean "heart" in the scriptural rather than the superficial sense.

The orphan heart is accordingly a condition caused by the loss of a father's love and which affects the very core of one's being. This primal wound affects just about everything in a person's life – from their thoughts and feelings to their words and actions. The orphan heart is therefore not a spirit that you can cast out with a prayer. It is a profound rupture in the human soul that needs healing over time. And the need for healing is urgent. The orphan heart condition is the number-one undiagnosed disease of our day. Millions of children are growing up without the love of a father and this has resulted in a generation of sad and aimless young people. Like the poor poet of Shakespeare and Company, far too many live with distressed and disintegrated centres. Their cry is the cry of the writer of Psalm 109:21–22:

> *But you, O Sovereign Lord, deal well with me for your*
> *name's sake; out of the goodness of your love, deliver me. For I*
> *am poor and needy, and my heart is wounded within me.*

The sharpest sorrow

Let's look a little more closely at the orphan heart condition. What is the nature of the wound which creates a fatherless or an orphan heart? What is it that causes this debilitating condition of the soul?

To answer this question I am going to enlist the help of perhaps the greatest preacher of nineteenth-century Great Britain. I am referring to Charles Haddon Spurgeon, a Baptist pastor who was known as "the Prince of Preachers". Spurgeon led the Metropolitan Tabernacle in London for over thirty-eight years. In its heyday it had a membership of over 10,000 and was situated in the largest church building of its era. Spurgeon not only preached; he also established the Stockwell orphanage in 1869 near the grounds of his church. He frequently visited the place, much to the joy of the children there, who always cheered when he arrived. Spurgeon's love for orphans was one of the hallmarks of his extraordinarily fruitful ministry in London. Indeed, his biographer William Fullerton remarked at the time that "the orphanage was the greatest sermon Mr. Spurgeon ever preached".[28]

> The orphan heart is not a spirit that you can cast out with a prayer. It is a profound rupture in the human soul that needs healing over time.

Spurgeon once delivered a sermon entitled, "Till He Come". It was based on Jesus' great promise in John 14:18: "I will not leave you as orphans; I will come to you." In this powerful message, Spurgeon turned his attention to the heart of the orphan. His work at Stockwell orphanage gave him profound insights into the orphan heart condition. In this sermon he memorably described the aching grief of an orphan's loss. In words that Charles Dickens would have been proud of, Spurgeon paints a picture of a father becoming sick and then dying:

The dear father, so well beloved, was suddenly smitten down with sickness; they watched him with anxiety; they nursed him with sedulous care; but he expired. The loving eye is closed in darkness for them. That active hand will no longer toil for the family. That heart and brain will no longer feel and think for them. Beneath the green grass the father sleeps, and every time the child surveys that hollowed hillock his heart swells with grief.

Then, having described this scenario, Spurgeon turns to the pain at the core of the orphan heart, describing it with almost unbearable precision:

The orphan has a sharp sorrow springing out of the death of his parent, namely, that he is left alone. He cannot now make appeals to the wisdom of the parent who could direct him. He cannot run, as once he did, when he was weary, to climb the paternal knee. He cannot lean his aching head upon the parental bosom. "Father," he may say, but no voice gives an answer.[29]

It is hard to improve on Spurgeon's eloquence. What the Prince of Preachers identified in these words is the primal wound at the root of the orphan heart condition. That wound is the "sharp sorrow" of *separation*, and specifically, *separation from a father's love*. This separation may come in different ways. In the scenario above, Spurgeon gives us two out of a number of potential causes of separation – disease and death. No doubt in the nineteenth-century urban context in which he was living, these were a constant reality.

In the twenty-first-century context the number of potential separation scenarios is much greater. As we saw in Chapter 2, a child can also be separated from his or her father's love because a father has deserted his children, or because the father is away from his children for large amounts of time (either willingly or unwillingly), or because the father is emotionally absent. A very common cause of separation in our times is divorce. When a father and a mother are separated from one another there is almost invariably a distancing of the father from his children, at the very least physically. In worst-case scenarios this separation may be one which the father actually welcomes. In other situations the father may long to be close to his children and, like Robin Williams in the award-winning movie *Mrs Doubtfire*, may go to any lengths to have greater legal access to them. Though the individual circumstances vary, one thing remains constant – the pain of being separated from a father's love. This is what lies at the root of the orphan heart, what Spurgeon called the "sharp sorrow" of being left alone.

The two kinds of breach

The primal wound that lies at the core of the orphan heart condition is accordingly separation from a father's love. I should add at this point that this rupture of relationship can occur in different ways, so it is important not to generalize. Sometimes the breach in a relationship between a father and his children can be gradual. It takes place over a period of time. This is especially true when a father is physically absent a great deal, perhaps because of his work. Then when he is physically present, he is not emotionally engaged with his children. If this goes on long enough, the children almost inevitably begin to feel a sense of detachment from their father. The father consistently sends the signal that he loves his work or his hobbies more than his children. This grows over time until there is really no relationship at all. When the children grow up to become adults the relationship may consist of nothing more than a few strained telephone calls each year, or fleeting emails. Or there may be complete silence as all communication breaks down and the relationship ends in all but name.

When a breach occurs gradually like this, it is like a tiny, invisible fault in one of the systems in a commercial aircraft. Something goes wrong with a particular part of the aircraft and over time, a miniscule fault begins to grow until it becomes a massive problem. One example among many is the fatal crash of China Airlines 611 on 25 May 2002. This Boeing 747 aircraft was on a regular route to Hong Kong when the aircraft broke up into pieces in mid air and then crashed, killing all 225 on board. The final investigation into this tragedy revealed that the accident was the result of metal fatigue that had begun after an incident in 1980 (over twenty years before). Inadequate maintenance had been carried out on some damaged skin on the tail strike after that first incident and, as a result, repeated flights had put great pressure on the weakened hull until it gradually began to crack. This led to the in-flight breakup of the aircraft twenty-five minutes after take-off in May 2002. A tiny piece of damaged skin ended up leading to a fatal crash.

Not all breaches are gradual. Some are sudden, like air disasters that happen without any warning, such as the one involving Pan Am 103. On Wednesday, 21 December 1988, a Boeing 747 carrying 259 passengers and crew blew up over the town of Lockerbie, Scotland. The tragedy was caused by a bomb that had been masterminded by a Libyan called Abdelbaset Ali Mohmed Al Megrahi. The plane was on its way to John F. Kennedy airport in New York from London Heathrow when the bomb went off in the aircraft's hold. This resulted in the plane disintegrating at 31,000 feet. Eleven inhabitants of the town of Lockerbie were killed on the ground, bringing the total number of fatalities to 270. Every house in Sherwood Crescent was destroyed by fire except that of the local Roman Catholic priest, Father Patrick Keegans.

Breaches in the father–child relationship can happen gradually over time, or they can happen very suddenly, without warning. One of the most poignant examples of the latter was the death of head teacher Philip Lawrence on 8 December 1995.

Philip Lawrence saw an incident outside his school gates and went to intervene. Seeking to help one of his students, he was stabbed in the chest by fifteen-year-old gang leader, Learco Chindamo. Chindamo's father was himself a criminal. Known as the Acid Man, he was a Mafia gangster in Italy with a grim history of violence. Philip Lawrence died later that evening in hospital. As Christmas drew near, Philip's eight-year-old son Lucien wrote a letter to Father Christmas, which was subsequently published in the newspapers. He wrote:

> *Dear Father Christmas,*
>
> *I hope you are well and not too cold. I hope you won't think that I am being a nuisance but I have changed my mind what I want for Christmas. I wanted to have a telescope but now I want to have my daddy back because without my daddy to help I will not be able to see the stars anyway. I am the only boy in the family now but I am not very big and I need my daddy to help me to stop my mummy and sisters from crying.*
> *love from*
> *Lucien Lawrence, age 8*

Sudden breaches like this are always traumatic. But even more than murder, the suicide of a father can be especially devastating because a surviving child is often left with not only confusion but also a sense of blame. When American theologian Frederick Buechner was ten years old, his father took his own life. His dad left a note to his mother: "I adore and love you, and am no good… Give Freddie my watch. Give Jamie my pearl pin. I give you all my love." He then killed himself by filling his car with carbon monoxide.

Frederick's father committed suicide on a Saturday morning when he was due to take both his sons out to watch a football game. Frederick never really got over this tragedy. Many years later he wrote a book called *The Sacred Journey* in which he wrote these telling remarks:

A child takes life as it comes because he has no other way of taking it. The world had come to an end that Saturday morning, but each time we had moved to another place, I had seen a world come to an end, and there had always been another world to replace it. When somebody you love dies, Mark Twain said, it is like when your house burns down; it isn't for years until you realize the full extent of your loss. For me it was longer than for most, if indeed I have realized it fully even yet; and in the meantime the loss came to get buried so deep in me that after a time I scarcely ever took it out to look at it at all, let alone speak of it.[30]

When fathers leave their children's lives – either suddenly or gradually – a profound sense of father loss grips the soul.

Whether sudden or gradual, the breach that occurs between a child and their father is always tragic. The pain of separation is acute, whether the trigger for that pain is a sudden crisis or a drawn-out process. A child mourns for his or her father because the longing for a loving father is the deepest need that a human being has. Everyone yearns for the protecting, guiding, self-giving, generous, involved, fun-loving and affectionate love of a good father. When fathers leave their children's lives – either suddenly or gradually – a profound sense of father loss grips the soul. An aching hunger for a father's love begins to overwhelm the person's life. Joy and peace are replaced by grief and anger as the orphan heart condition sets in. From this time on the child lives out his or her life from a fatherless centre, looking for love, direction, security, affirmation and self-worth in all the wrong places. Ultimately, only a spiritual experience will displace the negative experience of father loss, and that, as we will see later, requires the experience of receiving the love of God the Father. Only our Heavenly Father's love can fill the father-shaped void in the human soul.

> Below is the text of Lucien Lawrence's prayer that he prayed at his father's funeral, complete with spelling mistakes:
>
> *God in Heaven,*
>
> *Help us to think for a minit about the time when we all met my daddy. Help us to think of his kindness. Not only was he a headmaster but he was my daddy too. I remember the time he bort me something… Even thow it was too expensif. The time he lernt me to spell words. How gentle he was. We played football in the hallway… even when he had lots of work to do.*
>
> *Loving God, help us to pray that we will meet my daddy again.*
>
> *Amen.*

The entrance of shame

The orphan heart is a condition caused by separation, specifically separation from a father's love. But there is more to this condition than separation alone. As if this wasn't enough, in addition to separation the orphan heart often suffers a deep sense of shame. Indeed, when fathers leave by the front door, shame creeps in by the back door.

To understand how this happens we need to remember how shame works. It is now widely recognized that there is a big difference between guilt and shame. Many people tend to treat these two words as if they mean the same thing, but in reality they need to be distinguished. To put it as simply as possible, guilt is a negative feeling I experience about what I have done. Shame is a negative feeling that I experience about who I am. Guilt is about doing. Shame is about being. When a person feels guilty, they regret what they've done. When a person feels shame, they regret who they are. As the old

Only our Heavenly Father's love can fill the father-shaped void in the human soul.

71

saying goes, "Guilt says, 'I've made a mistake.' Shame says, 'I am a mistake.'"

It is vital to make this distinction because the orphan heart condition is made up of two things, separation and shame. Separation is usually something objective – an event or a chain of events in which a painful and tragic breach has opened up between a child and their father. Shame is usually something far more subjective – it is the feeling or the cluster of feelings that this breach creates in the human soul. The orphan heart condition is a combination of separation (from a father's love) and a sense of shame that this separation produces.

Why does shame enter when a father leaves? There are at least two reasons why this happens. The first is because the negative experience of separation leads a child to embrace negative beliefs about himself or herself. These negative beliefs are lies that go something like this: "If only I had been more lovely and lovable, then my father wouldn't have left me." Or, "If only I had been worth loving and worth staying for, my dad would still be here."

Negative beliefs are invariably false and toxic but in the absence of a loving father's affirmation, the child very quickly

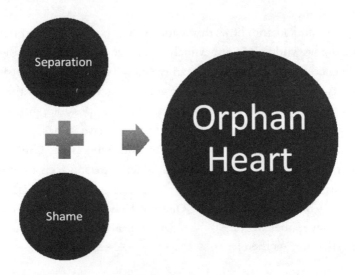

begins to believe these lies. These lies then begin to create negative expectations. These expectations are usually prefaced by the words "I will never" or "I will always". The kind of negative expectations that a person adopts can be anything from "I will always be left behind by someone I love", to "I will never be able to trust another person not to walk out on me." The trouble with these negative expectations is that they then become self-fulfilling prophecies that lead to the whole cycle beginning all over again with a negative experience. To take one scenario among many, we can picture a daughter, abandoned by her father, growing up believing the lie that she wasn't worth staying with. That child then becomes an adult and lives with the expectation that history will repeat itself in her relationship with her husband. This then creates the fertile conditions for history to repeat itself, and now she finds herself being left by her husband. Trapped in the prison of unhealed shame, the cycle begins all over again.

A second reason why shame creeps in the back door is because of the unique role of a father in the home. I have come to the conclusion that mothers can do most things – that mums are simply amazing. There is a Jewish proverb that goes something like this: "God couldn't be everywhere, so he invented mothers." Now, of course, there is a fair degree of heresy in that statement; God can, after all, be everywhere because he is omnipresent! Nonetheless, the sentiment is a good and noble one. Mothers are indeed a reflection of the nurturing, comforting, caring heart of God. A caring, selfless mother leaves a great legacy to her children and bears more than a passing likeness to the sacrificial love of God, especially the nurturing heart of God.

Having said all that, I have also come to the conclusion that there is at least one thing that a father can do which a mother cannot (at least, not to the same degree of effectiveness). A father can give honour to his children. Over 2,000 years ago the Jewish sage Jesus ben Sirah (second century BC) said this: "a person's honour comes from their father".[31] What does that mean? It means that a child derives their sense of value and significance from the words their father speaks over them. When a father says to his son, "Son, I am so proud of you. You make me smile. I am so glad you're my boy", it echoes around every chamber of the boy's soul, reinforcing a sense of security, identity, significance and masculinity that is priceless. When a father says to his daughter, "You're beautiful; you're a princess. You're a wonderful young woman and I love you", this again transmits honour to the daughter's soul and strengthens her growing sense of security, identity, significance and femininity. A father is accordingly vital in the home. He is the primary transmitter of honour in the family.

What happens when fathers become absent? The answer is not hard to find. When fathers leave the scene (for whatever reason), then children stop believing the truth about their worth and start to believe lies. Put another way, in the absence of a father's words of honour, the child begins to embrace shame. There is such power in a father's words of unconditional affirmation. There is astonishing strength in a father's words of approval, especially when that approval is based on who the child is rather than what the child does. Words are potent. As it says in Proverbs 25:11, "A word aptly spoken is like apples of gold in settings of silver." When a child is separated from their father's love, they are separated from the main source of honour in their lives. When that happens, the child begins a slow descent into the opposite of honour, which is of course shame.

The orphan heart condition is accordingly a combination of two things – separation from a father's love (an objective or external reality) and a profound, toxic shame (a subjective or internal reality). Both the wound of separation and the wound of shame need to be healed if a person is to move from the slavery of the orphan condition into the liberty of a true, new self.

Even before I was born, my mother – having been abandoned by her boyfriend – knew that she wasn't going to be able to cope with looking after my twin sister and me. Even within the womb, messages were being sent from the mother's heart to our hearts. Signals of separation were being communicated all the time. When we were born, Claire and I were separated from our mother when we were placed in an orphanage.

But this wasn't all. Through the door of separation, shame entered in. My father and mother hadn't been married, and so Claire and I were illegitimate children. The word "illegitimate" literally means "unlawful". As I became aware of this, I know there were times in my childhood when I felt that I had no right to exist: that it was in some sense or other unlawful for me to be on the earth at all.

Both of these things – separation and shame – were part of my life for many years. In fact, they controlled my life for decades. The good news is, however, that the wound of separation can be healed and the effects of shame can be removed from our hearts.

Mark Stibbe

Naked and ashamed

Before finishing this chapter, it is worth mentioning that I have sometimes had two negative reactions when speaking about "the orphan heart". The first arises from my exclusive emphasis on fathers. Some people have had good fathers but inadequate and even harmful mothers, so for them, my emphasis on the father wound can be problematic. Let me just say that although it is true that my focus is on fathers, this does not mean that it is fathers alone who wound us. Mothers can wound us too. Mothers can abuse and abandon their children willingly. Mothers can get sick and die and leave their children unwillingly. The wounds left by our mothers can be just as devastating as those left by our fathers, and so the need to forgive our mothers may be as intense as the need to forgive our fathers. While my focus is confined to fathers in this book, I am acutely aware from my counselling experience that there are people today who have deep mother wounds as well. I would encourage you to order our CD series on The Nurturing Heart of God (subtitled "The Healing of the Mother Wound"), if you want to deal with any hurts deriving from your mother.[32]

The second negative reaction I sometimes receive arises from the use of the word "orphan". Some people switch off when they hear this word. If their father is alive and they are therefore not literal orphans, they figure that the orphan heart condition is irrelevant for them. This is especially true where a person has a good relationship with their father. Whenever anyone is tempted to think that the orphan heart is not pertinent to them personally, I remind them of what I wrote in Chapter 1, that the orphan condition applies to every human being at a spiritual level. Every one of us has been implicated in the original sin of Adam and Eve. That first sin resulted in a fall into a state of spiritual fatherlessness. Sin separated us from God the Father's love. We had enjoyed intimate union with the Father in the Garden of Eden, but all that was lost and humanity fell into the orphan condition. What I am writing about here is therefore not restricted to literal orphans. It applies to every human being, because the Bible portrays us all as spiritual orphans. Until we are reconnected to the Father's love through Jesus, all of us live with an orphan heart in the spiritual sense.

All this is confirmed by a closer look at what actually occurred in the Garden of Eden at the beginning of the Bible. After creating a perfect world, the Father creates a perfect environment, the Garden of Eden. In this Garden he places Adam, whom he has formed by his own hands. Adam is unique in all creation; he is a living, speaking soul that enjoys intimate communion with his loving Heavenly Father. The Garden which he inhabits is an exceptional and exquisite home and it has two remarkable trees in it – the tree of life and the tree of knowledge. As the writer says in Genesis 2:8–9:

> *Now the Lord God had planted a garden in the east, in*
> *Eden; and there he put the man he had formed. And*
> *the Lord God made all kinds of trees grow out of the*
> *ground – trees that were pleasing to the eye and good*
> *for food. In the middle of the garden were the tree of life*
> *and the tree of the knowledge of good and evil.*

The tree of life is a tree whose fruit confers everlasting, immortal life. The tree of knowledge is a tree whose fruit confers the knowledge of good and evil. The Father specifically instructs Adam not to eat of the tree of knowledge because if he does he will surely die.

Having warned Adam, God creates Eve out of one of the ribs from Adam's side. Adam rejoices that he has a helper and that he can now become one with his companion, lover, friend and wife. For a season they live in complete

Until we are reconnected to the Father's love through Jesus, all of us live with an orphan heart in the spiritual sense.

harmony with the Father, with each other and with the created world around them. As the writer says in Genesis 2:25: "The man and his wife were both naked, and they felt no shame."

Then everything changes. A talking serpent enters the Garden. He is Satan, the adversary of God, who has been cast out of heaven for rebelling against God. Separated from God the Father's love, he has now fallen into the orphan state. In an attempt to retaliate against the Father, he heads for the Father's two children in the Garden of Eden, and tempts them to eat the fruit of the tree of knowledge. They yield to the temptation and immediately they enter the orphan condition themselves. What is the evidence for that? Remember that the orphan heart is a combination of separation and shame. This is exactly what we see in Genesis 3. The sin of Adam and Eve causes a sudden and devastating breach in their pristine, innocent and intimate communion with the Father. As we read in Genesis 3:8–9:

> *Then the man and his wife heard the sound of the Lord God as he was walking in the garden in the cool of the day, and they hid from the Lord God among the trees of the garden. But the Lord God called to the man, "Where are you?"*

Tempted into sin, Adam and Eve are now hiding from God in the Garden. Hiding, as we will see in Chapter 7, is one of the classic signs of an orphan heart. This is precisely what we see in Adam and Eve's behaviour. Their sin has separated them from their Father, who now calls out to them in the Garden, asking "Where are you?" The reply that Adam gives in Genesis 3:10 is very revealing:

> *He answered, "I heard you in the garden, and I was afraid because I was naked; so I hid."*

Not only have Adam and Eve experienced separation from their Father, they have also now begun to feel shame. Formerly they were naked and unashamed. Now, having experienced the first agonies of separation from the Father's love, they are naked and ashamed. Not only are they ashamed, they are also afraid. Fear (as we will see later) is another classic symptom of the orphan heart condition. Adam and Eve were a son and a daughter but they have now, through their own wrong choices, become orphans. They have been deceived by Satan, the original orphan, and have now fallen into the orphan state themselves.

The truth is, every single person who has ever lived (bar one, Jesus) has been born into the orphan condition. Since Adam and Eve, every human being has been separated from the Father's love and living in a state of shame. This is the human condition. We were created for sonship but we have fallen into slavery. We were created to be children but we have become orphans instead, spiritually adrift and alone in a far from perfect world. Since the fall of humanity in the Garden of Eden, we have been living as homeless orphans. As we saw in Chapter 1, the story of Genesis 1–3 ends bleakly (3:21–24):

> *The Lord God made garments of skin for Adam and his wife and clothed them. And the Lord God said, "The man has now become like one of us, knowing good and evil. He must not be allowed to reach out his hand and take also from the tree of life and eat, and live forever." So the Lord God banished him from the Garden of Eden to work the ground from which he had been taken. After he drove the man out, he placed on the east side of the Garden of Eden cherubim and a flaming sword flashing back and forth to guard the way to the tree of life.*

Why does the Father expel Adam and Eve from the Garden? Isn't this inconsistent with the Father's love? Isn't this abandonment, or even worse, rejection? The answer is no. This is in fact a loving parent's act of mercy. We must not forget that there were two trees in the Garden – not just the tree that conferred knowledge but also the tree that conferred everlasting life. Had Adam and Eve gone from eating from the fruit of the tree of knowledge and then eaten from the fruit of the tree of life, they would have been eternally fallen and therefore eternally unredeemable. They would have been forever in the orphan state. But the Father desires to rescue Adam and Eve and their descendants by sending Jesus, his only Son, to deliver them from the slavery of the orphan state into the position of daughters and sons. So they must leave the Garden and they must experience the full consequences of their disobedience until that momentous day comes when a child will be born in Bethlehem who will be the Saviour of the world. When that day comes, the curse of the orphan state will begin to be reversed at last.

Everyone's an orphan. Everyone's an orphan *spiritually*, insofar as we have all become separated from God the Father's love through our sinful choices. It is, however, also true that countless people in the world today are literal, not just spiritual, orphans. Millions of children are growing up separated from their earthly father's love, and feeling naked, vulnerable, ashamed and frightened as a result. Millions are entering into adult life like the poor poet of Shakespeare and Company, not knowing their earthly father, desperately looking for someone to stand in the place of their absent dad. This is why fatherlessness is not just a social reality; it is also a spiritual condition. We live in an orphan generation where the majority of people are now growing up with wounded, orphan hearts. The social problems that fatherlessness causes will never be alleviated until the spiritual condition is first healed. As Dr Billy Graham has always been fond of saying, "The heart of the human problem is the problem of the human heart." And the human heart is an orphan heart. Until orphan hearts are healed spiritually, the social problems of our time will never be solved. As Dr Martin Luther King once remarked, legislation can restrain the heart but it cannot transform the heart.[33] Our hearts need changing and they first need changing spiritually. Fatherlessness is a spiritual issue, not just a social issue, and we all of us need rescuing and leading to the arms of the true Father.

Chapter 4

LONGING FOR DADDY

The longing for a father is the deepest longing in the world today. All over the world children are growing up without the presence and affection of their father. In his closing speech at the 2009 Conservative Party conference in the UK, Conservative leader David Cameron spoke movingly about the death of his six-year-old son Ivan and the effect of this tragedy on his sense of perspective. He publicly stated that he now knew there were more important things in life than politics, referring to his love as a father for Ivan and for his other children. He then went on to add that he was saddened by the fact that so many children in the UK today are growing up without the love of a father.[34]

The truth is, every child needs a father's love. The God who created us all is known by the name "Father" and he has placed within each and every one of us the need for a father's love, both in a spiritual and a literal sense. We are created to know the embrace of our Heavenly Father and we are created to know the embrace of our earthly father. As long as we do not know this paternal, affectionate and reassuring love, we are incomplete, insecure human beings. We live with a profound father-shaped void in our hearts. When we miss out on a father's love, or when we lose a father's love, there is a sense of aching emptiness within the soul that can last an entire lifetime.

I am forty-nine now. I never knew my natural father. That is a source of great sadness to me. But I did know and love my adoptive father, Philip Stibbe. He died in 1997. It has been over thirteen years but I still miss him. I miss sitting down at the family meal table and hearing him chuckle. I miss going for walks with him and benefiting from his years of experience and wisdom. I miss going into the great outdoors with him, fishing for trout in Scottish lochs and English rivers. I miss his letters, with their words of affirmation and gentle offerings of advice. I miss my father's love.

And I am not alone. More and more people are giving public voice to their sense of father-loss. Recently a newspaper ran an article entitled "My Father Was an Anonymous Sperm Donor", written by an eighteen-year-old girl named Katrina Clark whose mother was artificially inseminated. Katrina described how she was angry for many years about the fact that she did not know even minor details about her father:

> *I was angry at the idea that where donor conception is concerned, everyone focuses on the "parents" – the adults who can make choices about their own lives. The recipient gets sympathy for wanting to have a child. The donor gets a guarantee of anonymity and absolution from any responsibility for the offspring of his "donation". As long as these adults are happy, then donor conception is a success, right?*

Katrina answers this question with a simple "no". She says that when she was young she would

> *daydream about a tall, lean man picking me up and swinging me around in the front yard, a manly man melting at a touch from his little girl. I wouldn't have minded if he weren't around all the time, as long as I could have the sweet moments of reuniting with his strong arms and hearty laugh. My daydreams always ended abruptly; I knew I would never have a dad.[35]*

The cultural lie

Human beings need the love of
a father. It is a fundamental fact
about the human condition. Yet
while the majority of people know
and accept this, many of us live in
countries where the cultural elite
have sold us the lie that fathers are

> We are created to know the
> embrace of our Heavenly Father
> and we are created to know the
> embrace of our earthly father.

now non-essential, like disposable plastic razors. In fact, during
the course of the twentieth century there has been a campaign in
Western culture to present fathers as peripheral or even redundant
figures in the home. This is a lie and yet it has been dogmatically
promoted as if it is the truth. Over the last fifty years in particular,
there has been a social marketing strategy to devalue the idea of
fatherhood, and this campaign has directly fuelled a mistrust of
fatherhood. It has also led to countries like the United States and
the United Kingdom becoming un-fathered societies. In my view,
this campaign is demonic and derives ultimately from the Orphan
Maker, Satan, who is the father of lies (John 8:44).

How has this lie been effectively sold to so many people?
David Blankenhorn's book *Fatherless America* gives us some helpful
insights. He spends much of his book exploring the way in which
the American cultural elite has worked hard to foster the view that
fathers are no longer essential to a child's healthy development. He
argues that US culture has time and again promoted seven images
of fatherhood, all of which are highly destructive to fathering. He
talks about these seven types of father as characters in the stories
that are pervasively narrated. These characters appear in the "texts"
of American culture – scholarly books and journals, popular non-
fiction books and magazines, children's books, movies and TV
shows, professional conferences, political hearings, national family
and children's commissions, national newspaper commentaries
and interviews with professionals.

These seven characters do not all receive equal attention.

The first three – the Unnecessary Father, the Old Father and the New Father – are in fact major or leading characters, while the remaining four – the Deadbeat Father, the Visiting Father, the Sperm Father and the Stepdad/Nearby Guy Father – are really minor characters.

Let's have a look at Blankenhorn's seven images of fatherhood that re-occur in America's cultural narrative.

The Unnecessary Father

Over the last fifty years in particular, there has been a social marketing strategy to devalue the idea of fatherhood and this campaign has directly fuelled a mistrust of fatherhood.

The primary story in American culture is one which assumes that fathers are superfluous. It is now regarded as morally unquestionable for a woman to choose to have a child on her own, without the involvement of a father. It is widely assumed that single mothers can bring a child up just as effectively as a married mother. The Unnecessary Father therefore plays a lead role in the contemporary cultural script. He is regarded as non-essential. When actress and film star Michelle Pfeiffer decided to raise a child on her own, she stated, "I don't want some guy in my life forever who's going to be driving me nuts."[36] What lay behind her comments was a strong and unyielding belief in the cultural lie that fathers are now entirely unnecessary for bringing up a child.

The Old Father

The Old Father is the old-fashioned or traditional father. He is ultimately the hunter-gatherer of the ancient plains. More recently, he is the father of the 1950s in America, always busy as the breadwinner but often emotionally distant from his family.

This father became a part-time influence on his children and his wife's primary role was that of housekeeper.

This post-war father was a commuter-dad. He was physically absent and emotionally unavailable. He funded his family but kept his distance. At his worst, he became an abuser of power within the home. Instead of loving his wife and children with tenderness and intimacy, he acted as if he was a tyrant and engaged in control and manipulation. This Old Father then often became an abuser of his wife and his children. He was the Big Daddy of Tennessee Williams' *Cat on a Hot Tin Roof*. He was a male predator when he was called to be a loving father.

The Old Father succeeded in pouring paraffin on the fire of the feminist critique of fatherhood. Many feminists, having suffered from the controlling and abusive behaviour of a destructive and overbearing father, proceeded to argue that we should do away with the words "mother" and "father" altogether and use new terms, such as "child-bearer" and "child-rearer", "sperm donor" and "gestator". This feminist critique has been in many ways understandable. Daughters who have been the victims of male selfishness and aggression have justifiably railed against their abusive and shaming fathers. Thanks to their critique, our culture rightly demonizes the extreme version of the Old Father, but it makes a great and fatal error in assuming that this abuse of fatherhood means that fatherhood itself is now outmoded. Just because some fathers have oppressed their wives and their children does not mean that all fathers behave this way. Nor does it mean that fatherhood itself is now irrelevant.

The New Father

The New Father is the opposite of the Old Father. The New Father is a friend to his children. He is nurturing. He expresses vulnerability. He is not ashamed of his emotions and wears his heart on his sleeve. He is truly a man in touch with his feminine side. He is deeply involved. He is a companion and colleague to his wife. He gets up at all hours of the night to change the diapers (nappies) and he shares the family responsibilities equally. He is a cultural hero because he has relinquished the power and control of the Old Father and has embraced half the work of raising a child from the time of that child's birth. The New Father is the cultural ideal.

So what's wrong with this story? This kind of father is surely every child's dream – certainly every mother's dream. While there are positive aspects to the New Father, Blankenhorn also argues that this story is ultimately destructive to fatherhood. In fact, he proposes that the New Father ironically contributes to fatherlessness. How can this be so? The reason is because the story of the New Father is one in which fathers are so indistinguishable from mothers that the concept of fatherhood is effectively emasculated. This New Father is really a "like-a-mother father" – so like a mother, in fact, that he is no longer a father in any meaningful sense. The New Father creates an androgynous image of fatherhood. In that respect he is a mixed blessing. While the tenderness of the New Father is an essential quality of authentic fathering, it is wrong to treat paternity and maternity as synonymous. Insisting that men become more like women is not the answer to fatherlessness. As American psychiatrist Frank Pitman has said, "Fathering is the most masculine thing a man can do."[37]

In the final scene of the movie *Mrs Doubtfire*, Robin Williams (dressed as Mrs Doubtfire) is hosting a new TV show for children. She is asked a question by a girl whose parents have separated. This is her reply (a reply that says so much about contemporary culture):

"You know, some parents, when they're angry, they get along much better when they don't live together. They don't fight all the time and they can become better people. And much

better mummies and daddies to you. Just because they [your parents] don't love each other any more doesn't mean they don't love you. There are all sorts of different families, Katie... And some live in separate homes and separate neighbourhoods in different areas of the country. They may not see each other for days, weeks, months or even years at a time. But if there's love, dear, those are the ties that bind. And you'll have a family in your heart forever. All my love to you, poppet. You're going to be all right."

The Deadbeat Dad

The Deadbeat Dad is the dad who is never there, who refuses to pay for his children's upkeep, and who is often in prison. He is a villain in the cultural script. He is an ex-father and a failed father who crops up frequently in our cultural stories. He contributes massively towards fatherlessness because he does not care for his children on a regular, daily basis.

The Visiting Father

The Visiting Father is the father who no longer lives with his children. He is most often the divorced husband who tries to keep in contact with his children by visiting them when the courts allow. He visits but he doesn't stay. He is a weekend dad or a holiday dad. He is a telephoning or texting dad. He is a father once removed.

The Visiting Father is not a villain in the way the Deadbeat Dad is. He tries hard. He visits. He keeps up the payments. He remembers birthdays. But he cannot raise his children. He can only call round.

In spite of his best efforts, the Visiting Father contributes towards fatherlessness. This is because, from a child's perspective, "visiting" and "fathering" cannot be the same thing. It is the unity of the home and the intimacy of daily contact that a child needs. When a husband and wife divorce, the husband often ends up divorcing his children as well. Visiting Fathers are disempowered fathers. A father is one who lives with his children. His authority in the home derives from his presence as loving protector and caretaker. When he is reduced to the role of visitor his status as father is changed and undermined. The Western nation's readiness to settle for divorce – or what has come to be called "better divorce" – has created the story of the Visiting Father, who ironically undermines fatherhood even in the act of trying to be a good father.

The Sperm Father

The Sperm Father completes his fatherhood prior to the birth of his child. For him fathering is simply a matter of spreading his seed, nothing more. He doesn't know his child. His child doesn't know him. He is the originator of his child but he is also a contributor to the story of fatherlessness. This Sperm Father is becoming increasingly a bigger actor – more of a major than a minor character – in our public discourse. At the time of writing *Fatherless America* Blankenhorn could call this father a minor character, an understudy to the three leading star roles – the Unnecessary, Old and New Fathers. But with the advances in IVF, the Sperm Father is attracting more prominence.

The Stepfather and the Nearby Guy

The Stepfather and the Nearby Guy are both similar to each other yet different. They are similar in that both are substitute fathers; they fill in for the biological fathers of the children they care for. Biology plays no part in their fatherhood. But they are also different. The Stepfather is married to the mother so lives with the children, but they are not his children. His commitment goes deeper than that of the Nearby Guy. The Nearby Guy does not live with the children, but they regard him as a father figure. The Nearby Guy can be a family friend, a neighbour, a teacher, a Scout leader, and so on. He is any adult male who is prepared to take a fatherly interest in a fatherless child.

Both kinds of father fill the fatherhood vacuum created by the absence of the Deadbeat, Visiting and Sperm Fathers. They are replacement dads. They fill the vacuum functionally (through what they do), but they cannot ultimately fill this vacuum relationally (through who they are). They offer a simulation of fatherhood because neither can claim to be the biological father of the children for whom they have assumed responsibility. They are biologically and legally unrelated to the child.

Why do kids need dads?

David Blankenhorn's book has had a huge impact in North America and has generated a great amount of debate.[38] The seven fathers that he has identified in America's cultural narrative are very clearly drawn and backed up by an impressive amount of academic and anecdotal evidence. His claim that the intellectual elite of America have effectively committed cultural patricide has been well argued and his assessment of the tragic social consequences of this patricide is undeniably accurate. He has shown that there is a direct cause-and-effect relationship between fatherlessness and youth crime, domestic violence, child sexual abuse, child poverty, educational failure, economic insecurity, and teenage pregnancy. It is quite simply a non-negotiable fact that every child needs the love of their father if they are going to grow into stable, confident contributors to society.

> It is quite simply a non-negotiable fact that every child needs the love of their father if they are going to grow into stable, confident contributors to society.

Why are fathers so important in child-rearing? We should

never underestimate the power of a father's unconditional love towards his children. As someone has said, "The love of a father is one of nature's great masterpieces." Actually, the love of a father is more than nature's masterpiece. It is something deeply supernatural or spiritual. The love of an earthly father is a reflection of the love of our Heavenly Father. God is supremely Father. He is the world's greatest Father – the Father we have all been waiting for. When men act as loving fathers they reflect the very core of the divine love, the Father's love.

Why is it then that kids need dads? Let me briefly offer ten reasons why I personally believe fathers are not disposable but rather essential to a child's life – whether that child is three, thirteen, or thirty. Some of the qualities that I am about to describe can also be said of mothers. But the following are particularly true of good fathers.

What does a good dad do?

A good dad values fatherhood

Someone once made the wise and telling remark that "No man on his deathbed ever wished that he had spent more time at the office." Most men, looking back on their lives, wish they had invested more in their relationships – in particular their relationships with their wife and with their children.

A good dad is someone who gives supreme importance to being a father. He is someone who does not sacrifice his wife and children on the altar of his work or other interests. Rather, he places fatherhood right at the top of his priorities and puts his family first. The great film star, singer and dancer Fred Astaire made this memorable and very powerful comment: "Being a father is the best thing that ever happened to me in my life. It kind of makes any success I have on the stage or screen very unimportant by comparison."

A good dad displays affection

A good dad also engages in natural displays of his affection for his children. C. S. Lewis used to talk about the four loves in ancient Greek writing. *Agape* is the Greek word for sacrificial love. *Phileia* is the Greek word for demonstrated natural affection. *Eros* is the word for sexual love. *Storge* is the word for nurturing, tender love. A good dad displays *phileia* love for his children. He demonstrates his affection for them in hugs and kisses. Again, whether they are three, thirteen or thirty, a good dad will always want to show tender, intimate, and holy affection.

Isobel Field, stepdaughter of Robert Louis Stevenson, once said this: "My dear father! When I remember him, it is always with his arms open wide to love and comfort me."[39]

Good dads are not afraid to tell their children that they love them. They are not ashamed of showing their emotions and revealing their affection. They are free to embrace their children.

A good dad gets involved

A good dad is quite simply involved with his children. He plays a full part in bringing up his children, helping his wife in the privilege and the challenge of rearing his children. A good dad is physically and emotionally present to his children, spending time with them and talking with them. When a dad gives his time and attention to his child, it is immensely powerful for that child's sense of well-being and worth. From a child's point of view this is never time wasted. As Hilda Bigelow (an American school teacher) once tellingly remarked: "My heart is happy, my mind is free; I had a father who talked with me."[40]

A good dad gets involved with every part of his children's lives, especially their education and leisure time. Good dads read and study with their children. Good dads love to play with their children. In the rough and tumble of a father's play there is a great release of joy.

A good dad provides security

A good dad makes his children feel secure. Of course this refers to material security – a good dad provides for his children materially. This is still an important part of fathering, even if mothers are today just as likely to be the breadwinners as the fathers. The provision of material security remains a vital aspect of genuine fatherhood. But even more important than this is emotional security. Good dads give a sense of safety and assurance to their children's hearts. Raniero Cantalamessa has written:

> *If a child is certain that his father loves him, he will grow up sure of himself and able to face life. A child out walking holding his father's hand or being swung around by his father with shouts of joy or talking to his father as man to man is the happiest and freest creature in the world.[41]*

I remember one time travelling back from America on a Jumbo Jet. I was sitting next to my son Johnathan who at that time was about seven years old. The journey was marred by the worst turbulence I have ever experienced on an aircraft. Winds of up to 230 miles an hour were raging behind the tail-plane, propelling the aircraft to speeds of over 800 miles an hour. Flight attendants were strapped into their seats. Passengers were crying as the aircraft was being shaken like a tiny twig in a great gale. But while all this was happening my son slept through the entire course of the storm, with his head resting on my shoulder. In his young mind, there was simply nothing to fear. He experienced peace in the storm because he was absolutely sure of his safety while he was in the sheltering care of his dad.

No wonder Sigmund Freud once wrote, "I cannot think of any need in childhood as strong as the need for a father's protection."

Charles Francis Adams, the nineteenth-century political figure and diplomat, kept a diary. One day he wrote: "Went fishing with my son today – a day wasted."

His son, Brook Adams, also kept a diary, which is still in existence. On that same day, Brook Adams made this entry: "Went fishing with my father – the most wonderful day of my life."

A good dad sets an example

Italian novelist Umberto Eco wrote: "I believe that what we become depends on what our fathers teach us at odd moments, when they aren't trying to teach us."[42]

Good dads model healthy and virtuous values to their children. These values, as Eco's statement reveals, are more caught than taught. They are picked up in the informal settings of everyday life rather than the formal context of a lesson.

Good dads model how to put God first in their lives. They set an example in prayer. They model what it is to have a healthy spiritual life, passionately pursuing the Father's purpose for their own lives and, indeed, the lives of every member of their family. Good dads are men of prayer. This is something that General Douglas MacArthur clearly believed and practised. He movingly remarked: "It is my hope that my son, when I am gone, will remember me not from the battlefield but in the home repeating with him our simple daily prayer, 'Our Father who art in Heaven.'"[43]

Good dads set an example in their relationship with God. They also set an example in their relationship with their marriage partner. The Bible says in Ephesians 5:25: "Husbands, love your wives, just as Christ loved the church and gave himself up for her." Jesus gave up his life for his bride, the church, on the Cross. Good dads set an example to their children in the way they selflessly love their wives. Good dads set an example in all areas of life.

Mario Cumo said this: "I talk and talk and talk, and I haven't taught people in 50 years what my father taught by example in one week."[44]

A good dad gives affirmation

I have already written about this in Chapter 3 but there is, I believe, a unique power in a father's gift of honour to his children. When a father praises his son verbally and sincerely, it has an immense impact on a boy's soul, especially when it is not based on the son's performance but simply on his position as a son. It greatly strengthens him in his identity and masculinity. As Jim Valvano beautifully put it, "My father gave me the greatest gift anyone can give to another person, he believed in me."[45]

Good dads know the power of praise. When a father praises his daughter openly and genuinely, it has a great impact on her soul too. As the novelist John Gregory Brown once said, "There's something like a line of gold thread running through a man's words when he talks to his daughter."[46]

Unconditional love, expressed in the love language of affirmation, has immense power in the building of a child's stability, self-worth, security and significance. A good dad is a child's best cheer-leader and their primary encourager. Laurie Beth Jones once confessed, "My father was always there for me when I lost. But then, I never really lost when my father was there."[47] Good dads praise their children frequently and give them the blessing of honour.

A good dad shares wisdom

A good dad is a good listener. He listens to his children when they ask him the questions that are burning on their hearts. When asked, he offers his children the wisdom that he has acquired over years. This wisdom is not the wisdom of someone who has never made mistakes but rather the wisdom of one who knows what it is to be fragile and falter and yet who has also soared above failure to the high place of redemption. This is not the transient and so often flawed wisdom of the world but rather the timeless and perfect wisdom of God.

In this respect, good dads share godly advice from the Word of God. They store up the treasures of the Bible in their own hearts and then place these treasures in the hands of their children when the children most need them. This is why the Bible itself makes such a big point of reminding fathers in particular to teach the Word of God to their children on a regular basis (Deuteronomy 6:4–9; Proverbs 4). As the Apostle Paul says in Ephesians 6:4: "Fathers, do not exasperate your children; instead, bring them up in the training and instruction of the Lord." Good fathers revere the Bible and bring its eternal wisdom to their family. As one child said to their dad, "The word 'Bible' stands for 'Basic Instructions Before Leaving Earth'."

A good dad establishes boundaries

Good dads set reasonable boundaries for their children and are prepared to exercise loving discipline when their children transgress them. In this respect, good dads are like our Heavenly Father. In the Bible, God the Father has given us clear guidelines about how to live our lives. If we stay within these boundaries, then we remain within the place wherein his love can reach us. If we ignore or cross these boundaries, then we can expect his loving discipline. These boundaries do not exist for our punishment but for our protection. If we stay within them, we will live life more abundantly. If we reject the Father's laws and choose to live by the moral relativism of the world, we will find not only that we suffer from the consequences, but our relationships will suffer too.

Boundaries are accordingly a vital part of bringing up a child, especially today when children and teenagers are often surrounded by peer groups that have few boundaries. God our Heavenly Father disciplines those whom he loves. Good dads must sometimes discipline their children when necessary as well. As the writer to the Hebrews puts it (12:9–10):

> *We have all had human fathers who disciplined us and we respected them for it. How much more should we submit to the Father of our spirits and live! Our fathers disciplined us for a little while as they thought best; but God disciplines us for our good, that we may share in his holiness.*

The important thing to remember is always this, that good dads exercise discipline with compassionate love, not with uncontrolled anger and aggression.

Paul Dwight Moody, son of the great evangelist D. L. Moody, told how his dad reflected the love of the Heavenly Father in the matter of discipline. The incident took place when Paul was only ten. His dad had instructed him to finish talking to a friend and go to bed. But Paul wrote:

A little later he came into the room again and saw that I had not obeyed him. Speaking with that directness of which he was capable, he ordered me at once to bed. His brusque tone of voice was new to me, and I retreated, frightened and in tears. But before I had time to fall asleep, he was at my bedside. He explained that he had reprimanded me because I had disobeyed him, but this in no way indicated that he didn't love me. As he knelt to pray with me, I noticed that tears were falling down over his rugged, bearded face... I'll never forget the scene. My father had unknowingly awakened within me the consciousness of the love of God.[48]

A good dad releases hope

The actress Liza Minnelli once said, "My mother gave me my drive, but my father gave me my dreams."[49] A good dad enables his sons and daughters to identify their gifts. He then helps to empower them to use their gifts so as to fulfil their true potential.

A good father will not only work towards this great goal. He will also be regularly in prayer asking the perfect Father to enable his children to fulfil the God-given purpose for their lives. Good dads pray on a very regular basis for their children, not just interceding for them in their own personal, devotional lives, but also praying for them in their presence when asked and releasing their blessing to them. As Jacob says in Genesis 49:26, "Your father's blessings are greater than the blessings of the ancient mountains, than the bounty of the age-old hills."

One of the best examples of this kind of prayer is in Luke's Gospel. In the first chapter, Zechariah prays the most wonderful blessing over his son, John (who will grow up to be the forerunner of Jesus the Messiah). This is what Zechariah says in Luke 1:76–79:

> *And you, my child, will be called a prophet of the Most*
> *High;*
> *for you will go on before the Lord to prepare the way for*
> *him,*
> *to give his people the knowledge of salvation*
> *through the forgiveness of their sins,*
> *because of the tender mercy of our God,*
> *by which the rising sun will come to us from heaven*
> *to shine on those living in darkness*
> *and in the shadow of death,*
> *to guide our feet into the path of peace.*

Good dads do not force their children to live out a dream that they themselves desire. Nor do they coerce their children into fulfilling some ambition that they themselves failed to achieve.

Good dads watch prayerfully over their sons and daughters to see what God has planned for their lives. They constantly encourage their children to seize their unique destinies and do everything within their power to facilitate the creative outworking of that divine purpose. In this respect they release hope to their children, reassuring them that there is a plan and a purpose for their lives and that they will complete the assignment for which they were put upon this earth.

The Apostle Paul says, "Fathers, do not provoke your children, lest they become discouraged" (Ephesians 6:4). Paul says this because he knows that fathers are meant to promote, not provoke, their children. They are to be encouragers, not discouragers. They are, more than anyone, dealers in hope.

A good dad leaves a legacy

Finally, good dads exert a godly and positive influence that goes beyond their own children to their children's children. This is why the Jewish Talmud says that "when you teach your son, you teach your son's son". The impact of a good father can be generational.

You don't have to be wealthy to leave your sons and daughters a legacy that is truly rich. As Ruth Renkel has rightly pointed out, "Sometimes the poorest man leaves his children the richest inheritance."[50] Good dads have a lasting effect not only on their own children but also on their grandchildren and beyond.

The cry of the fathers

Good dads are in short supply today. Pope John Paul XXIII once said, "It is easier for a father to have children than for children to have a real father."[51] Reading the list above, it may feel as if becoming a good dad is impossible. As a father of four children, I have to be honest and say that I don't measure up in the ten characteristics I have just mentioned. Being a good father requires selfless, *agape* love and the problem is that I am fundamentally a selfish person. Most people are. However, I do know this: children are very forgiving and so is our Heavenly Father, from whom true fatherhood is derived.

There aren't enough good dads today. In addition, one of the greatest tragedies is that so many good dads who are divorced are denied proper access to their children. The family law courts in the United Kingdom make it very hard for good dads to father their children effectively, especially when they award custody of the children to the mother. When Bob Geldof produced his very moving TV documentary on this issue in October 2004 he reported that there were at that time 15,000 custody cases a year in the family courts and that 93 per cent of them ended up with the children living with their mother. In these scenarios the father almost invariably becomes what Geldof called "A Sunday Dad", a weekend-only visitor. Geldof was so incensed by this that he described it as "state-sanctioned kidnapping".[52]

Geldof's own story is that he was married to Paula Yates. The couple had three daughters – Fifi, Peaches and Pixie. When Paula fell in love with Michael Hutchence, the lead singer of the band INXS, she left her husband. She and Michael had a daughter and in that same year, she divorced Bob. When this happened, Bob lost custody of his three daughters. He fought through the courts to get them back and eventually succeeded. He wrote a famous thirty-page reflection on this journey which he called "The Real Love that Dares not Speak its Name: A Sometimes Coherent Rant". The title came from a comment made to Bob by a well-meaning court clerk who told Bob, on his way into court, "Whatever you do, don't say you love your children." When Bob asked why, the clerk told him that the courts regard it as extreme if a man articulates his love for his child.[53]

Geldof maintains that a father can love his children just as much as a mother and yet nine times out of ten there is insufficient access to the children given to the father after court cases. Good dads are not allowed to see their children except at some weekends. Geldof eloquently described this as "love in a measured fragment of state-permitted time". In his documentary he speaks about "children stripped of their fathers, and fathers stripped of their children".

Some of these fathers are interviewed in the documentary and are shown weeping on camera as they describe their torment at not being able to see their children as much as they want to. The documentary (still available on the internet under the title *Geldof on Fathers*) is almost too poignant to watch. In it Geldof courageously rounded on the family courts for their secrecy and injustice, condemning them for the fact that four out of ten fathers lose contact with their children forever. He described their work as "state-sponsored child abuse". Their injustices left fathers feeling utterly worthless. They ignored the completely unequivocal evidence that children who have further contact and involvement from their fathers do much better at school and in life generally.

Geldof's documentary lifted the lid not only on a defunct and abject family legal system but also on the hordes of weeping fathers and traumatized, fatherless children in the UK. Today we are much more aware of the cry of these good dads because of organizations like Families Need Fathers and Fathers 4 Justice. But Geldof's lament was important at the time because it gave a voice to dads who barely had one. Many of them didn't even go to court to try to fight for their children because they knew that the law was tilted against men and that it had created an environment in which mothers could become adept at manipulating the system. So they had simply given up. Geldof argued for a much fairer and more just approach, on the basis that it is in the best interests of the children to be allowed to continue their relationship with both parents. Unless circumstances indicated otherwise, Geldof advocated a 50:50 division of time between both parents.

Geldof speaks passionately and with integrity on this issue. Not only did he fight for the custody of his three daughters after Paula divorced him. He also adopted the daughter of Paula Yates and Michael Hutchence after Hutchence hanged himself in a hotel room in 1997. His death left Paula Yates devastated. Several years later she was found dead in what appeared to be an accidental drug overdose. Four-year-old Tiger Lilly became an orphan but Bob applied for and won temporary custody of her. From that time on Tiger Lilly lived with Geldof's three other daughters. She was formally adopted into the Geldof family in 2000 (though she has kept her surname).

> We have far too many children growing up without the love of a father and far too many fathers not allowed to express their love for their children.

Bob Geldof brilliantly articulates the real love that dares not speak its name, the love of a father for his children. The truth is this: the picture in countries like the United Kingdom is deeply disturbing. We have far too many children growing up without the love of a father (as David Cameron pointed out in September 2009), and far too many fathers not allowed to express their love for their children (as Bob Geldof pointed out in October 2004). The United Kingdom is a fatherless country in a fatherless world. This truly is the orphan generation. The wounds go very deep indeed – both the wounds of the fatherless and the wounds of the fathers. Where will our help come from?

PART 2

THE SCARS

Chapter 5

CALLING GOD "FATHER"

When I was a little boy I would often go into the bathroom while my adoptive father was shaving. He used to shave without his shirt on and I would stand nearby watching him methodically remove the stubble from his face. I would also stare at his back at a mark behind one of his shoulders. This was the scar of a bullet that had been fired at him while he was fighting behind enemy lines during World War II. It had passed through his chest, a centimetre away from his heart, and come out the other side of his body. I used to look with fascination at this wound of war and try to imagine what it must be like to be shot in action.

So far in this book I have tried to show that we are a world at war. There is an arch-enemy at work in the cosmos trying to spoil and destroy what the perfect Father created. At the beginning of time he rebelled against *Abba*, Father and became the original orphan. He fell from heaven into the orphan state and immediately sought revenge against God by tempting Adam and Eve to enter the orphan state too. This they did and since that time he has been conducting an intensive campaign all over the planet to make orphans wherever he can. When Matt O'Connor wrote *Fathers 4 Justice* he started by saying, "in the time it takes you to read this book at least 100 children will have lost contact with their father".[1] He added that today's children are "the first fatherless generation, the lost generation".[2] Millions of people all over this planet have experienced the trauma of fatherlessness. Many carry the scars. They manifest symptoms and signs of hurts experienced years before. The enemy specializes in fatherlessness.

He has wounded countless souls. Truly there is a war on, and the battle is against fatherhood.

Why has the enemy been so hard at work creating fatherlessness? The reason is because he wants to make it as difficult as possible for people to call God "Father". If he can succeed in making the very idea of fatherhood something negative, then he will have gone a long way towards making it next to impossible for a person to have an intimate friendship with the world's greatest Dad. People who have been wounded by their fathers end up finding it very hard indeed to know God as Father. At best they relate to Jesus, but they fail to enjoy what Jesus came to achieve, which is an eternal communion with their divine Dad. This stands to reason. If you have been let down by your father, then there will be a lasting mistrust of fathers within your heart. If you then commit your life to Jesus, you will find it easier to relate to the second person of the Trinity (the Son) than to the first (the Father). You will always have a worry that if you entrust yourself to your Heavenly Father, history will repeat itself and he will walk out on you as well. Our work at the Father's House Trust has revealed that a huge number of Christians feel this way. The *scars* of the father wound are severe indeed.

My story is this: for ten years after my conversion I knew Jesus but I didn't know the Father. My own biological father walked out on me before I was born. The use of the word "Father" in connection with God was not helpful to me. It led me to see God as a dad who would one day abandon me like my father had.

This is the primary spiritual consequence of our father wounds. Countless Christians still have pain in their lives caused by a father. Consequently they know the Son but not the Father. They love Jesus and have a Jesus-centred spirituality, but they don't know God as *Abba*, as Daddy, as Papa.

Mark Stibbe

One of the few writers to discern this is John Eldredge. In his latest book, *Fathered by God*, he has described the effect of the father wound on boys. Like me, he regards the separation of boys from their fathers as one of the devil's main schemes today. In fact, he regards it as the main plan that the enemy has. This is what he says:

> *This is the enemy's one central purpose – to separate us from the Father. He uses neglect to whisper, "You see – no one cares. You're not worth caring about." He uses a sudden loss of innocence to whisper, "This is a dangerous world, and you are alone. You've been abandoned"... And in this way he makes it nearly impossible for us to know what Jesus knew, makes it so very, very hard to come to the Father's heart towards us.[3]*

Eldredge has given eloquent expression to the very heart of the enemy's plan. He has also brilliantly described the number-one cause of the crisis in masculinity in countries like the USA. But this strategy is not just confined to boys; it is also targeting girls. It is not just restricted to the USA; it is rampant all over the earth. There is not a country that I visit where fatherlessness is not an issue. On every continent throughout the world, the enemy has been driving fathers and children apart. Though the scenarios are diverse, we now have to wake up to the fact that there is a global pandemic of fatherlessness. Even though human beings have to bear the responsibility for this, it is ultimately a demonic master plan that has been behind this social tragedy. Many nations are now reaping the whirlwind of decades of collusion with this strategy, and the fruit from this is not just social disintegration but also spiritual disease. This spiritual disease is evident everywhere. In a moment we will see the fruit of this among Christians. But the fruit of this is also in the lives of unbelievers.

The anger of the atheist

One of the most telling signs of our times is the rise of the militant unbeliever. Of course there is a sense in which agnostics and atheists have been with us for over 200 years, at least since the dawning of the so-called Age of Reason or Enlightenment. But in the last decade there has been a noticeable and marked increase in vocal and aggressive atheism. The angry atheist is on the rise. In fact, our generation has seen the emergence of the anti-theist. If an atheist is someone who doesn't believe in God, an anti-theist is someone who actively believes against God. Such anti-theists are becoming more and more vocal in contemporary, Western culture.

Why have we witnessed the advent of the angry anti-theist? Although there are many answers to this question, one of the main reasons is because of fatherlessness. Most anti-theists have experienced great pain in their relationships with their fathers, or with father figures in their lives. Their anger against God is really anger against their father. In unleashing their wrath against the God whom they deny exists, they are in fact giving voice to a gut-level resentment against their absent or abusive dads. In most cases, when you hear about the pain they have experienced at the hands of their dads, you can understand why.

> **In the last decade there has been a noticeable and marked increase in vocal and aggressive atheism.**

I remember when I first realized this. I was doing some research for a presentation with my friend, G. P. Taylor, the best-selling Christian novelist. Graham and I were planning an evening responding to the first movie version of the *Dark Materials* trilogy by Philip Pullman. The three novels written by Pullman are fantasy stories written primarily for children, and they are brilliantly written too. Pullman, who lives in Oxford, is an atheist. In fact, he is an anti-theist. He sees it as his mission to be the opposite of C. S. Lewis (who was also based in Oxford when he wrote the Narnia Chronicles). In fact, Pullman's narrative world is a kind of anti-Narnia. It is a world designed to destroy the very notion of God. His theme is the destruction of the church and the overthrow of God. As Pullman has famously remarked, "I'm of the devil's party."[4] Elsewhere he has said, "I'm trying to undermine the basis for Christian belief."[5]

Why is Pullman so angry? Pullman claims that his anger derives from history, from the record of the church's wrongs against others (from the Spanish Inquisition to the burning of Catholics by Protestants). But is this really the reason? Here Pullman's past is as instructive as his prose. Tragically, his father died when he was seven years old. Pullman was deeply hurt by his father's death, as is clear from the following statement: "Naturally I was preoccupied for a long time by the mystery of what he must have been like."[6] On another occasion he remarked, "I'd love to meet him."[7] It is impossible not to feel sympathy for Pullman.

I believe the real reason for Pullman's anti-theism is not so much the obvious blemishes in church history but rather the painful wounds in his personal history. If you read Pullman's works, you will see that time and again he chooses to have fatherless children as his main characters. These orphans are everywhere. On the one hand they are present in his stories for literary reasons. If children don't have parents, then they are much freer to engage in the kind of adventures that a children's fantasy writer wants to describe. This tactic is older than Charles Dickens! On the other hand, these orphan protagonists give Pullman an opportunity to articulate his own father wound. Listen to how he describes Will's sense of father loss at the end of *The Amber Spyglass*:

> *He longed for his father as a lost child yearns for home. It had been five years now since that Saturday morning in the supermarket when the pretend game of hiding from the enemies became desperately real, such a long time in his life, and his heart craved to hear the words, "Well done, well done, my child, no one on earth could*

have done better; I'm proud of you. Come and rest now…" [8]

Could Pullman have been so hauntingly precise had he himself not lost his father when he was only seven years old?

I believe Pullman's angry anti-theism has less to do with the occasional abuse of power in church history than it has to do with the loss of his father in his own history. In other words, I am convinced that his anger against God has psychological roots. I am also convinced that even though fatherlessness is not the only reason for atheism, it plays a very much more significant part than has been recognized. As we will see here in Part 2 of this book, anger and rebellion are classic signs of the orphan heart condition. [9]

The faith of the fatherless

Shortly after the presentation on Philip Pullman, I went out for a coffee with my friend Jo Gill, a member of the church that I was then leading. Jo is a sharp thinker and a writer. She had done a PhD on the father figure in twentieth-century French politics. Over coffee, she and I began to talk about the relationship between fatherlessness and atheism. She pointed me in the direction of a book I hadn't heard of by Paul Vitz called T*he Faith of the Fatherless*. [10] I subsequently bought a copy and it confirmed everything I had concluded about the atheist's rage against God.

Paul Vitz argues that atheism of the strong or intense type is mainly driven by the psychological needs of its advocates. As a result of careful study of the leading atheists of the twentieth century, Vitz spotted what this psychological need was. It was the need for a father, caused by the loss of their own father. This, Vitz argued, is the coherent psychological explanation for atheism.

Vitz cleverly plays the atheists at their own game here. We need to remember that it was atheists like Sigmund Freud who argued that believers are fulfilling a psychological need when they put their trust in God. That need is the need for a father. Desperate for closeness to a father, believers embrace the supreme fiction of the fatherhood of God. When people choose to believe in God, they are in fact projecting their need of a father onto God.

Vitz does two things here. He first of all exposes the fallacy of this argument. If Freud's reasoning was right, then pre-Christian and indeed non-Christian religions would paint a picture of God as a loving Father. But this is exactly what we do not find. As we will see in a moment, it is only Christianity that prioritizes the name "Father" in relation to God. So Freud's projection theory is seriously flawed. Secondly, Vitz brilliantly points out that the atheist's use of psychology is in fact a double-edged sword. It can far more effectively be used against the atheists themselves. In fact, Vitz concludes that it is really the atheists who are guilty of projection. Having lost their relationship with their earthly father, they now rage against the divine Father. With angry atheism, the personal becomes political.

What Vitz is saying is that the main barriers that prevent an atheist from believing in God are not rational – they are psychological and emotional. It is here Vitz proposes a projection theory of atheism. He advances what he calls "the defective father hypothesis".[11] He argues that it is an atheist's grief and anger over their own father that lead them unconsciously to reject God.

Vitz brings many cases to show the compelling nature of his thesis. You will need to read the book to go through them all. I will just mention the one whom Vitz calls the world's most famous atheist, Friedrich Nietzsche (1844–1900). Nietzsche himself hinted at the psychological roots of atheism when he confessed, "I have no knowledge of atheism as an outcome of reasoning." For him it was "obvious by instinct".[12] But where did this instinct come from? Vitz says it came from Nietzsche's agony at losing his father. His biographers make clear that Nietzsche was closely attached to his father. Friedrich's father, Pastor Ludwig Nietzsche, died on 30 July 1849 after a long illness, aged thirty-six, when Nietzsche was two month's shy of his fifth birthday. Nietzsche later wrote about the moment of his father's death:

> *When I woke up that morning I heard weeping all round me. My dear mother came in tearfully, wailing "Oh God! My dear Ludwig is dead!" Young and innocent though I still was, I had some idea of what death meant. Transfixed by the idea of being separated forever from my beloved father, I wept bitterly. The ensuing days were taken up with weeping and with preparations for the funeral. Oh God! I had become an orphan and my mother a widow!*[13]

It is hard not to be moved by this account of the sharp sorrow Friedrich felt at being separated forever from his father's love. For Nietzsche, this was the wellspring for his later arguments for the death of God. Later on in his life, Nietzsche would remember his father's sickness, describing his father as delicate and morbid, and as lacking in "life force". He would then also say of Christianity that as a religion it lacked "life force" and that "God is dead". As Vitz demonstrates, Nietzsche's attack on Christianity was a projection of his weak, sick and finally dead father onto God. Nietzsche's atheism was a reflection of his orphan heart and the result of a catastrophic father wound.

The Father heart of God

There are many scars that come from the loss of a father's love but the most serious of all is the inability to relate to God as Father. This is, as we have just seen, one of the roots of atheism and especially anti-theism. This is a deeply tragic result because the core message of Jesus was that God is the strongest and most loving of all fathers. As Raniero Cantalamessa, preacher to the Papal household, puts it:

Every preacher has a special topic close to his heart, which he never gets tired of talking about and through which his ability is best expressed. Jesus has the "Father"! When Jesus talks of the Father, the eyes of the disciples open wide… But the Father is more than just a "topic" for Jesus, he is his "Abba", his Father, he who gave him his glory and his name "before the world existed"; he to whom he is infinitely attracted, even as a man.[14]

There are many scars that come from the loss of the fathers love but the most serious of all is the inability to relate to God as Father.

We could go to many places in the four Gospels of Matthew, Mark, Luke and John to prove the point. But perhaps the most helpful place to start (because it's arguably the best known) is the prayer that Jesus taught his disciples, commonly referred to as the Lord's Prayer. In Matthew's version the stage for the teaching of this prayer is set in verses 5–8 of chapter 6:

And when you pray, do not be like the hypocrites, for they love to pray standing in the synagogues and on the street corners to be seen by men. I tell you the truth, they have received their reward in full. But when you pray, go into your room, close the door and pray to your Father, who is unseen. Then your Father, who sees what is done in secret, will reward you. And when you pray, do not keep on babbling like pagans, for they think they will be heard because of their many words. Do not be like them, for your Father knows what you need before you ask him.

What is immediately striking from this scene-setting is the picture Jesus paints of prayer. For Jesus, prayer is about relationship much more than it is about requests. Prayer is not primarily the presentation of a list of petitions to God. God already knows what we need because he is all-knowing. Prayer is much deeper and more joyful than this. Prayer is a child's communication with their Father in heaven. It involves finding a "secret place" where you can close the door and be alone with the Father. It is not the public, ostentatious display of religious hypocrites. It is the private, authentic expression of a child's heart. It is not the endless babbling of those who use many words without emotion. It is the heart's cry of those who have only a few words but great passion. For Jesus of Nazareth, praying meant going to a place where he would be undisturbed and pouring out his heart to the world's greatest Father. Prayer is intimate connection with a holy, loving Father.

After describing *where* to pray, Jesus now turns to *how* to pray, and shares the most famous of all prayers in Matthew 6:9–13:

> *This, then, is how you should pray:*
> *"Our Father in heaven,*
> *hallowed be your name,*
> *your kingdom come,*
> *your will be done*
> *on earth as it is in heaven.*
> *Give us today our daily bread.*
> *Forgive us our debts,*
> *as we also have forgiven our debtors.*
> *And lead us not into temptation,*
> *but deliver us from the evil one."*

The most important thing to notice about this prayer is how it begins. Before anything else, Jesus encourages his apprentices, his disciples, to address God as their Heavenly Father. Before they can pray "your kingdom come", they have to pray, "Our Father". Before they can become those who will bring the kingdom, the rule, of God to the earth, they must be those who know God as their Father. Before they can use the authority and the power of the kingdom (in preaching and the ministry of healing, for example), they must be firmly rooted and grounded in the Father's love. The greatest priority of all is to know God as Father and call him Father in authentic, relational prayer. There is no higher priority than this. Even the great message of the kingdom of God must step aside for this greater truth. God is our Father in heaven and we must learn, before anything else, to love and adore him as the world's greatest Dad. Only then can we seek first the kingdom of God and his righteousness (Matthew 6:33). Only when Jesus' Father has become our Father can we legitimately and, indeed, safely petition for the invasion of heaven's rule here on the earth.

A Father like no other

The statement, "Our Father in heaven" presents us with possibly the four most important words ever spoken. With this brief opening address, Jesus opens up a whole new landscape. A whole new vista of revelation is brought into view. No longer is God the remote deity of so many religions, the distant Creator who demands submission. He is now the loving Father of Jesus of Nazareth who invites us into his everlasting arms of love. In these four words a whole new God-image lies before us like the most majestic portrait ever painted. God is our Father. He is our Papa. He is our Daddy. And he loves us dearly.

> The statement "Our Father in Heaven" presents us with possibly the four most important words ever spoken.

Three things need to be said if we are to plumb the depths of this great and surprising truth. The first is that Jesus portrays God as an *intimate* Father. Jesus of Nazareth spoke primarily in Aramaic. The Aramaic word that he would have used in the first words of the Lord's Prayer is the word *Abba*. I don't know anyone in the world who knows more about the Middle Eastern context of Jesus' teaching than my friend Kenneth Bailey. Ken is the Emeritus Research Professor of Middle Eastern New Testament Studies in Jerusalem at the Tantur Ecumenical Institute. He spent forty years living and teaching the New Testament in Egypt, Lebanon, Jerusalem and Cyprus. He has written many books in Arabic and in English and is most famous for the books he's published about the Parable of the Prodigal Son in Luke chapter 15 (a parable which he rightly points out is much more to do with a father than with a son).[15] His comments on the word *Abba* reflect the most up-to-date and insightful commentary on this word on the lips of Jesus.

Ken Bailey points out in his latest book, *Jesus through Middle Eastern Eyes*, that the word *Abba* is still used today.[16] In at least four countries in the Middle East, *Abba* is in fact the first word that a child will learn. It is a word that can be translated "Father", understood in an intimate and respectful sense. In some cultures the word "Father" may come across as too formal. *Abba* may therefore best be translated as "Daddy" or "Papa". If a child falls over in a street in Israel and hurts his knee, he is likely to cry out one of two things: *"Abba!"*, which means "Daddy!", or *"Imma!"*, which means "Mummy!" *Abba* denotes a close and very personal relationship, as does *Imma*.

The use of the word *Abba* in the opening statement of the Lord's Prayer is critical and indeed radical. It would have surprised the disciples in at least two ways. First of all, it would have surprised them that Jesus chose to speak in Aramaic. He did not choose the sacred prayer language of the religious, pious people of his day. That language was Hebrew. He used everyday Aramaic. This in itself tells you a great deal. It signifies that Jesus saw prayer as an everyday act of communication. Secondly, Jesus chose to use the Aramaic word *Abba* in addressing God. While it is true that the Old Testament uses the Hebrew word for "Father" in relation to God, it does so infrequently. And while "Our Father" appears in the famous Jewish prayer of Jesus' day (the Tefillah), it is only used twice and it is rendered in the Hebrew language (*Abinu*). What Jesus was doing was distinctive and unusual even if it wasn't absolutely without precedent in Judaism. He was teaching the disciples to address the God who created the universe as their *Abba*, Father, their Daddy-God, and their Heavenly Papa. As William Barclay once wrote, Jesus is teaching his disciples that "we come to God with the simple trust and confidence with which a little child comes to a father whom he knows and loves and trusts."[17] That was a new departure for Jesus' apprentices.

In the eighteenth century, a man by the name of John Harwood attempted to paraphrase the first line of the Lord's Prayer. This was the result of his efforts:

> *O Thou great governor and parent of universal nature*
> *– who manifestest thy glory to the blessed inhabitants of*
> *heaven – may all thy rational creatures in all the parts*
> *of thy boundless dominion be happy in the knowledge*
> *of thy existence and providence, and celebrate thy*
> *perfections in a manner most worthy by nature and*
> *perfective of their own.*[18]

I don't think it's possible to imagine a less appropriate reflection of what Jesus was trying to convey! Harwood has succeeded in doing the very opposite of everything Jesus intended. He has turned the simple and affectionate word *Abba* into the verbose and ostentatious "babbling" that Jesus was criticizing. Harwood has turned a loving Father into a distant monarch who has to be addressed with elaborate language. He has failed to see that *Abba* points to an *intimate* Father.

Secondly, *Abba* points to an *inclusive* Father. The Aramaic word *Abba* can be translated "The Father", "My Father" or "Our Father". Scholars are agreed that the opening of the Lord's Prayer should be translated as "Our Father". The disciples of Jesus are encouraged to enter into a deeply personal and intimate relationship with their Heavenly Father. But they are also urged to remember that God is Father to all who put their trust in his Son, Jesus. Whatever a person's nationality or background, they can enter an affectionate relationship with *Abba*, Father if they choose to love and honour God's Son. The word *Abba* therefore has an inclusive sense to it. It is emphatically "Our Father" that we come to in prayer. This Father is a Dad who believes in embrace, not exclusion. His love is for everyone. His invitation is for all people. He wants the spiritual orphans of this earth, whether Jew or Gentile, to come to a place where they can cry out to God, "You are our *Abba*-Father!" As Kenneth Slack beautifully puts it, "none of us can approach the Heavenly Father as an only child."[19]

Thirdly, *Abba* points to an *infinite* Father. Jesus qualifies the word *Abba* with the words "in heaven". This Father is a Heavenly Father. He is not an earthly father. In fact, earthly fathers fall far short of this Heavenly Father. We are not to make this Father in the image of our fathers. He is far greater. He is in fact perfect. He is majestic. He is omnipotent. Our Father is the King of Kings and the King of Kings is our Father. The word *Abba* therefore does not just denote relationship. It also denotes respect. The Father that we come to in prayer is no imperfect, earth-bound daddy. He is the everlasting Father who reigns on the throne of heaven. Like the Aslan the Lion in C. S. Lewis' Narnia stories, he is not just affectionate like a kitten – he is powerful like a thunderstorm.

What does it mean that our Father is in heaven?

It means that there's no one bigger than our Dad – our Dad rules

He flung stars into speckled space
He fashioned the blazing sun and deep lagoons of cloud and cluster
He created the planets, the constellations, and the galaxies
He conceived the Milky Way, the Helix Nebula, and the Pleiades
He made bubbles and arcs, nebulae and auras
He paints supernovas in effervescent colours
And stellar jets of iridescent glory
He out-thinks the physicist
And he dazzles the theologian
He preoccupies the astronomer
And inspires the poet with abundant wonder
He is beyond the reach of the Hubble telescope
Or the probing range of any Orbiter
He is what Einstein called "the Superior Reasoning Power"
And the Bible calls "the Father of Heavenly Lights"
He is my Dad, and he is your Dad
Our Dad, who is in Heaven, the Third Heaven,
Who dwells in unapproachable light
And who will one day make his home with us, on this tiny dot that is Earth

Mark Stibbe

Respect and relationship

It is really important to keep this note of respect when speaking of the *Abba*-Father revelation. We are not to domesticate God into a sentimental Daddy figure, robbed of all his royal glory. The truth is this: the God who is revealed by Jesus is both transcendent and immanent; he is both far away and close at hand. Moreover, he combines the two qualities that all good fathers must have – authority and affection. He has authority in his capacity as the High King of Heaven. He has affection in that he is the very epitome of what a loving father should be. We must therefore approach this Father with reverence as well as love. He deserves our respect because he is the radiant King of glory who is seated upon his eternal royal throne. He deserves our love because he has first loved us. And what love he has shown! In Jesus, this Father has demonstrated and bestowed the love of all loves.

When we think of the Father heart of God we must try to keep these two things in balance – affection and authority. Too much emphasis on his loving affection may cause us to fall into compromise. We may start believing the lie that if he is such a gracious Dad, then we can do what we like. But that is a grave error of judgment – one that will surely end in tears. Likewise, too much emphasis on his royal authority may cause us to fall into fear. We may end up thinking that God is like some of the toxic authority figures that have abused us in our lives. This also is a great lie and will almost always lead us into religious servitude. There is a delicate balance to get right here. The key is to be like Jesus, sure of the Father's affectionate love, and submitted trustingly to his authority. As Bill Hybels puts it:

> *Not only did Jesus live in constant awareness of the Father's affection for Him, but He lived under the Father's authority. Jesus wasn't worried about the*

The key is to be like Jesus, sure of the Father's affectionate love, and submitted trustingly to his authority.

Father's authority being destructive or manipulative or negative. You see, when you are absolutely convinced of the Father's affection for you, you have no fear whatsoever of the Father's authority.[20]

One of the passages of the Bible that best speaks to this theme is Psalm 62:11–12. Here King David has a revelation of both these aspects of God's character and expresses this insight in the simplest of ways. He exclaims, "one thing God has spoken, two things have I heard: that you, O God, are strong; that you, O Lord, are loving." Strong and loving – those are the words to think of. *Abba*, Father is truly a loving Dad. He is the most caring of fathers, who is always there for us, who never abandons us, who will always keep his promises and loves to show us his affection. But *Abba*, Father is also a strong Dad. He is omnipotent and all-knowing; his voice is powerful and majestic, striking with flashes of lightning and shaking the desert (Psalm 29). He is both loving and strong. Anything less and we limit him.

One of the pictures I find most helpful when thinking of this is a photograph of American President John F. Kennedy in the Oval Office in the White House, sitting at the Resolute Desk. At the time of this photograph he is the most powerful man in the world. People have to make an appointment to see him and they have to go through guards, secret-service checks and various secretaries to get near him. Yet at his feet there is a small boy.

Who is this boy? It is the President's young son, John Junior. I love this photograph for many reasons, but most of all for the fact that JFK's son feels completely safe to play at his father's feet. John Junior knows that his dad is the most important man in the world but he plays happily in his presence because he is absolutely sure of two things: that John F. Kennedy is his father and that he is his son. John Junior knew that his dad was strong, full of authority and powerful because he was the President. But he also knew that the President was affectionate, tender and safe because he was his dad.

It is important for us to remember both the authority and the affection of God when we relate to *Abba*, Father. We need a "both-and" picture of God – both King and Father. But the revelation of the Fatherhood of God needs to come first. Once we know that we are dearly loved by our Father, we can without fear submit to him as our King. As a lady called Helen exclaimed in one of our conference meetings, "I'm a Princess and my Daddy is the King of Kings!" The entire audience burst into cheering and applause when they heard Helen say this. Only the week before

Helen had tried to commit suicide and was well known for her depressed and desperate state of mind. But at the conference she encountered the Father's love and was taken on a journey from shame to honour. Her suicidal depression was healed and she was able to relate to God as her Daddy for the first time. Not only that, but she was able to submit to her Father's royal authority and to acknowledge him as her King. I have seen her several times over the last few years since her healing and she has grown in the joy of this revelation of who God really is, and who she really is too. Now she cannot do enough for the Father because she has seen how greatly she is loved.

A fatherless faith

But here's the point. Helen was a Christian. At the time of her healing, she was a church member. Yet she was sitting broken-hearted in the pews. She was a believer, but she was bound. She had been forgiven when she put her trust in Christ, but she was not free. She was so hooked into her past hurts that she could not walk joyfully into her future destiny. She was empty in the Father's house. She knew God existed, but for her he was a far-away deity whose love had to be earned. Weighed down by the heavy burdens of her broken, orphan heart, she knew Jesus but not *Abba*, Father. And the sad fact is that Helen is the rule, not the exception. In the church today, many Christians find it difficult to enjoy a sense of security and identity in the Father's love. Having been wounded by their earthly fathers, they find it hard to acknowledge that God is Father, Daddy, Dad or Papa.

These are the scars of the orphan heart, of being separated from a father's love. For the unbeliever, this primal wound more often than not leads to a great rage against the very idea of a divine being, especially one described as "Father". For believers, the spiritual consequences of the father wound can be equally damaging. For them the scar of the orphan heart will often be revealed in that person's inability to relate to God intimately as *Abba*, Father. They will invariably leave the Father out of the equation and relate only to Jesus. If they hear any reference to God as Daddy or Dad they will experience immediate discomfort. The spiritual scars run deep. While atheists embrace the faith of the fatherless, wounded believers embrace a fatherless faith.

Why does this happen? The simple answer is because of *projection*. Those who have been poorly fathered often transfer the face of their earthly father onto the face of their Heavenly Father. They hear that God is Father but their experience of pain at the hands of their earthly father means that the true Father's face is obscured by their pain. Regina Barecca put it very honestly when she wrote:

> *Drummed into me from an early age was the fact that God was "Father", which led to my thinking of God as somebody home only at the weekends. Thinking about God as a Father also meant thinking of him as a distant sort, one who wasn't to be disturbed because he was busy – one who was concerned with rules and punishments, and one having a short temper.*[21]

There are many ways in which projection can happen. Some of these story arcs can be seen in the box headed "Classic Projection Scenarios". One of the commonest today has to do with *disappointment*. The fact is, countless young people are growing up today with fathers that are absent. Many of these absent fathers accentuate the sense of separation by making promises that they then fail to keep. They promise to be there for their children, but they are not. They promise to take their children out for a day, but they do not. They promise to bail their children out when they get into trouble, but they do not. They promise their love, but they do not love their children. Promises are often made but equally often broken, and the wound of disappointment in the child's soul runs very deep indeed.

What happens to a child who grows up in this atmosphere of dashed hopes and dreams? They become mistrustful and profoundly sad. They grow into adults who long for someone to be there for them, and yet at the same time are profoundly suspicious of anyone's reliability. The heart's cry of these young adults is, "Will there ever be anyone who is truly there for me? Is there anyone who will really stay around and fulfil their promises?"

The orphan generation that is emerging today is a broken-hearted generation. So many young people have had fathers who have let them down, who have broken promises, who have failed and forsaken them. What happens when such a person becomes a Christian? Does this scar stay or go? It may often stay. Becoming a Christian doesn't mean that all your wounds are instantly healed. It means embarking on a lifelong journey of healing. For a person who has been badly disappointed by their father, a process of inner healing will be needed if they are to see God as a loving, covenant-keeping Father rather than as a divine promise-breaker. Becoming a Christian is the beginning of the healing journey, not the end of it. A person who has become a Christian will be forgiven but not necessarily free. The church has a responsibility to help the walking wounded to come to a place where they can truly call God "Daddy".

Classic Projection Scenarios

Desertion

If you have been abandoned by your father, it will be all too easy to embrace a toxic belief that your Heavenly Father will abandon you too, so you relate to Jesus but not to *Abba*, Father.

Disease

If you have seen your father deteriorate and become weak and unable to love you, then this may also affect your image of God the Father, especially his omnipotence (his all-powerful nature).

Detachment

If your father was detached emotionally, you may find that you lack intimacy with God because you have projected onto him the picture of your earthly father's lack of demonstrated affection for you.

Death

If your father died when you were young, this may well affect your image of God the Father. The root of much recent atheism lies in the unresolved grief and rage over the loss of a father.

Distance

If your dad was always away from home, maybe on important business, you may have a picture of God the Father as always distant, doing something more important than you.

Divorce

If your dad left you because of divorce, so that you were brought up by your mother alone, you may have a father-shaped void that leads you to appreciate the maternal but not the paternal aspects of God.

Disappointment

If your dad made promises to you that he never fulfilled – like promising to give you a gift, or promising to be at an event – you may develop a view that God the Father cannot be trusted.

Daring to call him "Daddy"

I was recently lecturing on the Fatherhood of God to a class of thirty students. I asked them how they found calling God "Daddy". Their replies were interesting. There was a noticeable split between the boys and the girls. The boys preferred the word "Father" or "Dad" because they felt that "Daddy" robbed God of some of his strength. The girls, on the other hand, preferred the word "Daddy" because they felt that the word "Father" and even "Dad" robbed God of his intimacy. There were some other interesting reactions too. Some found the word "Daddy" a non-starter because it reminded them of posh, upper-class English people who call their fathers "Daddy" even when they have grown up and left home. Others found the word "Father" a non-starter because it denoted nothing more than a biological figure in their lives. One young woman from America said she felt that neither "Father" nor "Daddy" were the best words; she preferred "Papa". Many tilted towards the word "Dad" because it somehow represented a middle ground between security (implied by the word "Daddy") and strength (implied by the word "Father"). A few said that "Daddy" was acceptable when you are a very new Christian but that "Father" is a better word for when you have become a more mature believer. What was abundantly clear from the whole exercise was the emotive nature of the word "Daddy". Everyone had a reaction to it! A few absolutely loved the idea of calling God "Daddy". Many found it made them feel deeply uncomfortable.

When my researcher Catriona Reid took a poll of how the students referred to God in their personal prayer life, the results were revealing:

- *Abba* (4)
- Father (9)
- Papa (3)

- Father God (1)
- *Abba* Papa (1)
- Daddy (3)
- God (4)
- Lord (1)
- Dad (2)
- Friend (1)
- Daddy God (1)

Clearly, there was a great uncertainty and even discomfort about calling God "Daddy". Some of this discomfort derives from the fact that there isn't one English word that could be usefully deployed to translate *Abba*. But the most telling reason why it was all so uncomfortable was because at least some of the class had been poorly fathered. The father wound in the students radically influenced the exercise.

People carry deep scars today. These are the scars caused by the global pandemic of fatherlessness. For the unbeliever, the scar of the orphan heart is often evident in the angry denial of the very existence of a divine Father. For the believer, it is often revealed in their inability to relate to God as their *Abba*, Father and to enjoy true intimacy with God. The believer knows Jesus as their best friend, their Saviour and their Lord, but they do not know God as their *Abba*, Father, their Daddy, their Dad, their Papa.

Although these scars are very visible and very common among Christians, this is no reason for the church to give up hope. While no one should underestimate what it takes to heal the orphan heart, there is great cause for encouragement. There are many Christians who have been impacted by the revelation of the Father's love and who have opened their hearts for healing. That healing process has brought about lasting transformation and turned slaves into sons, orphans into heirs. The key in every case has been a process in which the negative experience of an absent earthly father has been displaced by the positive experience of the love of our *Abba*, Father in heaven. We will look in more detail at what that experience actually entails, but for now – in the remainder of Part 2 – we need to continue to look at the scars of the orphan heart condition. We need to address the symptoms and the signs that provide the telling evidence that someone has been separated from their father's love. It is to that task we now turn.

When I was little, my *abba* was Ronald Reagan. He was my Daddy. That was the only name I had for him. For eight years during the 1980s, almost everyone else in the world was required to call him "Mr President" – but not me. If I called him on the phone, I called him dad. Being a son gives you an intimacy with your father that the rest of the world can't have. To me, Ronald Reagan was always my *abba*.

Michael Reagan,
adopted son of US President, Ronald Reagan

Chapter 6

SYMPTOMS OF PAIN

Charles Dickens' *A Christmas Carol* is the greatest Christmas story in English literature. A large reason for its continuing success and abiding popularity is Dickens' brilliant portrayal of the miserly old man, Ebenezer Scrooge. Scrooge absolutely detests Christmas with all the bitterness he can muster, crying "Bah! Humbug!" in response to his clerk Bob Cratchit's Christmas greetings. He hates the idea of charitable giving and festive merrymaking. He is angry, greedy, lonely, sad, mistrustful and self-absorbed. Like the Grinch, he hates Christmas.

We all know the story, not least because of all the film adaptations (the best of which is still, in my view, *A Muppet's Christmas Carol,* starring Michael Caine as Scrooge). Scrooge is visited first of all by the ghost of his old business partner, Jacob Marley, who warns Scrooge to mend his ways. He also tells Scrooge that three ghosts are about to visit him. The first to arrive is the ghost of Christmas past.

One year ago I re-read this part of the story as I prepared for a December at church based around *A Christmas Carol.* It was while reading the events involving the ghost of Christmas past that I began to see something that I had never noticed before – something from Scrooge's past that explained so much about his controlling, manipulative and hateful behaviour.

The first ghost appears in the form of an old man who looks like a child. The spectre announces himself as the ghost of Christmas past and leads Scrooge to various places and scenes from his childhood, youth and young adult life. The most telling of these is Scrooge's boarding school. Before they arrive at it, the ghost tells Scrooge, "the school is not quite deserted". He adds, "a solitary child, neglected by his friends, is left there still." Dickens reports, in his typically terse way, "Scrooge said he knew it. And he sobbed."[22]

With this, the ghost takes Scrooge to a large brick mansion that had seen better days. This is Scrooge's school where he had been sent away to be educated. His mother has died and his father, strict and cruel, has simply abandoned him to the schoolteachers. The storyteller then describes the scene in vivid and heart-breaking prose:

> *They went, the Ghost and Scrooge, across the hall, to*
> *a door at the back of the house. It opened before them,*
> *and disclosed a long, bare, melancholy room, made*
> *barer still by lines of plain deal forms and desks. At one*
> *of these a lonely boy was reading near a feeble fire; and*
> *Scrooge sat down upon a form, and wept to see his poor*
> *forgotten self as he used to be.*[23]

Why is Scrooge so desperately alone? The explanation comes next as the ghost shows Scrooge a scene from a later Christmas. The school is now more run down but one thing remains the same. Scrooge is all alone as the Christmas holidays begin. All his friends have gone home. He is once again left behind. But this time something changes. The boy's sister enters, telling him that she has come to bring him home. She repeats the word, "home, home, home". She adds:

> *Home, for good and all. Home, for ever and ever.*
> *Father is so much kinder than he used to be, that home's*
> *like Heaven! He spoke so gently to me one dear night*
> *when I was going to bed, that I was not afraid to ask*
> *him once more if you might come home; and he said*
> *Yes, you should; and sent me in a coach to bring you.*[24]

"Father is so much kinder than he used to be." What a revealing line!

Why did Scrooge become Scrooge? That is a question we should ask when reading *A Christmas Carol*. What makes a person turn into such a sad and angry man? The answer is in these scenes from Scrooge's childhood. Scrooge is an abandoned child. He has an absent father and a dead mother. He stays at the boarding school during the Christmas holidays when everyone else goes home. His father has for many years been an unkind and cruel man whose children are fearful of him. Separated from a father's love, ashamed and alone, Scrooge becomes the man he later is because he has an orphan heart. In many ways, the young Ebenezer is yet another one of Dickens' orphans.

But all is not lost. Scrooge is visited by three spirits and he has an awakening. By the end of the story, this fatherless man has had a spiritual transformation and becomes a father figure to the handicapped child, Tiny Tim. As a result of what we can only call a series of supernatural interventions, Scrooge chooses to change from being a wicked and hurtful man to being a good man. Look at how the storyteller describes him right at the end of the tale:

> *He became as good a friend, as good a master, and as good a man, as the good old city knew, or any other good old city, town, or borough, in the good old world. Some people laughed to see the alteration in him, but he let them laugh, and little heeded them; for he was wise enough to know that nothing ever happened on this globe, for good, at which some people did not have their fill of laughter in the outset; and knowing that such as these would be blind anyway, he thought it quite as well that they should wrinkle up their eyes in grins, as have the malady in less attractive forms. His own heart laughed: and that was quite enough for him.*[25]

On 16 September 1968, on my eighth birthday, I went to my first boarding school. I remember to this day (over forty years later) the feeling of indescribable pain I felt as my adoptive father and mother left me in the hall of an old country house in the presence of a headmaster of whom I was instinctively scared – and later, justifiably so. I remember him standing next to me as my father and mother got into our family car and started to make their way out of the driveway of the grounds. My trunk containing my possessions, clothes and school equipment lay beside me on the ground. It felt like this was all I had left as I waved to my parents. I fought back the tears. I so wanted to cry but I also didn't want to show the headmaster any weakness. All I can remember was the feeling of utter abandonment. I knew in my head that my parents were doing what was best and right for me, but in my heart I felt desperately alone. Having been abandoned as a baby, this felt like another similar rupture. To this day I recall the smell of the heavy oak hallway and stairs in that old mansion. Whenever I detect that smell again the memories come rushing back to me and I am right back in that school, remembering the pain of being separated from home and feeling left behind. And I know I'm not alone in this; there are thousands and thousands of grown men and women today just like me, still feeling the wound of the breach in the relationship with their parents from their boarding-school days.

Mark Stibbe

The wound and its scars

I have begun this chapter with a reflection on Ebenezer Scrooge because he furnishes us with a helpful example of how easy it is to become preoccupied with a person's outward behaviour and to neglect the real issue of their inner pain. Most of us, if we are honest, tend to focus on the outward appearances of a person, whether their behaviour or their looks. Scrooge's faults are very much on view from the start of *A Christmas Carol*. He is angry, rude, self-preoccupied, greedy, controlling, mistrustful, lonely and sad. All these and many more adjectives could be used to describe him. But in many respects these are not the most important things about Scrooge, though in some ways Dickens makes them the most memorable. The most important thing about Scrooge is why he behaves in this way. What is the engine driving these observable weaknesses?

The answer to that question lies in the boarding school episode briefly touched on by the ghost of Christmas past. From this cameo we see that Scrooge was separated from his father's love and left alone at school. He was denied the security and familiarity of "home", a vital word in a child's heart. He was not allowed to enjoy the Christmas holidays with his family, and a great resentment towards Christmas was born in his soul as a result. Scrooge's childhood provides the clue. Abandoned and ashamed, the tragic circumstances that create the orphan heart were established in his life. This orphan heart becomes the warp-core of Scrooge's later weaknesses. His manipulative and materialistic character in later life was his way of protecting his own heart from acknowledging the primal wound of abandonment. Although this in no way excuses his actions as a grown man (for Scrooge chooses to become this way), it does begin to explain them as we seek to ask the question, "What made Scrooge become Scrooge?"

The lesson we learn from all of this is the importance of being able to discern the vital clues which indicate that a person suffers from an orphan heart. It is particularly important that people in the church become adept at this. If the world is to be healed of its father wounds, then Christians need to be healed of them first.

> If the world is to be healed of its father wounds, then Christians need to be healed of them first.

As the influential church leader Bill Hybels is fond of saying, "the local church is the hope for the world". Yes it is. The local church really is the hope for a fatherless world because it carries the premier message and ministry of God the Father's love. But the church can only fulfil its destiny to rescue this orphan generation if Christians recognize and deal with their own father wounds. How can fatherless Christians be good news to the great swathes of fatherless people outside the churches? The simple answer is, they cannot. Those of us who are Christians need to attend to our own wounds first. We need to heed Jesus' words, "Physician, heal yourself!" (Luke 4:23).

It is for this reason it is so vital that we are wise and observant when it comes to the scars of the orphan heart condition. These scars are the clues that someone has a father wound – or, as in Scrooge's case, both father and mother wounds. Christian pastors and counsellors need to be especially discerning in this area. They need to be able to spot the tell-tale clues that a person is wounded and needs help and healing. If the church is to be the main vehicle of *Abba*, Father's healing in this fatherless world, then we need to get our own house in order first. We need to help those with orphan hearts to admit that they are exhibiting the classic symptoms and signs of this condition and to become receptive to the healing power of *Abba*, Father. Only then will the church fulfil its destiny to be the hope for the world. Only when we have learned to receive the Father's love and healing will we be able to give it away to the broken-hearted ones who surround us every day.

"I'm fine, thank you."

The problem, however, is that Christians cover up really well. In other words, we aren't always as honest, open, real and vulnerable as we should be. We wear masks. We disguise our frailties. In an attempt to look good, and to make others think well of us, we develop strategies for concealing our true, wounded selves. In English culture, when someone at church asks us how we are doing, we give the conventional reply, "I'm fine, thank you." Our whole world may be falling apart, our emotions may be imploding, but we reply, "I'm fine," sometimes adding, "praise the Lord!" This is our default way of living. Like Adam and Eve in the garden, we hide. We paper over the cracks in our souls. We present outwardly as if we have got it all together while internally we are fragmented people. Thus we busily create a culture where – to use Tom Harris' famous phrase – "I'm OK, you're OK", and all the while we do this, we have little to offer a hurting world that longs for depth and reality.[26]

Christians cover up well, especially when they are suffering from the orphan heart condition. Yet there are times when the scars begin to show, when the clues become obvious, and when the wounded soul is laid bare. My late friend Jack Frost once put it beautifully and very insightfully when he wrote this:

> *Often within the church, it is difficult to tell whether a person walks in the heart attitude of an orphan or a son (this includes daughters). Outwardly, a person may have a pattern of service, sacrifice, discipline, and apparent loyalty, but you do not know what is inside a person until he or she gets bumped. Then the attitude of the heart overflows at a time when they feel they are not getting the recognition or favour they deserve.[27]*

This is exactly my experience as well. It is my experience in the sense that this is precisely what I have witnessed when I have "bumped" others. It is also precisely how I have behaved when I myself have been "bumped"!

Bumping can happen in a number of ways. It may involve a significant person in our lives failing to recognize and value us. It may involve that person denying us what we think we rightfully deserve and need. Whatever way it comes, when it happens we react strongly and we react negatively. We also react disproportionately. Our negative reaction to the bumping is one which is totally out of proportion to the issue at stake (which may be quite trivial). We do this because the person who has bumped us has unwittingly stirred up the buried pain of our orphan hearts. Why does Scrooge respond so hatefully to his nephew saying "Merry Christmas" at the start of *A Christmas Carol*? It is because the Christmas holidays were very far from merry for Scrooge when he was a boy. Abandoned and alone during the Christmas holidays, the young Scrooge learned to hate Christmas and all it stands for. As an old man, his intense and seemingly irrational reactions to the words "Merry Christmas" will be one of the main clues that he has an orphan heart. They will be the scars that he unwittingly wears on his sleeve.

In the light of this, we can see how important it is to discern the tell-tale scars of the primal wound of fatherlessness, not just in other people's lives, but in our own as well. We need more wounded healers in the church to become doctors of the heart, people who understand the way our emotions can be damaged by the wounds from our fathers (and indeed our mothers) and who are able to lead others on a journey of healing that they themselves have travelled. In fact there are few challenges more important than this for the church today.

> As a pastor for twenty-five years, I was the spiritual father in several of the churches that I led and served. As the "father figure" in the congregation, I was an obvious target for anyone with father wounds in their lives. Most of the time, hurting people would not be a problem. But when they were "bumped", all hell would sometimes break loose. All the deep feelings of resentment and sadness would be vented on me and I would be left thinking, "Your reaction is totally out of proportion to the issue!" What I didn't understand for a long time was that their issues with their earthly fathers were being visited on me as their spiritual father and pastor. They were letting what was buried deep within their souls out into the open. The wrong way to react to such a person is with anger, because anger just breeds more anger. The right way to react is with love, the Father's love.
>
> Mark Stibbe

Studying the scars

What, then, are the scars of the father wound? What are the tell-tale indications that a person has experienced a breach in the relationship with their father? Over the course of this chapter, and indeed the remainder of Part 2 of this book, I am going to list the clues that you and I can look out for. But there are a number of things I need to say before I begin the process of describing these.

First of all, I want to pay tribute to a man who helped me to discern what the clues are. That man is called Paul Kusuubira and he lives and works in Uganda. In March 2007 I visited Uganda and spent part of that time in an orphanage ministering to 300 Ugandan orphans in an inspiring Christian organization dedicated to bringing the Father's love to the fatherless. I was invited by their leaders because they had read my book *From Orphans to Heirs* and used much of its contents to help Ugandan orphans experience the Father's love. They now wanted the author to come and teach the material in person.

One of the most memorable moments in my visit was when I had the opportunity of meeting Paul Kusuubira, who had been brought up in the orphanage and had learned – over a long and sometimes painful journey – to call God *Abba*, Father. The two of us spent a whole afternoon together sharing about our experiences of being orphaned. Over the course of several hours, Paul and I discussed the evidence of the orphan heart and shared our own experiences of it. We looked at twenty-one tell-tale indications of the orphan heart. It was an amazingly illuminating experience and I have to say that the things I am about to describe would probably never have come to light had it not been for Paul. I want to honour him here before I list those twenty-one pieces of evidence we discussed.

Secondly, in developing the insights from that conversation, I have felt it necessary to separate the twenty-one clues into *symptoms* and *signs*. In medicine, symptoms are distinguished from signs. A sign is something objective, that a doctor can observe. A symptom, on the other hand, is far more subjective. It is something that a patient feels. With a sign, the doctor can say, "I discern you have this disease." With a symptom, the patient can say, "I feel as if I have this disease." A bloody nose would constitute a sign, observable to the doctor. A feeling like an ache or a pain, anxiety or fatigue, would constitute a symptom, felt by the patient but not necessarily evident to the doctor. Symptoms and signs are therefore different. When it comes to the condition of the orphan heart, some of the tell-tale clues are felt internally by the wounded person. Others are exhibited outwardly in their behaviour. We need to know about both the symptoms and the signs.

Thirdly, it is really important to be honest as you read the remainder of this chapter and the following two chapters. As I list and briefly describe the twenty-one symptoms and signs of the orphan heart, it is vital to reflect on the state of your own heart. This is an opportunity for you to conduct a heart-scan on yourself. It would be very easy to think about other people in your life who might have these symptoms and signs. You might be tempted to think these clues perfectly describe your father, your boss, your spouse, your friend. But the important thing is not to think about other people but to examine yourself. The ancient Greeks used to say, "Know thyself." Knowing who you are and why you are the way you are is essential if you and I are to become whole and integrated people. I encourage you to use the words of Psalm 139 as your prayer as you conduct this inventory: "Search me, O God, and know my heart; test me and know my anxious thoughts. See if there is any offensive way in me, and lead me in the way everlasting."

Fourthly, it is possible to use this list as a guide to revealing

> **Knowing who you are and why you are the way you are is essential if you and I are to become whole and integrated people.**

other conditions, such as the widow's heart. If the orphan heart is defined primarily by a separation from the love of a father, the widow's heart is defined primarily by a separation from the love of a spouse. I remember the first time I shared the symptoms and signs with my staff team when I was leading St Andrew's Church, Chorleywood. We had about thirty people in the room. One of them was Helen Clark, who now heads up the intercession team at the Father's House Trust. She had recently lost her husband Phil. When I went through the list she commented that she could relate as a widow to many of these symptoms and signs. She is now working on a unique teaching called the Healing of the Widow's Heart in the light of her experience. So it is possible to benefit from this inventory even if you feel that your presenting issue is not the orphan heart condition.

Finally, you will notice as you go through the list that some of the symptoms and signs may be due to factors other than the wounds from our fathers. A sign like "anger", for example, may have a different cause in your life. In your story it may be the case that several of these symptoms and signs actually have a different explanation. The key here is really whether you have enough of the symptoms and signs to suggest a syndrome – that syndrome being the orphan heart condition. Only you will know the answer to that question. The vital thing is to hold up the mirror to your own life and to be honest.

The ten classic symptoms

In this chapter we are going to consider the symptoms of the orphan heart. Symptoms are internal clues; they are feelings or attitudes that I may have. Here are the ten symptoms commonly associated with the wounds from our fathers:

Abandonment	Rejection	Loneliness	Hopelessness
Worthlessness	Sadness	Insecurity	Hyper Sensitivity
	Fear	Poverty	

Abandonment

To abandon someone is to leave and desert them. There are different levels of abandonment. A child may feel a sense of abandonment when their father goes out to work, when he drops them off at day care, or when he leaves them for a long period of time at a relative's house, a school or a camp. These are temporary acts of abandonment which can cause a measure of pain. But when a father abandons his child permanently, the wound that is inflicted on the child's soul is immense. That child will often grow up with a sense of abandonment in their heart, a feeling of having been left behind and left alone. Having been utterly forsaken by their father, they will frequently bottle up their emotions and find it tough to form healthy and strong relationships. The feeling of abandonment leaves a lasting legacy of poor self-esteem and an inability to express feelings.

I was abandoned by my parents as a baby. My father left my mother before my twin sister and I were born. My mother then had my sister and me put in an orphanage, in the hope that we would be adopted. This experience of abandonment wounded my soul. Even though I had no consciousness of what was going on at the time, the primal wound was buried deep for decades.

Do you live with a deep sense of abandonment?

Rejection

Rejection, like abandonment, can refer to both an act and a state of being. Rejection can refer to what someone does to me. It can also refer to the position I find myself in. In relation to the act of rejection, this can be either active or passive. It can be either an act which denigrates me (like bullying) or a concentrated neglect ("the silent treatment"). In relation to the state of rejection, when a person is deliberately excluded from a relationship it results in a sense of isolation and pain.

The word "reject" (in the verb form) literally means to throw back. When someone rejects me, I am wilfully cast aside and thrown away. The feeling of having been rejected is extremely painful. It often results in very low self-esteem and aggressive behaviour. It can lead to a heightened expectation of being rejected again in the future.

The difference between abandonment and rejection is significant. Abandonment as an act is usually done without malicious intent, and is often done unwillingly. For instance, my birth mother left my twin sister and me but we know from a letter she wrote that there was no harmful intent and that she had not wanted in her heart to forsake us. This is nearly always true of abandonment. Abandonment as an act is not intended to be harmful for the person who is left behind, even if that person subsequently feels a traumatic reaction to that act. Rejection, on the other hand, is always intended to harm. It is deliberately cruel. It is the entirely conscious and intentional act of discarding someone as useless and defective.

When a father rejects his child he treats his child as if he or she is of no worth whatsoever. This then leads to the child living constantly with a feeling of having been rejected and an anticipation of being rejected again. This in turn robs the child of the conditions in which he or she can grow up into a healthy, stable, confident adult. As John Powell says, "human beings, like plants, grow in the soil of acceptance, not in the atmosphere of rejection."[28]

Do you live with the pain and the expectation of rejection?

Loneliness

My friend James Jordan – who runs a ministry dedicated to the Father's love in New Zealand – often says that loneliness is not the condition of being on your own. You can be in a family and still feel lonely. You can be in a large crowd and feel a crushing sense of loneliness. Loneliness is not the state of being on your own. Loneliness is having no one to share your heart with. Loneliness is having no one to relate to at the level of true intimacy. Loneliness is accordingly much more than the physical state of being without people.

People who have experienced a breach in their relationship with their father will often live with a profound sense of loneliness. They will feel dislocated, uprooted and isolated – an outcast or outsider in the world. They feel utterly alone even in the midst of many people.

Claretta Miller was one of thousands of street children in New York in 1853. These children were taken by train to families in other parts of the United States. The trains were called "The Orphan Trains". Aged nine, Claretta was put on one of these trains and taken to live with a family in the West. She later reflected:

I knew that this was going to be my home from then on, but it seemed like it just kind of hit me when I got here that I had left everything behind, which I had. I didn't have my sister anymore. I didn't have my parents anymore. I didn't have any friends. It just caught up with me all at once. But she was with me, Mrs. Carmen. She never left me for a minute. And she helped me get into bed. I still felt all alone and yet I knew there was someone around me, but they were strangers. I didn't know them from Adam.[29]

Loneliness is one of the clearest symptoms of the orphan heart condition. With the growing problem of fatherlessness, the break-up of the family, and the widespread loss of community, loneliness is one of the most devastating diseases in the world today. As Kurt Vonnegut puts it, "What should young people do with their lives today? Many things, obviously, but the most daring thing is to create stable communities in which the terrible disease of loneliness can be cured."[30]

Do you live with a sense of loneliness?

Hopelessness

A person who has been separated from their father's love may often feel a sense of despair. A true father's love is a hope-giving love. A father helps his child to identify their gifts and to seize their potential. A true father is his child's greatest cheer-leader, urging them on to fulfil their destiny and to achieve their dream. When a child experiences a painful breach in their relationship with their father, it can often lead to a sense of hopelessness. The dream-giver has now been snatched from their lives and with him a sense of meaning, purpose and future direction. This kind of despair can lead to a reckless love of danger and a belief that only today matters. As one orphan wrote, "When you don't see any future, you just want to grab this moment and live it to the max – even if it kills you." This kind of despair is rampant in today's youth culture.

Are you a hopeful or a despairing person?

> A person who has been separated from their father's love may often feel a sense of despair. A true father's love is a hope-giving love.

Worthlessness

A person with an orphan heart will feel deeply ashamed. As I wrote in Chapter 3, guilt is a negative feeling I have about what I have done. Shame is a negative feeling

I have about who I am. When a child is separated from their father, they are separated from the primary transmitter of honour in their lives. The father is no longer present to tell his son that he is proud of him. He is no longer present to tell his daughter that she is beautiful. In the absence of this radiant language of acceptance, the child begins the slow drift downwards into a pit of worthlessness. Often the child will begin to believe the lie that if they had been more valuable, then their father would not have gone.

The power of this negative thinking is very destructive. I often retell the story told by Norman Vincent Peale, who went into a tattoo shop. He had been looking at the tattoos in the shop window. One of them said "Born to Lose". Horrified, Peale asked the Chinese tattoo artist whether anyone would ever have that toxic statement tattooed on their skin. The man said yes. Peale then exclaimed, "Who in their right mind would ever have 'Born to Lose'?" The body artist tapped his forehead and replied, "Before tattoo on skin, tattoo on mind."[31]

Children who grow up with this sense of worthlessness often end up believing lies about themselves. Some end up rejecting, hating and even harming themselves. Worthlessness is a painful and destructive emotional state and it is a symptom of the orphan heart.

Do you feel a sense of shame about yourself?

Sadness

A person with an orphan heart can sometimes appear like a comedian but underneath their hearts are melancholy and sad. Their outward appearance is the typical happy mask of the clown. But the face behind the face is not a happy one. A deep sense of grief is lodged within the soul – grief for the unconditional love and affection of a good father that the person has missed. This father-shaped void is a place of sadness and anguish, hidden from public view, but felt daily in private.

Peter Sellers, a comedic genius if ever there was one, provides a graphic example of this symptom. To this day my whole family can sit around the TV and watch the Pink Panther films and howl with laughter. Sellers had a unique talent for making people laugh. But his biographers have revealed that there was a tragic sadness behind his funny characters. These characters were in fact masks for Sellers to hide behind. The real face was a very sad one indeed. Sellers thought his life was meaningless and empty. He had four marriages and three divorces, many affairs, and engaged in drug and alcohol abuse. Like so many others, this clown was really crying on the inside.

When did this great sadness enter Sellers' life? The answer lies in his childhood. Peter was named after his older brother who had been still born – a fact which explains why Peter was later to grow up with a great insecurity about his true identity. Sellers' father, William ("Bill"), was frequently absent from the home. He was a poor, weak, ineffectual, uneducated man who was often compelled to move from house to house in order to avoid paying the rent. Peter would later recall that one of his most vivid memories from his childhood was sitting in the back of a car as they drove from one home to another. Peter was sent to a Catholic school where his sense of isolation increased; he was the only Jewish boy there. His father eventually walked out on the family and left Peter to be brought up by Peg, his doting mother (whom he always called Peg, never Mum).

As a successful actor, Sellers once remarked, "If you ask me to play myself, I will not know what to do. I do not know who or what I am." On another occasion he said, "I'm a classic example of all humorists – only funny when I'm working." And perhaps most revealingly, "There used to be a me behind the mask but I had it surgically removed."[32] Peter Sellers was a profoundly sad man. His friend and fellow actor Graham Stark recalls:

I remember one time he drove me and my wife around north London in his new Bentley showing us all the

houses he once lived in. When we got to Highgate,
where he lived as a child, he just put his head on the
steering wheel and cried. "Whatever happened to Peter
Sellers?" he asked us, weeping.[33]

Do you present outwardly as happy when internally you are sad?
Are you a person who cries frequently on the inside?

Insecurity

A person with an orphan heart will often live with feelings of
profound insecurity. Having lost the reassuring and affirming love
of a good father, the fatherless soul ends up feeling unsure about
whether they're valued, accepted and capable.

The orphan heart needs constant affirmation from others.
People with an orphan heart tend to ask repeatedly, "You do
still love me, don't you? You do like me, don't you?" This arises
from a deep-seated sense of insecurity about oneself. The orphan-
hearted person is unsure of their true identity. "Who am I?" they
cry. Having never really known and accepted their true selves,
they then find it hard to believe that they are accepted by others.
This often results either in emotional withdrawal and chronic
shyness or in compensatory behaviour patterns like bullying and
aggression. Furthermore, lacking confidence in their value and
their capabilities, fatherless people also often find it hard to hold
down a job and pursue a successful career path.

Insecurity is a symptom of the orphan heart condition. Are
you unsure of yourself? Do you need a lot of reassurance from
other people?

Hypersensitivity

Related to the issue of insecurity is a hypersensitivity towards the
words, body language, tone and actions of others. A person who
grows up with an unhealed father wound will often become overly

sensitive to the signals being sent by those around them. These are almost invariably subjected to an emotional interpretation which transforms them from harmless, innocent signals into harmful gestures.

Hypersensitivity is a toxic feeling that an orphan heart experiences on an everyday basis. Someone suffering this set of emotions can become allergic to life. Normal stimuli like sound, scent and touch become so overwhelming that the person concerned becomes over-stimulated. This can lead to the person feeling that their lives are unmanageable and becoming reclusive. Or it can veer in the opposite direction and lead a person to become obsessive in their relationships. This can result in frequent and highly destructive bouts of jealousy, especially if the person becomes a relationship addict.

Hypersensitivity almost always derives from the loss of a warm and secure environment of attachment in childhood, either with a mother or a father. This disrupted attachment is the wound behind emotional hypersensitivity.

Are you often hypersensitive to other people's signals?

Fear

One of the commonest emotions felt by the orphan heart is fear. Having become separated from a good father's love, a person is torn from the person who symbolized safety in their lives. A good father is a strong and loving father who protects his children. When this figure is taken away from a child's life, they grow up experiencing not only insecurity but also fear.

The orphan heart lives with a constant state of fear. Fear is the state of apprehension and dread about a possible, harmful, future situation or event. The kinds of fear that are experienced in the orphan heart condition are many. But some of the most frequently reoccurring fears that I have found are:

- Fear of abandonment

- Fear of rejection

- Fear of betrayal

- Fear of the disapproval of others

- Fear of sickness

- Fear of redundancy

- Fear of failure

- Fear of death

- Fear of being replaced

- Fear of isolation

- Fear of homelessness

- Fear of not being good enough

The kinds of fear are many but the most common of all is known as "separation anxiety". Separation anxiety is an excessive worry that I feel about being separated from someone I love or a place that I love (for example, home). It almost always derives from a separation in childhood from a father or a mother (or both). Separation anxiety is an emotionally crippling fear that can paralyse your life and shipwreck your relationships. It is a common symptom of the orphan heart.

Having said that, you don't have to be a literal orphan to feel the kinds of fear I've listed here. These "orphan feelings" can be experienced by anyone, whether they have been literally orphaned or not. They can occur in anyone's heart.

Do you live in a state of fear – especially the fear of separation?

Poverty

Poverty is the feeling of scarcity, of never having enough. This is a frequent emotion experienced by fatherless people. The good father is, after all, a provider. While good mothers provide as well in today's world (they too are breadwinners), good fathers have an important role in providing shelter, food, and other essentials of life. Good fathers not only provide these bare essentials, they also provide gifts for their children. They give generously to their children as an expression of their love.

When a child is separated from a good father's love, they will often grow up with a feeling of poverty and scarcity. Even in the midst of plenty they will have an attitude that says, "I had better hoard as much as possible, just in case there is nothing tomorrow." People with a father wound accordingly have a constant poverty mind-set. They worry that there is never going to be enough. They believe deep down that someone is going to come and take away what they have. Often they become self-centred, not caring whether someone else has what they need, just so long as they themselves have enough. As a survivalist instinct kicks in, the person with a father wound can become almost apocalyptic in their thinking, wanting to bunker down with plentiful supplies against the nightmare of a future day when everything has run out.

Do you suffer from a poverty mind-set?

Thinking and feeling

These, then, are ten of the symptoms of the orphan heart condition. They are emotions felt by those who have experienced separation from a father's love. A person with a father wound may not experience all of these emotions. But they will experience some. And to those who have to run the daily gauntlet of these toxic feelings, it can feel like they are no longer living at all, just surviving or merely existing.

Before we finish this chapter on symptoms, there are a couple of things to add. The first has to do with the growth of these feelings over time. The truth is, the negative emotions that I am calling "orphan heart symptoms" evolve and intensify gradually. One famous orphan (adopted by Ronald Reagan, former President of the USA) remarked:

> *I grew up with a big hole inside me. Most adoptees grow up sensing that same hole inside them. That hole is our missing sense of identity, of belonging, of knowing our own unique place in the world. It starts small, but it grows year by year and experience by experience into a gnawing emptiness that we seek to fill any way we can. Many people spend their whole lives searching for something to fill that hole.*[34]

This is an important observation because it shows how the negative feelings associated with the orphan heart condition do not remain the same. From the moment of separation from a father's love, these emotions develop and intensify over time. Some we succeed in burying. But most of them eventually come to the surface, leaping uninvited from our subconscious minds into the foreground of our experience, causing havoc as they do.

Many people with an orphan heart may know something to be true in their heads but feel completely differently about it in their hearts.

A final comment relates to the difference between thinking and feeling. Many people with an orphan heart may know something to be true in their heads but feel completely differently about it in their hearts. For example, they may know that their father abandoned them because he sincerely believed that they would have a better chance in life if they were adopted into a stronger family. A child may grow up knowing this in their head and even giving intellectual assent to it. Yet at the same time they may well continue to feel a desperate sense of abandonment in their heart. Others may even criticize them for these feelings, saying "You weren't abandoned at all. You were put up for adoption because your father wanted the best for you." But even with the weight of this critique, an orphan-hearted child will still experience abandonment in his or her heart because that is what it felt like and still feels like.

It is vital therefore to make a distinction between thinking and feeling when it comes to orphan heart symptoms. A wounded person may try to accept the reasoned arguments of others and even themselves. They may try to change their thinking about the details of the rupture in their relationship with their father. But they may equally find that emotions are stronger than logic, and that feelings frequently trump their thoughts.

These are some of the primary and most obvious symptoms of the orphan heart condition. They are internal feelings felt by the person with a profound father wound. If the church is really to be the hope for the world, then Christians need to begin by having their own hurts healed. Christians need to become alert to their own symptoms and the symptoms of others in the Body of Christ. In addition, we all need to become more astute and aware when it comes to the external clues, the signs of the orphan heart condition. It is to these that we now turn in Chapter 7.

A prayer

Loving Father, I pray that you will help me now to be honest and real with you and with myself. As I look at the orphan heart inventory below, I pray that your Holy Spirit will illuminate those words that apply to me personally. I pray especially that you will expose the hidden hurts that I am not even aware of and help me to face the things that I may have buried for years. My prayer is the prayer of King David in Psalm 139:23–24:

Search me, O God, and know my heart;
test me and know my anxious thoughts.
See if there is any offensive way in me,
and lead me in the way everlasting.

I trust you now to bring any symptoms of a broken heart into the light. Save me, heal me, deliver me, my Father. I ask in Jesus' name.
Amen.

Chapter 7

INTERPRETING THE SIGNS

Recently my wife and I were invited round to a neighbour's house. We went because we have recently moved and we wanted to get to know the people who lived on our street. During the evening I engaged in conversation with a school teacher who was not a Christian but interested in the work we are doing at the Father's House Trust. She admitted that there is a chronic problem with fatherlessness right now in UK society and that school teachers are at the sharp end of this social problem, looking after children who have suffered the trauma of separation from their dads.

She told one particularly heart-breaking story of a fifteen-year-old boy in her class. Eighteen months previously he had been enjoying his fourteenth birthday at home. His dad offered to buy him, his brother and his mother some fish and chips as a birthday treat. The father walked out of the house to go to the local fish-and-chip shop but he never came back. He decided to use this moment to desert his wife and children and is now living on his own.

The teacher told me that a year had passed and that the boy had coped bravely with this sudden and tragic desertion but that on his next birthday the harrowing memories had come flooding back and he had been inconsolable. She then told me that this had been six months ago and that since then the boy had begun to behave badly in class. In particular, he had become disruptive and aggressive. He was getting more and more angry with teachers and other children at school and the school authorities really didn't know how to deal with him. Counselling had been offered but the destructive behaviour patterns were still appearing on a regular basis. "Is this something you could help us with?" she asked.

Whenever I hear these kinds of stories (and I hear them a lot) my heart goes out to those directly involved and especially to the child who has experienced the nightmare of a father's abandonment. The devastation a boy like this feels is indescribable. The truth is, there are thousands and thousands of children growing up today who have been separated from their fathers. As I have constantly reiterated throughout this book, there is now a global pandemic of fatherlessness that affects every continent. What happens to children who have been deprived of the love of a father? Sooner or later they begin to exhibit outward signs of the inner trauma of separation. At home, out on the streets or in school, they begin to manifest some tell-tale signs of what I call the orphan heart condition. The boy that I have just mentioned had been exhibiting anger. But anger is just one of the signs of the orphan heart condition. There are at least ten signs of a heart that has been devastated by father wounds, and this list may not be exhaustive.

Tell-tale clues

In Chapter 6 I made a distinction between the symptoms and the signs of the orphan heart condition. Symptoms are internal feelings that the wounded person experiences. They may or may not be detectable to others. Signs, on the other hand, are outward behaviour patterns. These are far more observable and discernible to the trained eye. Though they may be kept relatively well hidden for a while, sooner or later the growing sense of inner

> The truth is there are thousands and thousands of children growing up today who have been separated from their fathers.

anguish over father loss will result in the manifestation of these tell-tale signs. The trigger for this can be almost anything. In the story I have just told about the boy abandoned by his father, the catalyst was the following birthday, when the memories came flooding back. This was the moment when at least one of the tell-tale signs of the orphan heart became noticeable in the classroom setting – namely, anger. In the boy's case, it was a birthday that caused the pressure valves to blow and the pain to become visible. But the trigger can be almost anything. Every situation is different. Every story is unique, even if some of the overall scenarios are shared.

What then are the outward signs of the orphan heart condition? Again, having spoken with my Ugandan colleague Paul Kusuubira, I can suggest the following set of signs that a person has been wounded because of separation from a father's love.

Some of these signs could be classed as symptoms as well. For example, "mistrust" is both an inner, invisible feeling as well as an outer, visible behaviour. What is common about all of these, however, is the fact that they all become externalized in the words and actions of a person with an orphan heart condition. If you have an orphan heart, someone will have noticed these things in your behaviour. If you know someone with this condition, you will have seen these things in them as well.

So let's now look at these signs briefly. Again, I want to encourage you not to look at other people in your life but to use this inventory to assess your own heart. Remember that not all of these signs may be attributable to the orphan heart condition. For example, you may be mistrustful of men because your husband deserted you or cheated on you and not because you have an orphan heart. The wound in this case will be a wound from a husband, not a wound from a father. Similarly, you may not show all of these outward signs, but ask yourself whether you show enough to suggest an orphan heart syndrome.

Mistrust

Mistrust is a lack of trust in other people, deriving from a deep sense of suspicion concerning the reliability of their love.

People with an orphan heart have a very hard time trusting others. Having been abandoned or abused by their father, their trust in other people is seriously eroded. A father is supposed to be a source of constancy and stability in a person's life. His love is meant to be steadfast and sure, through thick and thin. This consistency of unconditional love strengthens the trust base in a person's life. It leads a person to believe that others, like their dad, will be there for them, come what may. When the opposite happens, and a breach occurs in the relationship with their dad, the trust base in a person's heart is greatly weakened. Further on down the road, the child comes to believe that no one can ultimately be trusted. Everyone is regarded with suspicion.

Orphan-hearted people exhibit noticeable behaviour patterns of mistrust. This is hardly surprising. If a father is a source of security and protection in a child's life, and the father then deserts or abuses his child, this child will find it hard to trust others in the future. "If I trusted my dad and he hurt me so, then who can I ever trust?" The "once bitten, twice shy" attitude kicks in and the wounded soul builds protective walls around the heart. An inner vow is made: "Trust no one."

The trouble with all of this is that the person with the orphan heart not only becomes mistrustful of others, they also become mistrusted by others. Mistrust breeds mistrust. The person wounded by his or her father finds himself or herself not only the subject of mistrust but the object of it too. Study of orphans in Japan confirms this pattern. In Japanese culture, orphans are regarded with great mistrust. They are not deemed reliable, especially by employers. For example, many Japanese banks will not employ orphans as workers. This succeeds in reinforcing the sense of mistrust in the orphan. "I don't trust others because they are not trustworthy" morphs into "I don't trust others because others don't trust me". This encourages what in Japanese is called *koji konjo*, the "orphan mentality", and this is a leading cause of depression and paranoia among Japan's fatherless citizens.[35]

Mistrust of other people is a key sign of the orphan heart, but it's not just people that are mistrusted. Mistrust of institutions is a further characteristic of our present "orphan generation". In the fatherless context in which many of us live today, institutions like the government, educational establishments and the church are regarded with great suspicion by many people. If your father abused or manipulated you, then it is quite likely that you will see institutions as agents of control. The church has suffered particularly from this prevailing attitude of mistrust. Hugh MacKay says: "in the present climate of mistrust of institutions, many people who yearn for a more meaningful and fulfilling life would regard the church as an unlikely place to go for guidance."[36]

So here are a few leading questions:

Do you easily trust other people?

Do other people see "mistrust" in you?

Do you have a mistrust of institutions, such as the church?

Hiding

The Greek poet Homer once wrote, "hateful to me as are the gates of Hell is he who hiding one thing in his heart utters another".[37]

People with an orphan heart conceal their true selves. They keep their real feelings hidden. This strategy of concealment can come in many different guises. There is first of all physical hiding. This is when the person wounded by their father becomes a recluse, withdrawing from all but a very few relationships. In an attempt to protect their hearts from further pain, they isolate themselves from human contact and live a life of secrecy. The trouble with this is that self-isolation proves a context in which loneliness can grow (see Chapter 6 and the section on the symptom of loneliness). The person who hides physically ends up with no one to share their heart with.

A second kind of hiding is perhaps more common. It is emotional in nature. The person wounded by their father may well resort to a lifestyle of emotional concealment. They hide their true feelings because their trust in others has been broken. They may be hurting badly inside, but they will keep all these strong emotions a secret, repressing their feelings and concealing the broken heart within. While this is very understandable, it is also deeply unhealthy. Bottling up emotions is bad for your health. It also leads to uncontrollable releases of pain at the wrong time with the wrong people. Emotional hiding is accordingly very common among those who have been wounded by their father, especially where shaming has been part of that wound. The person struggling with shame may hide their true feelings because they do not even know who they are any more. They may especially be tempted to hide through using humour.

A third kind of hiding is verbal in nature. Now the paradox is this: a person who hides by talking may not be quiet and say very little. In fact, the opposite may very well be true. They may say an awful lot – including a lot about themselves – but reveal practically nothing about who they really are or what they really feel. As German philosopher Friedrich Nietzsche once very insightfully remarked, "Talking too much about oneself may be a way of hiding oneself."[38]

Hiding is a very common sign of the orphan heart condition. When Adam and Eve fell from being a son and a daughter to being spiritual orphans, the first thing they did was to go into hiding. God came looking for them in the Garden of Eden. They were hiding from him because they were now naked and felt afraid and ashamed. This is such a telling picture. This is exactly what orphan-hearted people do. They default to hiding – hiding from God and hiding from others, and even hiding from themselves. They withdraw into a castle of self-imposed solitude, surrounded by a moat of their own making, and draw up the bridge until it slams shut.

Perhaps you may be thinking of someone you have known for many years. You have done many things together during that time. But even though he spoke a great deal and you laughed much, you now realize you knew little about who he really was. He hid from you. Later, after you unwittingly "bumped" him and he became dangerous to be around, you started to learn from others things that you had never been told – that he had been abused by his father and that he was in reality a broken and wounded man. By then, sadly, the damage had been done and there was no way back. But it taught you a lesson. Just because you hang around with people a lot, that doesn't mean you really know them. Someone with an orphan heart will most likely conceal who they really are and what they're really feeling. Sometimes you simply have to learn this lesson the hard way. As Ralph Waldo Emerson put it, "Society is a masked ball where everyone hides his real character."[39]

Christians are called to walk in the light, not hide in the darkness. Walking in integrity and transparency is the route to true and authentic community. As the Apostle John says in 1 John 1:7: "If we walk in the light, as he is in the light, we have fellowship with one another."

Here, then, are a few more leading questions:

Do you have a tendency to hide?

Do you conceal your real feelings?

Do you let people see "the shadow" – the part of your life where your hurts and hang-ups are found?

Do you conceal or reveal your true self?

Superficiality

Andy Warhol once famously remarked, "I am a deeply superficial person"![40] Does this describe you too?

The truth is, the person with an orphan heart lives life at a superficial level. In a sense, this is a sign very closely linked with hiding. The person wounded by their father may decide that it is safer to live life at the surface level. Delving too deep into the human heart may be seen as far too dangerous and painful. Therefore, as part of their survival kit, the fatherless resort to living life at a cosmetic, shallow level. Their relationships with others are formed not on the basis of what they can give of themselves but rather on the basis of what they can extract from the other person. If the other person is useful, attractive or pleasant to be around, then they will relate to them. If they are not, they will keep their distance and find other people they can use or who will entertain and excite them.

Richard Foster made this telling statement in his bestselling book *Celebration of Discipline*: "Superficiality is the curse of our age. The desperate need today is not for a greater number of intelligent people, or gifted people, but for deep people."[41] This is undoubtedly true but we need to ask why it is that our age is especially superficial. One plausible reason is because there are so many people now who have been damaged by their fathers. They know that there are deep places of the heart that they could explore but they choose not to go there because it seems too scary. They are like divers who choose to spend their time snorkelling in the safety of the shallows when they could go down to the deepest depths in a submersible. They prefer the bright security of the lagoon to the dark mystery of the ocean.

The trouble with this is that the orphan-hearted person never really gets to know who they really are and never really gets to know who others are either. Stephen Covey has said:

> the most important ingredient we put into any relationship is not what we say or what we do, but who we are. And if our words and our actions come from superficial human relations... others will sense that duplicity. We simply won't be able to create and sustain the foundation necessary for effective interdependence.[42]

That is really well said, yet many fatherless people fail to heed the advice. They live a life of superficiality and then wonder why their friends don't stick with them.

If you have an orphan heart, people may have noticed this about you. They may have spotted that you are quite a cosmetic person, that you live life only on the surface, and that you are quite shallow.

So here's another leading question:

Is this something others would say of you, or you of yourself?

Do you hide behind your persona or possessions?

Attachments

One of the commonest signs that a person is suffering from father wounds is attachment or addiction.

In 1995 I published a book called *Brave New Church*, subtitled, *Rescuing the Addictive Culture*. In it I wrote in depth about excessive attachments or addictions. I described the idea of addiction as follows:

*The word "addiction" comes from the Latin verb
addicere, which means "to hand over" or "to surrender".
This suggests that an addiction is something to which
I surrender, something to which my life is given over.
That indeed is the case: addicts are people who have
lost control of their lives and who are now controlled
by their addiction – alcohol, gambling, sport, cleaning,
drugs, whatever. Addicts are people whose lives have
become unmanageable as a result of their excessive
attachment to someone or something.*[43]

I went on to point out that the reason why we become addicted
is because the objects of attachment have an alluring, anaesthetic
quality that alters our moods and masks our pain. The problem,
however, is that these attachments are ultimately toxic; they never
satisfy the deep hunger within. I went on to define addiction as
"an attachment to a mood-altering agent that is excessive and
destructive, leading to feelings of powerlessness and eventually to
'hitting bottom'". I then identified five different kinds of addiction
in our escapist culture:

- **Substance addictions.** These involve taking a substance
  into the body, through the mouth or the nose, or into a
  vein using a syringe. I pointed to drugs (both illegal and
  legal), food (overeating), alcohol, caffeine, nicotine, etc.

- **Behaviour addictions.** This involves being hooked
  on a process or a specific set of actions. I pointed to
  shopping, danger (like joy-riding or riding the rails),
  violence, holidays, cleaning, perfectionism, gambling,
  materialism, sport, etc.

- **Technology addictions.** These involve an excessive
  attachment to various interactive technologies, such as
  computer games, virtual reality, internet gambling, and
  so on.

- **People addictions.** These involve excessive attachments to sex, romance and relationships. People today seek to fill the hole in the soul through a preoccupation with sex, pornography, romance and relationships defined by obsessive love.

- **Ideology addictions.** The final kind of addiction I identified was the excessive attachment to a philosophy. Mood-altering fixations to ideologies are commonplace today. People become hooked on ideologies like communism, capitalism, patriotism, feminism, paganism, occultism, militarism, consumerism, etc.

The causes of addiction can be many but one of the major ones is "love hunger" and specifically "father hunger". Where a person has become separated from a father's love they can start resorting to mood-altering anaesthetics in order to mask the pain of their father loss. This leads to a downward mobility towards the place of "hitting bottom" which follows a recognizable course. This journey begins with the experience of pain, say a breach in the relationship with your father. Then, later on, an addictive agent is sought (a substance, behaviour, technology etc.) which people resort to in order to cope with the pain. This brings temporary anaesthesia or pain relief. The problem is that this then becomes addictive and starts to control your life. Eventually this leads to you crashing or "hitting bottom" as your life becomes completely unmanageable.

> The causes of addiction can be many but one of the major ones is "love hunger" and specifically "father hunger".

A person with an orphan heart often has an addictive personality. Right at the centre of their lives is a deep, gaping void. Excessive attachments are attempts to feed the love hunger left behind by the primal wound of separation. All of us have a choice when we feel pain. Are we going to fill the container with

something created (such as a sexual relationship or a drug)? Or are we going to fill it with an attachment to the Father who loves us like no earthly father ever could?

Carl Jung once said, "Every form of addiction is bad, no matter whether the narcotic be alcohol or idealism."[44] Addiction is one of the most pervasive signs of the orphan heart condition. A loss of healthy attachment (to the father) leads to unhealthy attachments (to father substitutes).

A loss of healthy attachment (to the father) leads to unhealthy attachments (to father substitutes).

Here, then, is another leading question:

Have others noticed any excessive attachments in your life?

Manipulation

Manipulation is another sign of the orphan heart condition. Manipulation can be defined as the attempt to gain control over others through the use of underhand means.

The orphan heart is highly manipulative. This is really born from fear. The person wounded by a father is frightened of being hurt again. In order to protect themselves, wounded people seek to dominate and control others into doing what they want, in the hope that this will insulate them from pain.

Manipulation is a highly toxic form of influence. The orphan heart controls others so as to get as much from them as possible. The orphan heart knows what you want to hear and says it in order to get what it wants. Orphan-hearted people are expert manipulators. The kinds of tactic used can be positive or negative, constant or intermittent.

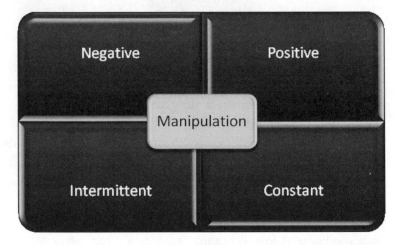

Negative tactics include deception, spin, shaming, exploitation, intimidation, evasion, blackmail, yelling, lying, denial, sulking, the silent treatment, projection of blame, and so on. Positive tactics include praise, charm, sympathy, gifts, approval, seduction, attention, and so on. Intermittent manipulation is occasional. Constant manipulation is ongoing.

Although the tactics may vary, there is a common theme. All manipulators aim for what I call our "buttons". These buttons are our own personal places of vulnerability. They may be any of the following:

- Need for approval
- Need for acceptance
- Need for love
- Need for protection
- Need for belonging
- Need for resources
- Need for control
- Need for position

Manipulators are very adept at finding these "buttons" and pressing them. I remember one occasion a number of years ago when I asked a man to come into my office and sit with an ordained colleague and myself. He was an arch-manipulator – a habit which arose from his orphan heart condition (a condition about which he was in complete denial). I watched as this man, within the course of a few moments, located and pressed every single one of our buttons. It was skilful and scary all at the same time. The man's motivation was power and control. While his tactics were extremely clever, what he was engaging in was really a form of bullying.

Manipulation is rife in society today. At its worst it is a form of bullying or "peer abuse". It can occur anywhere from schools to workplaces. It is particularly toxic in the church. Men and women with unhealed orphan hearts can become extremely destructive in Christian communities. They are like spiders that spin a web and then lure people in. They can deceive people into believing their side of every story and enlist others into movements of rebellion that are devastating in consequence. Many churches have been torn in two by such people.

So here again are some leading questions:

Are you a manipulative person?

Do you have a controlling temperament?

Anger

It is no surprise to hear that anger, resentment and rage are clues that a person is suffering from traumatic father wounds. Those who have been badly hurt by their dads are prone to anger. This emotion is directly related to the absence of a father's love.

There are at least two ways in which anger is related to and created by father wounds. First of all, a person who has been robbed of a father's love will feel a very profound sadness over what they have missed and an equally deep resentment against their father for not being there for them. This cocktail of grief and rage is very powerful and sometimes also confusing. Often a child will be simultaneously sad that the father is not there and angry that he is absent. This emotional ambiguity is so intense that it is often pushed down deep into the recesses of the subconscious life where it boils away like a subterranean hot spring. From time to time something will cause the anger to surface and become visible. When it does, it is a sign of the orphan heart condition.

A second way in which anger is related to father wounds has to do with abuse. When a father is abusive, this can lead to a child emulating their father's behaviour. The recent highly publicized case involving two young and violent brothers is a good, though extreme, example. I am referring to two brothers who were systematically beaten and shamed by their alcoholic father and who then went on to commit the worst crime by a British child since the Jamie Bulger case in 1993. These two brothers (who cannot be named) led two boys into a wasteland in the Yorkshire town of Edlington in April 2009. They subjected them to a ninety-minute ordeal of torture in which they struck the boys with bricks, stamped on them, and beat, choked and burned them. The older boy almost died from his injuries. The two offenders were sentenced to an indefinite time in prison, to serve a minimum of five years behind bars.

The trial at the start of 2010 revealed some startling and frightening details about the home life of the two children who perpetrated this awful crime. Both were the victims of an abusive, alcoholic father who not only severely and often beat them when he was drunk, but also struck them when he was sober. During the trial the mother commented that she had become worried about her two sons when they began to start acting violently towards other children. At times they would imitate the measured and sadistic voice of their father when he was beating them while sober. This highlighted the fact that the two boys had started to imitate their father. They regularly watched him punch and kick their mother. According to one of the barristers at the trial, these children were brought up in an atmosphere of "routine aggression, violence and chaos". It was, he said, "a toxic family life".[45]

There are therefore close and complex relationships between the emotion of anger and the wounds caused by fathers. Today, the global pandemic of fatherlessness is creating the ripe soil for crime and lawlessness. Fatherless teenagers are increasingly on the prowl on our streets. They are pumps primed for violent and aggressive behaviour.

Fathers who are fully involved in their children's lives help to form their characters. Boys especially need a father to reel in their aggressive and unruly tendencies – to challenge them when they're disrespectful and when they engage in bad behaviour. Boys in particular need dads to hold them accountable to a higher standard and to be a model for responsible conduct and healthy conflict management. This is a critical part of a father's role. Where this kind of loving guidance is missing – or where fathers model disrespect for authority – a child will often become an unbridled youth with no boundaries.

So here again are some leading questions:

Do you have an anger problem?

Are you aggressive?

Selectivity

Selectivity is the attitude of being selective. People with orphan hearts are often selective about what they remember; they block out painful memories, or memories that might produce a negative picture of themselves.

Charles Caleb Colton once remarked that "Pure truth, like pure gold, has been found unfit for circulation because men have discovered that it is far more convenient to adulterate the truth than to refine themselves."[46] This is all the more pertinent in the case of those with father wounds. Such people tend to covey an untrue version of past events by leaving out certain important facts.

Perhaps the best expression for describing this tendency is the one usually associated with politicians. I am referring to the idiom, "being economical with the truth". When someone in the political arena is economical with the truth, they omit information in order to create a false picture of a situation or a person. In their view they are not actually lying, but in the public's estimation they are sailing very close to the wind of deception.

So here again I need to ask some leading questions:

Are you selective in what you remember?

Do others find you "economical with the truth"?

Fantasy

A person suffering from an orphan heart condition will almost certainly have a tendency to indulge in fantasy.

Fantasy in general is neither good nor bad. It is morally neutral. Fantasy can be used for virtuous purposes. The psychologist Carl Jung said that "without this playing with fantasy, no creative work has ever yet come to birth. The debt we owe to the play of the imagination is incalculable."[47] Fantasy can be positive but it can also be put to negative use. People who have been wounded by their fathers will often indulge in unhelpful fantasizing because, as the poet T. S. Eliot once wrote, "human kind cannot bear very much reality".[48] This kind of fantasizing is a common characteristic of those suffering from an orphan heart condition. It involves avoiding the painful truth about our past by creating a fictional version of what has happened to us. In this version we become the innocent victims and our fathers, or father figures, become the ogres.

Here we are dealing primarily with the tendency to create a fictional version of one's past in order to protect ourselves from harmful emotions connected with our life script. I was certainly guilty of this for years in relation to my mother. Having been placed in an orphanage by my birth mother (along with my twin sister Claire), I built a mythology about what kind of woman she was. In the absence of any real information, I painted her in the worst possible light as someone who consciously rejected me in the most callous and wicked of ways. In effect, I constructed my reality when there were quite straightforward ways in which I could have discovered my reality (not least by asking my adoptive mother). It was only in my late thirties that I discovered that I had been indulging in fantasy to create a "bad mum, good child" mythology. The real truth, as I subsequently discovered, was quite different.

Michael Reagan, who was adopted by former US President Ronald Reagan and his wife Nancy, has recently written about a very similar experience. He was convinced for many years that his birth mother was a cruel woman. He then discovered more information about his mother and changed his mind completely. He had a kind of awakening in which he was not only able to forgive his birth mother. He was able to start honouring her as well. In addition, he renounced the lie of his own version of events (the fantasy he had created) and embraced the truth (the reality he had denied). In his autobiography *Twice Adopted*, he writes this about his change of heart concerning his birth mother, Irene Flaugher:

*For most of my life, I really couldn't grasp the depths of
my birth mother's love. I didn't understand how any
mother could love her baby yet give that baby away.
What now I see as love I used to see as rejection. It took
me decades of pain and anger to understand the loving
sacrifice Irene Flaugher made for my sake. Today I have
nothing but praise and gratitude for my birth mother.*[49]

When you are speaking with someone with an orphan heart, you
will find that they speak about past events in a way that does not
seem to correspond to what actually happened. This is because
orphan-hearted people are disconnected from reality. They have
to be constantly told, "I don't think that's really what occurred."

Winston Churchill once famously remarked that "Men
occasionally stumble over the truth, but most pick themselves up
and hurry off as if nothing had happened."[50] It is the truth that
truly liberates us. Only by embracing reality can we be healed
of our father wounds – the reality about ourselves, about others,
about our past, about our fathers and mothers. Sometimes this
will mean that we have to see things as they really are and break
ourselves free from the victim mentality that we have been living
with. It is reality, not fantasy, that brings freedom. This means
that we have to stop constructing our reality and we have to start
confronting our reality.

So once again we have to ask ourselves some leading
questions:

Have others discerned a fantasizing tendency in us?

Have we ever been accused of constructing reality, or of
being disconnected from reality?

Have you had a tendency to create myths about your past?

Ralph Waldo Emerson once said that "The highest compact
we can make with our fellow is 'let there be truth between us
for evermore'."[51] Is this the kind of value we embrace in our
relationship with our parents and with other people?

Misinterpretation

To misinterpret someone is to interpret or explain what they have said in the wrong way. Misinterpretation can refer to the act of interpretation or the act of explanation. For example, if I misinterpret what you say, that refers to a private act of erroneous interpretation. If I misinterpret what you say in relaying our conversation to someone else, that refers to a public act of erroneous explanation. People with orphan hearts constantly do both. For example, your spouse may say, "Please don't load the glasses that way into the dishwasher." You may hear, "You lousy good-for-nothing! You're so useless that you can't even do a simple job like that!" Harmless comments become devastating rejections which are then often relayed in gossip to other people.

So, once again we need to ask a few questions:

Do you have a tendency to misinterpret others?

Have others seen this in you?

Independence

Last, but by no means least, in our list of signs is independence. I define independence as the desire to be free from the control, guidance, oversight and influence of other people.

The widespread problem of fatherlessness has succeeded in providing a very fertile breeding ground for the independent spirit. Many people have grown up without the tender, unconditional love of a trustworthy dad. Or alternatively, they have experienced the nightmare of a cruel and abusive father. These two tragic realities have helped to create a dominant ethos in our culture – an ethos that is suspicious of authority figures and deeply cautious of any kind of submission. Independence and rebellion are consequently rife in society and, sadly, also in the church. Many churchgoers today have an independent spirit, a rebellious attitude that says, "I will not be accountable; I will do things my way." Much of this is rooted in the orphan heart condition.

How has all this happened? This really comes about because of one of two primary scenarios. First of all, the absence of a father causes a child to grow up without boundaries and without any healthy respect for authority. This leads them to enter adolescence and adulthood with no idea of how to submit to the reasonable, legitimate and appropriate oversight of teachers, police officers, employers, pastors, and others. The absent father leaves a legacy of destructive independence in their children. He creates generational havoc and social decay, spawning children who become more and more lawless. The failure to recognize and deal with these issues within the church is one of the main reasons why so many churches are vulnerable to division and splits.

Secondly, the abusive father leaves an equally damaging legacy. He either produces children who become passive doormats, ripe for further and repetitive experiences of victimization. Or he succeeds in shaping children who rebel aggressively, seeing the face of their abusive father in every authority figure they subsequently encounter. No wonder they stand with their fists raised high! Children who have been the victims of controlling fathers will have a very hard time being accountable in a trusting way to authority figures. This can reap a whirlwind within churches if the wound of abuse is not addressed.

Of course, not all acts of independence and rebellion are wrong or unhealthy. There is a spectrum from legitimate, justified independence to illegitimate, unjustified independence. What we are talking about here is the wilful, rebellious and destructive independence of those who have been wounded by their fathers. This is a very specific expression of independence and rebellion which causes fragmentation in communities, including church communities. That is a sign of a heart wounded by a father, and it needs healing.

I often say that leading churches can feel like trying to herd cats. I have been involved in church leadership for twenty-five years and have seen this many times. In previous generations, the authority of the spiritual leader of a church was pretty well assumed. Now it has to be earned and even then it cannot be guaranteed. If you feed, love and stroke the cats, then they'll most likely stay (though they may often find other places to visit where they can get additional feeding). If you challenge them too much, or call upon them to change, they'll often leave! It's a hard life being a pastor. Leading a volunteer-intensive community in a time of increasing independence is just about the most challenging job there is. But it is still infinitely worthwhile and eminently achievable, provided you deal with the issues of the heart that so often cause problems. That includes your own heart as well! You have to address your own "feline" tendencies if you're going to minister to others.

So independence is a sign of the orphan heart condition and one which requires honesty and courage if it is to be acknowledged and healed. So I ask these questions:

Have others discerned an independent attitude in you?

Do you have a history of being rebellious?

What is your attitude to those in authority – spiritual or otherwise?

Do you happily submit to trustworthy authority figures?

These, then, are the ten signs or outward behaviours that point to the orphan heart condition. They must now be confronted within local churches. Before churches can be agents of healing to a fatherless world, they must first begin by putting their own house in order. This means providing a safe place for new believers to become integrated disciples. It means teaching on the symptoms and signs of the orphan heart condition and providing opportunities within the local church for Christians to be healed of their father wounds and to encounter the love of their Heavenly

> **Before churches can be agents of healing to a fatherless world, they must first begin by putting their own house in order.**

Father. It means creating communities where believers know how to be transparent with one another and, indeed, accountable to one another as adopted brothers and sisters in Christ. Before there can be revival in a fatherless world, there needs to be a reformation within the church – a reformation based on the revelation of the Fatherly heart of Almighty God. We cannot go on marginalizing the revelation of the Father's love and neglecting the wounds from our earthly fathers. We need programmes and courses that enable us to become free. We will look at how this freedom can be experienced in Part 3. Before we do that, however, we have one last symptom and sign to address in Chapter 8, and this one is the most widespread and damaging of them all.

A prayer

Loving Father, I pray that you would help me to confess any of the signs of the orphan heart that are observable in my life and behaviour. I want to walk in my new, true self – recreated in Christ. I don't want to live out of the old, false self any longer. Help me to be real and truthful, for your Word says: "Do not lie to each other, since you have taken off your old self with its practices and have put on the new self, which is being renewed in knowledge in the image of its Creator" (Colossians 3:9–10). I commit to confessing and dealing with whatever your Holy Spirit now spotlights in the ten signs of the orphan heart.

Help me, *Abba*, Father, to be free from all of these behaviours in my life and to walk in the light from this day on. I pray that every one of them would now be crucified with Christ and put to death forever. Break the chains that have bound me for so long. I ask for *freedom* in Christ. I ask this in his mighty name. Amen.

Mistrust	Hiding	Superficiality	Attachments
Manipulation	Anger	Selectivity	Fantasy
	Mis-interpretation	Independence	

Chapter 8

THE PERFORMANCE TRAP

I have never been a fan of tennis, I'll be honest, but even I can appreciate a great tennis player when I see one, and one of the finest of all was the American champion, Andre Agassi. Agassi was at one time number one in the world. He won eight grand slam titles (including a Wimbledon title) and a gold medal in the Olympic Games. Born in Las Vegas in 1970, he turned professional at the age of sixteen and by the end of his first year was already ranked number ninety-one in the world. He ended his second year ranked number twenty-five, having won his first major title. By the end of the following year he was ranked number three in the world, behind Ivan Lendl and Mats Wilander. In 1992 he won his first grand slam title at Wimbledon, beating Goran Ivanisevic in a thrilling five-set final. In April 1995 – a year in which he won seventy-three matches – Agassi was ranked the world's number one player for the first time in his career. He subsequently won many tournaments before retiring in 2006 after suffering serious back pain brought on by sciatica. He won over 30 million dollars in prize money and was respected by all his peers for his unparalleled ability to return serve and his amazing capacity to dominate play from the base line. Married to another multiple grand slam tennis champion – Steffi Graf – Agassi remains to this day one of the most entertaining figures in modern tennis.

In spite of all this success, Andre Agassi has recently admitted to hating tennis. The very sport that made him so rich and famous was actually something he detested. Why did Agassi live in the tension of such a glaring paradox? The answer lies in his relationship with his father, Iranian-born Michael Agassi. Andre Agassi's autobiography *Open* gives us some profound insights into this troubled relationship. Mike Agassi regarded his son Andre as the means by which he could fulfil his own frustrated desire for great wealth. He aimed to do this by turning his boy into a world-famous tennis champion. From the very beginning of his life, Andre was consequently subjected to an intensive regime of practice in the tennis court that his father had built in the back yard of the family home in Las Vegas. Even while Andre was lying as a baby in a crib, he had tennis balls hanging in a makeshift mobile over his head. As he was later to say, "My dad was convinced that if my eyes were going to move around as a baby, I might as well be looking at a tennis ball."[52] His father was later to provide his own rationale for this and other extraordinary measures during his son's infancy and childhood: "I believed I could hardwire Andre's body to swing a racket to make contact with a secondary object, and in doing so boost his hand–eye co-ordination."[53] Andre was just six months old when this process of disciplined training started. By the age of two he was running round his back yard with a tennis racket that had been taped by his father to his arm. Andre was truly being groomed for greatness.

Michael Agassi's dream was that his son would be the world's number one, and as far as he was concerned, the end justified the means. And the means were harsh.

Later he would answer his critics by saying, "People say I pushed my kids too hard, and I nearly destroyed them. And you know what? They're right. I was too hard on them. I made them feel like what they did was never good enough. But after the childhood I had, fighting for every scrap in Iran, I was determined to give my kids a better life."[54]

To push his son further and harder, Mike Agassi now bought a machine called "the dragon" which propelled a tennis ball at a speed of 110 mph. Andre said that he flinched every time he heard the dragon roaring.

He added, "My father says that if I hit 2,500 balls each day, I'll hit 17,500 balls each week, and at the end of one year I'll have hit nearly one million balls. He believes in maths. Numbers, he says, don't lie. A child who hits one million balls each year will be unbeatable."[55]

There is little doubt that Mike Agassi's bullying succeeded. His son Andre did indeed become the world's best tennis player. But it all came at a cost – a permanently broken relationship between father and son. Perhaps the most telling moment of all came when Andre won the Wimbledon grand slam event. His father wasn't even there. When Andre phoned him to break the news of his astounding success, all his dad could say was that he shouldn't have lost the fourth set. No wonder Andre once said, "I hate tennis, hate it with all my heart, and still I keep playing, keep hitting all morning, and all afternoon, because I have no choice."[56]

The number-one sign and symptom

I've begun the final chapter of Part 2 with this sad story because it highlights the number-one clue that someone is suffering from what I call the orphan heart condition, and that is striving. By striving I mean the tendency to seek to earn love, acceptance and value through working tirelessly to perform well in one or more areas of one's life. The person who lives a life of striving is really the person who is unsure of other people's approval and who seeks to win that approval through doing well. Striving is another word for what I call "the performance orientation" or "the performance mind-set". It is an extremely common sign and symptom of the orphan heart. It is a symptom because it describes an inner feeling felt by the person who lives in this way. It is also a sign because it is something visible in a person's outward behaviour. The person who strives is a person driven to succeed. They are working for approval rather than from approval.

I have to be honest here and say that this was a problem in my life too. Having been separated from my earthly father's love, I started striving to earn love through performance. In fact, for more years than I care either to remember or admit, I was driven to succeed in order to be accepted. At first this was expressed through sport. I discovered when I was about eight years old that I was really good at soccer. Someone, for some unknown reason, made me the goal-keeper in a team game and I saved a penalty. I can still remember the moment, even today. I flung myself a long way to my left and caught a ball that was heading for the top corner. There was an audible gasp from all the other players, on both sides, followed by rapturous applause. I remember the rush and the thrill of that moment. It was intense. I felt esteemed and honoured. From that moment, for the next five years or so, I worked as hard as I could at improving my soccer skills, training harder than anyone. And it was rewarded. I got into the first team in my school (for the 14–18 year-olds) and stayed there for three years. I was recommended for trials with a top-flight English football team. I became well known in the school for this and I felt good about myself.

Then I turned to academic studies. I discovered that I had a particular aptitude for English Literature. I worked all the hours God sent – some days into the early hours of the morning – going the extra mile, exceeding all the efforts of my peers, writing essays that I hadn't even been asked to write! I remember one night staying up till four o'clock in the morning to write a twelve-page essay on John Milton's *Paradise Lost*. I hadn't been asked by my teacher to do this nor was I required to write it as part of my course. I just did it to earn plaudits. And again, as in the case of my sporting life, I excelled. In my success, the pleasure of knowing the applause of others was addictive. I lived for it and I sought to replicate it as often as I possibly could.

From academic striving, I turned to Christian ministry. By this time I had become a Christian and had trained for the ordained ministry in the Church of England. No sooner had I been released into church leadership than I began to strive again. The same driven, desperate need to achieve that had been my motivator in sport and academic studies now spilled over into church life as I tried to create the biggest and the best youth group in my city. I so wanted to have a reputation for being an anointed man of God and an effective and successful leader. I would go to almost any lengths to achieve this goal, not realizing that I was now performing for approval and striving for love. But now it was for God, so it had to be right, didn't it?

It is not healthy to drive ourselves to the point of exhaustion in order to win the approval we never had from an honour-giving father.

How easy it is to develop a performance mind-set which is based on striving rather than resting. Over the years I have come to the realization that much of this ultimately derives from father loss – from the honour deficit left by the absence of a loving father, or from the sense of not measuring up generated by an achievement-driven father. When we lack the unconditional affirmation and affection of a good father, we begin to believe the lie that we have to earn this love through tireless effort. Hard work in itself is not wrong, nor is the desire to succeed a negative thing. But it is not healthy to drive ourselves to the point of exhaustion in order to win the approval that we never had from an honour-giving father. This leads to burn-out and robs us of authentic relationship with others. In the end, it can even rob us of life itself.

Striving is accordingly the primary sign and symptom of the orphan heart condition. It is rooted in separation from a father's love. That separation can be caused by the father or it can be caused by the child, or it can be a combination of both. The scenarios are almost endless. But when this separation comes, it leaves a deep sense of worthlessness. This wound then opens the door to a lie, the lie that I have to work my fingers to the bone in order to earn the honour, value and affection that I never had from my biological father. People who believe this lie almost invariably become approval addicts – people addicted to the mood-altering pleasure of other people's applause.

The enigma of the orphan

How widespread is this problem of striving? In a book called *Creative Suffering*, Paul Tournier gave the answer. Tournier was a general practitioner in Geneva for fifty years, so he knew a thing or two about the human condition. Having counselled patients for half a century, Tournier came to the conclusion that human suffering doesn't have to break us. It can actually make us too. In other words, suffering doesn't have to be destructive. It can be creative or fruitful, if we allow it to be. Suffering is part of the mysterious fabric of our lives and Tournier's belief was that it can be used as a means of growth. It can be the driver for great artistic, scientific, and political advances.

To prove the point, Tournier began his book with a prologue entitled, "The Enigma of the Orphan". The starting point for his comments was an article published in 1975 and written by Dr Pierre Rentchnick. It was called "Orphans Lead the World". In this article the author had set himself the task of studying the life stories of the greatest political leaders in history in order to see whether sickness had played a part in their growth and development. What he discovered astounded him. In Tournier's words, "He was soon struck by the astonishing discovery that all of them had been orphans!" Here is Tournier's summary:

Some had lost their fathers in infancy or in early youth, others their mothers, and some both parents, or else they had been cut off from one or the other because they had separated; or else they had been illegitimate children

183

and had not known their fathers or anything about them. Yet others had been rejected or abandoned by their parents. Dr Rentchnick compiled a list of them. It contained almost three hundred of the greatest names in history, from Alexander the Great and Julius Caesar, through Charles V, Cardinal Richelieu, Louis XIV, Robespierre, George Washington, Napoleon, Queen Victoria, Golda Meir, Hitler, Lenin, Stalin, to Eva Peron...[57]

Tournier pointed out that all of these and many others had experienced emotional deprivation in their childhood, especially separation from the love of a father.

Tournier was particularly interested in this research for two reasons: first of all because he was an orphan himself – his father having died when he was two years old, his mother when he was five. The research helped to explain why he had felt so driven in his life – why he had been motivated by what he called "a quite exceptional will to power". Secondly, it helped him to understand how suffering can actually produce fruit in people's lives. Tournier realized that orphaned children grew up to become great leaders. This applies not just to the world of politics but also to the world of religion. As Dr Rentchnick said, "The great religious leaders were orphans too! Remember Moses floating in his basket on the waters of the Nile!"[58]

All of this might lead us to conclude that being separated from a father's love is actually a positive thing. In reality, of course, the picture is far more complex. On the one hand there is a potentially creative side to the orphan condition. It produces an unconscious drive to change the world in the lives of many eminent men and women. At the same time, this condition has a down side – a dark side. Such driven people prove exceedingly hard to live with. They become intolerant of others. They tend to put a much higher value on the attainment of their goal than on the enrichment of their relationships. Their sense of destiny becomes more important than intimacy. They are therefore capable of the lowest, not just the highest, actions.

The prologue to *Creative Suffering* is a confirmation of the claim I'm making here that striving is a widespread symptom and a sign of the orphan heart condition. Having been denied a father's love, orphans resort to performing for love. This can be expressed through politics, through religion, through the arts, through sport, through just about anything. Tournier has clearly demonstrated that people with father wounds tend to work for approval rather than from approval; they tend to rest from work rather than work from rest.

Even more significant, perhaps, is Tournier's statement that everyone is an orphan, which underlines what I claimed in Chapter 1 when I wrote about the big story of the Bible. He quotes a comment by the author

In a cold and fallen cosmos, we are all of us spiritual orphans, trying to find our way home into the true Father's arms.

Saul Bellow: "Everyone is born to be an orphan."[59] He argues that actual or literal orphans suffer more intensely what all human beings experience. We are all separated from a father's love. In a cold and fallen cosmos, we are all of us spiritual orphans trying to find our way home into the true Father's arms. On the way there, we so often resort to performance in our desperate attempt to feel value and affirmation.

Performing in the church

What happens when a person with an orphan heart becomes a Christian? Does this tendency to earn love through performance suddenly disappear? More often than not, it does not. If one of the problems we brought into the Christian life was the tendency to earn love through performance, this will not go away until it is displaced through divine healing. In fact, not only will a new-born Christian still strive to earn the love of others through performance. They will also strive to earn the love of God the Father through performance.

All this stands to reason, if we think about it. What we are talking about here is once again the problem of projection. If we had a father whose love had to be earned through doing well at school or sports, we may well end up transferring his face onto the face of our Heavenly Father. We then end up believing the lie that God is in reality a Master and we are his slaves. This Slave-Driver theology then robs us of our true identity and security as the adopted sons and daughters of our perfect, loving, Heavenly Father. We become driven people; driven in our relationships with other Christians and driven in the most important relationship of all, our relationship with *Abba*, Father.

The fact is, the absence of a loving, affirming, affectionate father in our lives can turn us into super-achievers who desperately try to make up the love deficit through performance, and this performance orientation can even spill over into our understanding of who God is and how we relate to him as our Father. It can lead us into a performance-based religious ethic, into the misery of fearful slaves rather than the intimacy of joyful sons and daughters.

Take Neil's story as an example. Neil recently wrote to us at the Father's House and has given us permission to use his story. It is worth sharing because, as Neil himself admits, it is so worryingly normal in the contemporary church. This is what Neil says:

> *My story is one that could be repeated a million times over, throughout this land. However, this is a story not of a broken home and the absence of a father, but rather of a broken heart and the absence of my ability to receive love.*
>
> *My father was a good man who doted on my two brothers and me, yet due to financial pressures he was forced to work many hours and thus was often absent.*

But he loved us, and loved us deeply.

My father was taken ill when I was ten years old with a heart attack, and he suffered one a year until he died just before my sixteenth birthday.

It is only in the light of recent discoveries that I can now see that what was lacking was his ongoing affirming presence. What was missing in my life was the knowledge that there was a loving, understanding authority presence that was for me and not against me. I have never been able to rest in the love of someone like that. I never knew it; I never knew that it could be experienced. Added to this there was the strong influence that my mother had on me. She was a loving but forceful character, who somehow or other, communicated conditional love. If I was good, clever, top of the class and the life and soul of the party, then I would be able to receive the consummation of my hidden inward need to be loved.

At the age of eighteen I gave myself wholeheartedly to the pursuit of pleasure, seen through the bottom of a beer glass, and very pleasurable it was too, but ultimately empty and unable to meet the deep needs within.

At the age of twenty-four I became a Christian, and my heartfelt gratitude to Jesus for my salvation led me to throw myself fully into the work of the Gospel. However, the love of God was simply something God had objectively shown to save me and not a personal experience. It was as if this side of my being was incapable of receiving His love. Yet my passion for Jesus and His Kingdom knew no bounds. But I remained a servant, not a son. And what a devoted servant I was! I read the Bible more, prayed more, witnessed more and attended church more than all my contemporaries. I had a gift for communicating, which led to preaching, but with hindsight I have come to see that my main emphasis throughout the years has been service. I never got to resting in the Father's love.

My burnout, which led to our return from our beloved field of service, France, enabled me to unearth the hidden childhood motivations that had driven me all my life, but they did not take me to Abba, Father's heart. Since April 2004 I have been in ministry again, having stepped out of it for four and a half years, ministry that has been blessed with saved souls, but still marked by this absence, until a month or so ago.

I don't quite know what happened; it hasn't been the result of prayer from others, nor of Conference attendance or anything else. I have simply had this growing awareness that I have at last discovered that I have a Father figure who is for me and not against me, who believes in me as a person, and who loves me.

Neil's story is a powerful tale of the toxic power of "striving". His background was one in which he had a father who loved him but who was not present to show that love. This love deficit led him in later life to believe the lie that no one was ever going to love him in an ever-present, unconditional and demonstrative way. This lie in turn led him to negative beliefs about God – the lie that God is a Father who is absent, not present, whose love has to be earned rather than simply received. In this kind of spirituality, God was Master and Neil was a slave. Instead of resting in his position as a son, Neil became a driven man, trying to earn the Father's love through performance.

The elder brother syndrome

And this brings us, of course, to the elder brother. I am referring here to a character in perhaps the most famous story that Jesus ever told, the Parable of the Prodigal Son in Luke 15. This story tells of a father who has two sons. The first, his younger son, rebels against him. He asks for his share of the inheritance while his father is still alive – an appalling insult in the ancient world. His father graciously agrees to his son's shameful request and the boy leaves home to squander his father's fortune on wild living. Eventually his money runs out and he crashes. Having lost everything, he is reduced to looking after the pigs in a Gentile homestead. Pigs are unclean animals in Jewish thought and this boy is a Jewish boy. He has therefore truly "hit bottom", as experts in addiction would say. In this pit of degradation the boy comes to his senses and experiences an awakening. He realizes that even the slaves in his father's estate have a better life than he does, so he hatches a scheme to return to his dad and plead for the status of "hired servant" in his house. He begins the long trek home from the "far country" (i.e. the non-Jewish, Gentile lands) and eventually comes home. His dad sees him, runs to him, embraces him and forgives him. In a stunning act of mercy and generosity, he refuses to even hear the boy's plea to become a servant. He wants a son, not a slave. So the son is reinstated and a great party is started in his honour, to which everyone is invited.

It is at this point – just when you think the story's over and everyone will live happily ever after – that another character emerges. We heard right at the start of this tale that the father has two sons. The younger son insulted his father while there was an elder son present as well. In fact, understood from a Middle Eastern perspective, this elder brother's silence condemns him. The elder brother should have stood up for his father and reprimanded his younger brother. But he said nothing.

This elder brother disappears from the story until the moment of the younger son's return and the start of the great celebrations instigated by the relieved father. In verses 25–32 of Luke 15 we read what happens when he appears:

Meanwhile, the older son was in the field. When he came near the house, he heard music and dancing. So he called one of the servants and asked him what was going on. "Your brother has come," he replied, "and your father has killed the fattened calf because he has him back safe and sound."

The older brother became angry and refused to go in. So his father went out and pleaded with him. But he answered his father, "Look! All these years I've been slaving for you and never disobeyed your orders. Yet you never gave me even a young goat so I could celebrate with my friends. But when this son of yours who has squandered your property with prostitutes comes home, you kill the fattened calf for him!"

"My son," the father said, "you are always with me, and everything I have is yours. But we had to celebrate and be glad, because this brother of yours was dead and is alive again; he was lost and is found."

A few years ago I wrote a book on this parable called *The Father You've Been Waiting For.* In it I concentrated on the father figure and what we learn about him. Clearly Jesus is using this character to portray the Fatherhood of God. The exceptional father in this story – who goes way beyond what any father in the Middle East would have been expected to do – is a symbol of the perfect Father, our *Abba,* Father in heaven. In writing this book I concentrated on the younger son's homecoming and the marvellous, extravagant, compassionate love of his father. What I neglected to write about was the elder brother, whose behaviour throughout the story is at best questionable. He is clearly a very sad and bitter boy. He doesn't stand up for his dad when his brother insults him and he is very angry when his brother comes home. As has often been said, it's a good thing that the father was waiting for the younger son when he came home, not the elder brother!

Why does Jesus include this elder brother? It is because the people he is telling the story to are just like this character. In Luke 15:1–2 we read:

Now the tax collectors and "sinners" were all gathering around to hear him. But the Pharisees and the teachers of the law muttered, "This man welcomes sinners and eats with them."

It is extremely important to understand what these men are muttering about. These Pharisees and teachers of the Law are moaning that Jesus welcomes broken people to his meal table. Jesus is having meals with the messed up and parties with prostitutes. Why is he doing this? It is because his meal table is in fact a powerful message. Eating with someone in the Middle East is a sign that you welcome and accept them. Jesus' meals were a strong signal about who God is and what his kingdom is all about. They tell us that God is a loving Father who believes in embrace, not exclusion. They tell us that God is a party-throwing Dad who loves it when his children come home in repentance.

> God is not a lawyer; he is a lover. He is not an angry and exclusive legalist; he is a forgiving and demonstrative Father.

Why were Jesus' listeners so mad about this? It is because they believed in exclusion, not embrace. They believed that only the righteous could come into the kingdom. Only those who meticulously kept the Law and observed all of their rules and regulations could be considered insiders. Everyone who didn't measure up to these standards was an outsider, and tax-collectors and sinners were the most excluded in that regard. In telling the story of the loving father in Luke 15, Jesus turns the tables on these self-righteous religious elders. In effect he castigates them for misrepresenting God. God is not a lawyer; he is a lover. He is not an angry and exclusive legalist; he is a forgiving and demonstrative Father.

Jesus introduces the elder brother in the story because he wants to challenge his hearers to renounce their life of religious slavery (which in turn was enslaving others). Even the word "elder" in the phrase "elder brother" is a clue here. The word "elder" points to the status of the listeners, especially the teachers of the Law, as the religious "elders" of Jesus' time. It is quite clear from this that the elder brother represents the religious elders. When he exclaims that he has been slaving away for the father all these years, he is giving voice to the performance-oriented ethic of the Scribes and the Pharisees. The elder brother in the story is a picture of all those who embrace a life of religious striving. He is the embodiment of that drive to earn God's love through endless acts of self-righteous religious observance. He is the very opposite of Jesus. If Jesus stands for the law of love, the elder brother stands for the love of law. While Jesus rests in the knowledge of his Father's love, the elder brother strives to earn his father's affection.

The performance mind-set

If we look at the character of the elder brother more closely, we can see a number of characteristics of the mind-set of someone with a Master–slave relationship with God. Here are seven that spring to mind:

1. Angry

The storyteller says that the elder brother became "angry" when his brother came home. Why is the elder brother angry? He is angry because the younger son has been reinstated without punishment. He thinks his brother deserves to be severely beaten. He certainly isn't expecting his father to forgive him and to reinstate him as his son. What is worse still is that this act of restoration has big implications for the elder brother. It means that his share of the inheritance has just reduced in size. If the younger son is now part of the family again, that means the younger son will inherit more of his father's fortune in the future and that will entail financial loss for the elder brother. He has been slaving away for his father in order to protect this portion of the estate. Now everything he's worked for is under threat. He becomes mad and resentful at his father's extravagant love. He may even be cross because he regarded the prime beef as his as well!

Anger is one of the characteristics of the performance mind-set. Those who strive to earn the Father's love, or the love of others for that matter, often become angry people. Anger is the emotion I feel when one of my goals is blocked. If I am driven to earn another person's love, some of my goals are inevitably going to be blocked. How can I ever actually measure up to the standards that I've chosen to adopt? In reality, I cannot. Christians who have a performance mind-set often exude anger.

2. Unloving

The storyteller says that the elder brother refused to go in. This is a moment fraught with tragic significance. The elder brother is expected to come in and welcome all the guests. That was culturally a given. By staying outside he refuses to act hospitably and thereby insults his father. Here we need to remember that the story began with the younger son insulting his dad. Now the same story ends with the elder son doing exactly the same thing (though not in the same way).

The elder son's rebellion is a very public act. Everyone at the party would have seen that the elder brother was not fulfilling his responsibilities as a son here. In effect, he was behaving in a very unloving way. He was in fact sinning against love. His father loved him and wanted him to play his part in the celebrations, but he refused.

At this point the father does something extraordinary. He goes out to his boy and pleads with him to come on in. Now this goes right against what would have been anticipated within a Middle Eastern culture. It was the son who was meant to come in to the father, not the father who was supposed to go out to the son. It was the father's right to punish his boy for his shameful behaviour, but the father chooses to entreat him to come in rather than exclude or discipline him. This is quite simply amazing. For a second time on the same day this extraordinary father shows mercy and chooses reconciliation rather than retaliation. His love is amazing, while the love of the elder brother seems to be non-existent.

This again provides a picture of the performance mind-set. The fact is, those who strive to earn God's love are often themselves unloving people. They are quick to judge and slow to show mercy. They care more about being right than being in relationship. They often have an unloving edge to their words and their conduct.

3. Rude

When the father pleads with his elder son, he gets short change. The elder son replies by saying to his father, "Now look!" This is extremely discourteous. The boy should have been far more polite. He should have begun with the words, "O my father". But instead he forgets his manners and launches straight into an impolite act of self-righteous remonstration. He acts like he isn't even a member of the family. Not only does he refuse to acknowledge his father properly, he refers to his own brother as "this son of yours" – not "my brother", but "your son"!

Those who strive are often rude. People with a performance mind-set are not good at treating other people with respect and honour. Very often they run roughshod over even their family members in order to achieve their goals. Driven by a great inner will to power, they regard others disdainfully and they speak dishonourably to and about other people.

4. Driven

The most telling moment in this last section of the parable is when the elder brother proclaims in verse 29, "All these years

I've been slaving for you and never disobeyed your orders." The elder brother's whole mind-set has been one defined by the word "slavery". The younger son was of course a slave. He was a slave to sin. But the elder brother is a slave too. He is a slave to earning his father's love through performance. Both kinds of slavery are destructive. We know that the younger son's kind of slavery proves to be toxic but the same can be said for the elder son's too. He understands his relationship with his father in terms of duty not joy, law not love, performance not position. This is tragic.

Those who strive are driven people. They see their success or failure in terms of whether or not they measure up to the standards they feel God sets, or others set. In relation to God, people who have fallen into the performance trap embrace a Master–slave rather than a Father–child relationship. They think like slaves ("I have never disobeyed you") and they demand their rights ("I've worked long hours and I deserve my reward"). People who strive think and act like slaves, not like sons or daughters.

5. Competitive

What does the elder brother say to his father? "I worked hard and didn't get a young goat so I could celebrate with my friends." There are a number of things going on here. Notice that he says he wants a party with his friends. There is no mention of the father here. Clearly he is not invited! Yet more rejection, then, for the poor, longsuffering dad! But what the elder son is also saying is this. He worked harder than his younger brother and didn't even get a young goat. The younger brother didn't do any work and was given the prime beef. What we are seeing here is a competitive streak in the elder brother. He is competing with his younger brother for his father's possessions. In effect, both of these boys make a great mistake. They relate to their father on the basis of what they can get out of him, not out of love. The younger son learns his lesson. He loses everything except one thing – the one thing that really matters, his daddy's love. The elder brother doesn't appear to learn anything at all. He exudes a competitive mind-set. He just wants to be first and to have the greater prize.

There is something horribly competitive about Christians who adopt a performance-oriented walk with God. They strive for pole position and work strenuously for approval and applause. They are fiercely competitive and make comparisons with others. They are promoters of sibling rivalry within their own family and within God's family too. They are often extremely jealous of other people and unable to celebrate when someone else succeeds and thrives. In the end they can only celebrate their own achievements and are intimidated by anyone else's.

6. Selfish

The elder brother continues his tirade against his poor father. He adds, "but when this son of yours who has squandered your property with prostitutes comes home, you kill the fattened calf for him!" There is an incredibly selfish note to this statement. He refers to "your property" when talking of his younger brother's share of the inheritance. He refuses to acknowledge that in fact it was his brother's property because the father had given it to him. He should have said "his property".

Note the inconsistency here. The elder brother is unwilling to admit that his younger brother had the right of ownership in regard to his share of inheritance. Nor did he have the right to choose what to do with that share, once the father had given it away. On both counts he is wrong. But he is even further beyond the pale because he claims that he himself doesn't have the right to choose to do what he wants with his own share of the property! In this he betrays an astonishing self-centredness that must have broken his father's heart.

People who strive are almost always self-centred. All they care about is their own goals and gains. When they see others prospering, they become negative and accusatory. Their world is one which revolves entirely around themselves and their rights.

7. *Proud*

A final characteristic of the performance mind-set is pride. Not much needs to be said about the elder brother here. He is clearly a very proud man. He has a proud attitude towards his own life. He makes claims about his own performance that are clearly rooted in pride. He tells his father that he has been slaving for him and that he's never disobeyed him (a comment that hardly rings true, now that he is refusing to come into the party!) But he also reveals a great deal of pride in relation to his younger brother. He assumes the moral high ground and accuses his brother of squandering his father's estate by spending it on prostitutes. Now why does the elder brother say this? Does he need to get this specific? Of course he doesn't. He is clearly assuming a note of self-righteousness that is entirely unwarranted. When were prostitutes ever mentioned? On what occasion has the elder brother had an opportunity to hear about this? The truth is, he has had no opportunity. He is simply trying to paint his brother in the worst possible colours so that his own moral rectitude will be given more visibility. In reality, the elder brother is not just being proud here. He is fantasizing and gossiping. Like all who strive, he is proud and arrogant. He assumes a stance of self-righteous superiority over other people.

And it is precisely here that we return at the end of the chapter to where it began, with the religious elders who have been "muttering" about Jesus eating with sinners. The Pharisees and the teachers of the Law have been complaining that Jesus has meals with messed-up people. No doubt this included prostitutes. When the elder brother starts muttering against his younger brother, the religious elders hearing the story are exposed. They too are proud and arrogant. They too have a self-righteous sense of superiority over others. They too have a critical and judgmental spirit. The elder brother in the story truly is the elders listening to the story.

Lost inside the house

To see what Jesus is really saying here, we need to leave this story for a moment and have an overview of Luke 15 as a whole. When Jesus replies to his critics, he doesn't just tell one story. He in fact tells three. He begins with a story about a lost sheep. A shepherd has one hundred sheep and one goes missing. The shepherd leaves the ninety-nine and goes out searching for the one out in the hills that has become separated from the rest. In leaving the ninety-nine unattended, he of course takes a risk, but his passion is to restore the one that has become lost. Joyfully he finds it, drapes it over his shoulders, and then goes home. The sheep that was lost has been found, so he has a party with all his neighbours.

The second story Jesus tells is of a woman who loses a coin. She has ten but now one is missing, so she goes round the house, sweeps and cleans, searching for the lost coin. Eventually she finds it and she calls all her friends and neighbours round to have a party with her. Her coin was lost but now it is found.

After two stories, you might have been tempted to think that the point has been made. But Jesus has one more story left to tell. Perhaps it is because sheep and coins are incapable of repentance that he tells a third story. In this third story a younger son rejects his father and leaves home. He goes to the far country, but then realizes his mistake and comes home. His father holds a party because his son had been lost but now is found; he had been dead but now he's alive.

At this point the third story feels like it has ended and a fourth story begins, the story of the elder brother. In reality it is still part of the third story – the final story in a trilogy of remarkable parables. But it feels like a fourth story in some ways because this elder brother is also lost. If the younger brother is lost in his slavery to sin, the elder brother is lost in his slavery to striving.

Let me put it this way. In the first story, the sheep is lost outside the house. In the second story, the coin is lost inside the house. In the third story, the younger son is lost outside the house (in the far country). In the final story, the elder son is lost inside the house. He is empty in his father's presence. He is lost within his father's house.

When we put it this way we can see the deeply tragic and heart-breaking nature of the elder brother's problem. He is lost in a life of striving, in an ethic of performance that never satisfies. How does he respond?

The coin and the sheep are found, and so is the younger son. But the chapter ends without any clue concerning the elder brother's response. The story is left open-ended, unfinished, and in the air. The younger son makes his response but the elder one does not. The one who slept with the pigs is saved but the one who kept his life clean is not. He is still lost at the end of the story, as are the religious elders who are listening to Jesus' storytelling. What will he do? What will they do? What will anyone who is caught in the performance trap do?

No more slavery

Striving is the number-one symptom and sign of the orphan heart and those who are inside the Father's house – Christian believers – are by no means exempt. It is quite simply amazing how easy it is to slip into the elder brother's shoes and start living a driven life based on performance rather than a joyful life based on position. The Bible calls this state "slavery" and we are told to avoid it like the plague. The Apostle Paul makes this very clear in Galatians 4:6–7:

> *Because you are sons, God sent the Spirit of his Son into our hearts, the Spirit who calls out, "Abba, Father." So you are no longer a slave, but a son; and since you are a son, God has made you also an heir.*

Paul was writing to people who were being deceived by a group of Jewish believers who were arguing for a return to a works or performance mentality. In other words, they were trying to seduce others into thinking that they had to earn the Father's love through striving. Paul counters this by calling that kind of behaviour "slavery". He clearly states that we have been saved for sonship, not slavery. We are not to live in the constant fear of God's disapproval and punishment, but we are to live under the Father's smile, knowing that he is our Daddy and that he loves us with amazing grace, with unmerited but extreme love.

> We are not to live in the constant fear of God's disapproval and punishment but we are to live under the Father's smile knowing that he is our Daddy.

I know of only one antidote to the slavery of the performance mind-set and that is an encounter with the Father's love. Those who are caught in the performance trap will only be set free by what Paul speaks about in Galatians 4:4–6 – an experience of the Spirit of adoption which leads to the "*Abba*, Daddy!" cry of worship from our hearts. Those who are imprisoned in a life of striving need the Father to come out to them and whisper his gentle words of love in their ears, just like the father did with the elder brother. They need to hear his tender words of love and affection. Only an encounter like this will bring us into the party. Only an experience of the loving Spirit of adoption will break us free from our slavery and bring an end to that awful nightmare of being on the outside looking into the party that we, deep down, long to attend ourselves.

I will finish Part 2 with a story that I pray will fill you with hope, as we move into Part 3, from the scars to the cure. Encountering the Father's love is the indispensible requirement for all those who want to leave the performance orientation behind and who want to learn to rest in their position as much-loved sons and daughters. This testimony is from Michael W. Smith, a brilliant Christian song-writer and worship leader. In it he tells of how he drifted into a life of striving but how he was rescued by an encounter with the Father's love. This encounter has released him into a lifestyle of worshipping the Father from a place of deep assurance. Now he is no longer driven by whips but led by cords of love. Now he no longer ministers out of law but out of love. As we prepare to look in Part 3 at how we might be healed of slavery, my hope and prayer is that the work will begin right now, as you read this:

> *I had a good home life. My mum and dad are my biggest fans. But somewhere along the lines I found out that my life started to be based on performance, and that was quite depressing in many ways. For some reason I believed the lie that if you did all the right things then maybe God would love you more.*
>
> *Then, a little over twenty years ago, I was shaving and looking in the mirror, and my knees buckled. I had to grab the sink to keep from falling down because I had a massive revelation. God said to me, "Michael, you know I love you. But you know what? I don't just love you, I actually really like you. And not only do I like you, I'm extremely fond of you." At that very moment I began to understand the Father heart of God – that he just wanted to be my Papa. And for the first time I believed – and knew beyond a shadow of a doubt – that he had my name written on the palm of his hands. For the first time I knew that his mercies are new every day. For the first time I believed without a shadow of a doubt that he came to give me a future and a hope. And it just changed my life, because all of a sudden, my life wasn't based on performance. My identity crisis was solved. I knew I was a son of the High King of the universe.*
>
> *My life has really never been the same since because my security and my identity are not wrapped in*

a piano or in selling records. They're not wrapped up in my job, my home, in my car.

That's the message and it's really never changed. And that's my prayer for you that you would come to know the Father heart of God. Ever since that moment and that revelation I've been writing love songs for Papa.[60]

A prayer

Abba, Father, I pray that you will break the chains of slavery in my life. Where I have been the victim of religious or any other kind of legalism, I pray now in Jesus' name that the curse of the Law will be broken and that the blessing of Grace would flow into my life.

Thank you so much for the Cross. Thank you for the great exchange that Jesus won for me – I get his blessings, he gets my curses (Galatians 3:10–14). I pray now that the religious, striving spirit would be cast out of my life and that I would be delivered from slavery into sonship.

Help me, Loving Father, to enter into your rest (Hebrews 4:11), to live in the Sabbath rest and rejoicing that is my birthright as a child of the High King of Heaven. Help me to move from wrestling to nestling, from performance to play. Put the joy back in my heart!

So now, let all striving cease. Help me from this day on to minister out of rest. Help me to know there is nothing I can do for you to make you love me any more than you do already. May ministry flow out of intimacy. May I work hard *because* I'm loved, not in order to be loved. I pray in the words of John Whittier's hymn:

Drop Thy still dews of quietness,
Till all our strivings cease;
Take from our souls the strain and stress,
And let our ordered lives confess
The beauty of Thy peace.

In Jesus' name. Amen.

PART 3

THE
HEALING

Chapter 9

THE ROAD TO FREEDOM

On 29 April 1945, my adoptive father Philip Stibbe was part of a large number of POWs (prisoners of war) being guarded by Japanese soldiers. They had recently left Rangoon jail where they'd spent many months in prison – years, in my father's case – and they were now being moved to a new location. Those who had survived the ordeal of torture and deprivation were exhausted, emaciated and confused. They headed north in columns, marching under the watchful oversight of the men who had been guarding and oppressing them. After a while the guards suddenly barked some orders and allowed the British soldiers a rest underneath the trees. Many of them, including my father, fell asleep, weary from the journey.

A few hours later the POWs all began to wake up, and as they did, they quickly noticed that all the Japanese guards seemed to have disappeared. Not one of them was to be seen anywhere nearby. They had simply left without any warning. As everyone scratched their heads in bewilderment, the Brigadier who was in charge of the British troops called everyone to attention. There was a quick and obedient response and then he began to utter words that took every soldier's breath away: "At last I can tell you something that you have been waiting to hear for years: we are all free men!"

My father describes what happened next in his moving and beautifully written book, *Return via Rangoon*, first published in 1947, when he had returned to Oxford University to study English Literature under C. S. Lewis:

There was an audible gasp of astonishment, and a few seconds passed while this amazing news sank in; then pandemonium broke loose. There was a great shout of joy as the full realization of what it meant came over us; then we all went completely crazy, patting one another on the back, shaking hands, laughing and weeping simultaneously.

Soon they became aware of exactly what had happened. Evidently the Japanese Commandant at Rangoon jail had realized that the War was all but over. The Allied forces were drawing nearer and nearer to their position and he knew that Rangoon jail would be recaptured. So he had summoned the Brigadier and come to an agreement, that his soldiers would march the POWs north towards their advancing Allied comrades and then leave them there to wait for the Allies to arrive. The Commandant had even written a signed document to this effect, in case the unguarded POWs ran into any retreating Japanese soldiers. This document would alert the enemy to the fact that the POWs had been released, that they were free, and were not to be harmed.

Now, with the guards having left, the Brigadier informed his soldiers that they were no longer POWs but free men. My father later wrote of the exhilaration that he and his comrades felt at this moment:

We were free. The strain under which we had lived for so long was suddenly lifted and the feeling of relief was almost unbearable. Now for the first time for years we could look forward confidently to the future we had almost despaired of, to our homes and families, to a civilised life instead of a bare existence... Four hundred of us had been lifted from utter wretchedness to unbelievable happiness on that Sunday morning in an unknown village about seventy miles north of Rangoon.

After these heady moments, there followed days of marching and waiting until they were reunited with their own forces. More days of recuperation followed, including several idyllic days of rest by the sea in Israel. My father was later to say, "we were free, we were safe, we were happy". Then there began the long journey home to Great Britain. In the last paragraph of his memorable book he tells of how the aeroplane that he and some of his comrades were flying in suddenly broke through the clouds to reveal the beautiful, green landscape of England beneath. He sums up "the unspeakable joy of homecoming" in a terse but memorable sentence: "There was no need for any speeches; it was enough to know that we were home."[1]

Legally free, actually free

It may seem strange for me to begin Part 3 of *I Am Your Father* with a story about prisoners of war, but there is a point to all this! Besides being a story about my adoptive father, it also provides a useful illustration. Throughout Parts 1 and 2 I have been proposing that the enemy has been conducting a war against fatherhood and that the worldwide pandemic of fatherlessness is evidence of this. Tragically, this demonic campaign has left a legacy in the church as well. Believers come to know Jesus and in that sense they are saved and going to heaven. But far too many don't really know God as *Abba*, Father. Bound by the wounds they have suffered at the hands of their earthly fathers (even the wound of indifference), they find it difficult if not impossible to relate to God intimately in a child–father relationship. Consequently, many inside the church are really in chains. They are prisoners to their past. They know they have been forgiven but they haven't really experienced true freedom. They have been pardoned legally and believe it. But they haven't yet entered into their full inheritance and started to live in the glorious freedom of the children of God. While this situation remains – and it pertains on a very wide scale – the church is part of the problem of fatherlessness rather than God's most potent solution.

The sad fact is that far too many Christians are not living as free people. If we remember the three stages of my father's liberation – legally free, actually free, and finally free – there are far too many who are legally free but not actually free. That was certainly my story. On 17 January 1977, I was walking down Kingsgate Street in Winchester, far away from God. But the Holy Spirit started to convict my heart and within minutes I was at a Christian teacher's door – at 11:15 at night – asking for salvation. He knelt down with me on the floor of his front room and led me in a prayer of confession and repentance in which I asked Jesus for forgiveness, thanked him for paying for my sins at Calvary, and invited him into my life as my Saviour, Lord and friend. That day I knew I was forgiven. Forgiveness is a priceless gift.

Bono, the lead singer of U2, has written a book simply entitled *Bono on Bono*. It is, in reality, a 300-page description of a series of answers he gave to his interviewer who co-authored the book. It is a fascinating book, not least because of Bono's clear stand for the Cross. He speaks very powerfully of the difference between the Hindu doctrine of karma and the Christian doctrine of grace. The essence of his argument is that Hinduism teaches, "you sin, you pay", while Christianity teaches, "you sin, Christ pays".[2] Bono confesses that he is holding out for grace because he knows what he is like. He admits he is a man in need of amazing grace, of the undeserved love of God revealed in the sacrificial death of Jesus. Then, at the very end of the book, the interviewer asks Bono a perceptive question. He asks, "Is there anything that makes you speechless?" This is a great question because Bono is an extremely articulate man and can talk with great passion and eloquence. But Bono now pauses and then says very simply: "Yes, forgiveness… especially, being forgiven."[3]

Every Christian needs to know this glorious gift of forgiveness. When Jesus died on the Cross, he cried out, "Father, forgive them, for they know not what they do." Those two words, "Father, forgive" are among the most powerful and significant ever uttered. At the Cross, Jesus released the Father's pardon to all those who would repent of their sins and put their trust in him. At the Cross, sinners like me were given the opportunity of receiving a full and divine pardon because of the self-sacrificial love of Jesus the Messiah. Near midnight on 17 January 1977, I went and knelt at the foot of the Cross and confessed my sin, my wilful independence from God and my self-centred life. I was immediately, totally, unconditionally forgiven. The next morning I woke up feeling speechless. I was no longer under condemnation and I no longer feared God's punishment. I knew that the previous night on Kingsgate Street, I had entered through a gate into the presence of the King. I knew that I was different, changed and fully alive. That cold, wintery evening in Winchester was the turning point in my life. Being forgiven revolutionized my life.

And yet, not everything changed. I was forgiven, but I wasn't free. For years after that momentous evening, I knew Jesus and loved Jesus. I had a Jesus-centred faith. But the Holy Spirit was not a personal, supernatural, experiential reality in my life and the Father was not even on my radar. There were a number of reasons for this, but the first was the fact that I was a part of a church that believed that the miracle-working power of the Holy Spirit was enjoyed by the New Testament church but not by Christians today. This meant that there was no expectation of the Spirit's power moving in our lives and that everything revolved around the Bible. Our faith was a bookish faith. It was cerebral, not experiential. The Holy Spirit was really replaced by the Holy Bible and emotional or inner healing was frowned upon.

A second reason why I had an incomplete understanding of God was because of my father wounds. While I had enjoyed a good relationship with my adoptive father, Philip Stibbe, I had had no relationship with my biological father. He had abandoned my birth mother before my twin sister and I were born. This meant that the word "Father" was not a positive one in my heart. While I was aware of people addressing God as "Father", I was not able to do that myself. Calling God "Father" meant that I was setting myself up for further abandonment – this time not by an earthly father but by God himself.

It took ten years to get to the place where I could cry out "*Abba*, Father" to God. That came when I had a powerful experience of the Holy Spirit during a time of worship in a youth celebration when a song began to strike up with the words:

> *Father God, I wonder how I managed to exist*
> *without the knowledge of your parenthood*
> *and your loving care.*
> *But now I am your son*
> *I am adopted in your family*
> *and I can never be alone,*
> *because Father God you're there beside me.*
>
> IAN SMALE, COPYRIGHT © 1984 THANKYOU MUSIC.

At that moment it was as if the lights came on. I suddenly understood that God is a perfect Father; that he never abandons his kids; and that he has chosen and adopted us to be his sons and daughters forever. At that moment, it was as if my chains fell off and I started to enjoy what Paul called "the glorious freedom of the children of God" (Romans 8:21).

In a nutshell, my experience is very common and it can be summed up in the following phrase: "forgiven, but not free". I was like the POWs I wrote about earlier. I was legally free but not actually free. Everything needed for my freedom had been achieved by Jesus at Calvary. I was legally free from the moment when I knelt and repented of my sins in 1977. But it wasn't until ten years later that I became actually free. For a decade I was living like a POW, as if guards were all around me, not realizing that I was a free man! It took a mighty encounter with the Holy Spirit to release me from a Jesus-only faith to a Trinitarian walk with God in which I knew *Abba*, Father through Jesus and in the power of the Spirit. That was truly a day of liberation!

Forgiven but not free

Freedom is the great hallmark of those who are the adopted sons and daughters of *Abba*, Father. Jesus said in John 8:36, "if the Son sets you free, you will be free indeed". Paul pronounced in Galatians 5:1, "it is for freedom that Christ has set us free". Jesus' death and resurrection have liberated every single person who has chosen to put their faith and trust in Jesus. As far as the New Testament writers are concerned, the followers of Jesus are supposed to live as sons and daughters, not as slaves to sin, because we have been set free from the enemy's rule and ownership. We are no longer the sons and daughters of the father of lies; we are the sons and daughters of a loving Father. We no longer strive to earn the Father's affection; we rest in the revelation that we are greatly loved. We no longer live by the lie, "I do, therefore I am"; we live by the truth, "I am, therefore I do". We are no longer fearful of punishment; we are assured of our position. We are no longer driven by whips of law; we are led by cords of love. We are no longer uncertain of who we are or where we stand; we know we are the royal children of the High King of Heaven and that we are welcome in his presence. We are no longer bound by guilt and shame; we are forgiven and we live as honoured members of God's family. Christians are supposed to be free people. Indeed, we of all people should know what freedom really means. As the great poet William Cowper once said:

Freedom has a thousand charms to show,
That slaves, howe'er contented, never know.[4]

> We are no longer driven by whips of law; we are led by cords of love.

Why is it that so many Christians are forgiven and yet still so bound? One of the main reasons I have discovered during twenty-five years of counselling and ministry is that the church has not known how to deal with the wounds inflicted by our fathers. The church has at best neglected the idea that people who become Christians are still wounded and in need of inner and emotional healing. To a cerebral church, this all seems far too sentimental and self-indulgent. What new Christians are taught is that they need to assent intellectually to the truths of the Bible. The idea that the deep hurts caused by the orphan heart condition somehow need to be faced and then displaced by a personal revelation of *Abba*, Father's love has been largely ignored or dismissed. While no one would want to disagree that esteeming and applying the truths of the Bible is absolutely central to the healing process, this denial of the toxic power of father wounds, along with a widespread suspicion concerning subjective encounters with the Father's love, has left many believers embattled and in chains. In fact, it has really only been in the last decade of the twentieth century that there have been any signs of a change in this situation. Since the mid 1990s there has been a fresh wind of renewal in the church in which believers have been given a revelation of the Father's love, resulting in forgiveness and freedom.

The sad fact is, however, far too many have had to wait such a long time for their freedom to come because of wrong theology and a suspicion of emotions. The following testimony, from a retired pastor called Terry, is typical in this regard:

> *My mother deserted us when I was four years old. My younger brother went to an aunt, my older sister went to our grandma and I went into a children's home where I was abused physically and emotionally. After a succession of foster homes and children's homes I was returned to my father seven years later. He never wanted children so I was either told to go outside or upstairs. Never was I held or told I was loved, just*

the opposite. I was regularly beaten for the slightest misdemeanour and one time put head first in a water-filled barrel. I thought I was going to die.

Now let's fast forward in time thirteen years. I had a "Damascus Road" conversion experience. But I had the faith of a servant, not a son. Obviously I could not relate to Father God but I was so thankful to Jesus for taking my punishment. I knew a lot about punishment.

I was married by this time and my wife had two sons from a previous marriage. They were one and nine years old when we got together. Both became Christians as did my wife, though one has now fallen away. I became a Methodist Minister at thirty-nine.

I took early retirement a few years ago. I wrote a book, unpublished, in response to Richard Dawkins' The God Delusion. It helped me sort a few things out. Either God is God and He knows what He is doing, or I pack it in. I couldn't deny all the blessings I had received, especially when I was told my wife was going to die. That was thirty years ago and she lives!

That first year of retirement was a time of great blessing. Then I hit a very steep decline, my "Dark Night of the Soul", for about a year. On the way up I read a book which said "If you don't love God, pray to Him and ask Him to help you to love Him." I did.

Two weeks later I received a letter from our older son and daughter in law. I had asked for a recording of a conference they held at their church on "Signs and Wonders". Instead I received a recording of another conference, "The Father Loves You", which you had given. I didn't connect it with my prayer and left it for some time. Then out of a sense of duty I thought I had better listen to it. It blew me away! I felt like new wine had been poured into an old wineskin and I was about *to burst! I have never experienced anything like it. Why oh why hadn't I heard this before? I subsequently bought your books* From Orphans to Heirs, *and of course* The Father You've Been Waiting For. *How I wish I was still in ministry. This is what the Church, the world needs to hear. There are still too many orphan sons and daughters.*

Thank You, Father. Thank you for waiting! I can now say, "I LOVE YOU, I LOVE YOU, I LOVE YOU" to the Father...

This is a really helpful testimony for several reasons. For one thing, it clearly highlights the deficiency of some of our theology. Terry had to wait much of his adult life for his freedom because the prevailing theology of his day was one which did not give primacy to the revelation of God as *Abba*, Father. Nor did it leave any room for inner or emotional healing for the deep issues of shame brought about by the wounds from a father and a mother. This is tragic. At the same time Terry's story encourages us because he did get healed. He eventually experienced freedom as well as forgiveness and found that God is indeed the Father he had been waiting for. One reason why Terry had this experience is because the Holy Spirit has recently been breathing afresh upon the church all over the globe, releasing many from a legalistic theology into a relational theology in which God is known as *Abba*, Father. Terry was set up by the Holy Spirit to receive this revelation and today he has a whole new foundation on which to build his walk with God. Now he is "rooted and grounded in God's marvellous love" (Ephesians 3:17, New Living Translation) – and not a moment too soon.

Far too many have had to wait such a long time for their freedom to come because of wrong theology and a suspicion of emotions.

Understanding how we're wired

Throughout this book I have stated that a vast number of us within the church are suffering from father wounds. We have been saved, yes, but we are still sick. We are legally free but not living actually free. Many of us in the church are children of God yet we still have an orphan heart condition. We have come to the Cross and been justified and pardoned but we continue to wrestle with the toxic legacy of wounds suffered at the hands of our fathers and our mothers earlier in our lives. This means that even though we are saved, we still live with a sense of abandonment and rejection, sadness and worthlessness. This leads to a paradox; we claim to be children of God on Sunday but we live like orphans on Monday – and indeed throughout the rest of the week until the next Sunday comes around.

How then are we to rectify this problem? One of the ways we can change this situation is by understanding how we are wired. By that I mean we need to appreciate how we have been created as human beings. Many of us operate on the assumption that we are bipartite human beings – in other words, that we are made up of two parts, the body and the soul. This leads to a strict division between the spiritual and the physical. The physical tends to be downplayed and the spiritual tends to be elevated. Becoming a Christian in this framework becomes a matter of "getting saved spiritually", of having our souls saved from eternal separation from God.

But this is really a Greek rather than a Jewish way of thinking. It owes more to ancient Greek philosophers like Plato than it does to Jewish Christians like Paul. The Apostle Paul has a much more Hebraic view of how we are wired up or designed by the Father. He sees us as more than just body and soul. In 1 Thessalonians 5:23 he presents us with a three-part, not a two-part, vision of human beings. In his remarks to the church that he's planted in the Greek city of Thessalonica, Paul says, "May God himself, the God of peace, sanctify you through and through. May your whole *spirit, soul and body* be kept blameless at the coming of our Lord Jesus Christ" (italics mine). Notice here how Paul speaks of the three parts our humanity; he speaks of the spirit, soul and body. There has been a lot of discussion about just how differentiated these are in Paul's understanding, but I believe that Paul sees these three as distinctive parts of our humanity. Just as God is three-in-one, so we have three parts to our humanity, all within the one person. Created in the image of the Triune God, we too are "three-in-one" beings. We are spirit, soul and body just as God is Father, Son and Holy Spirit.

What is the difference between these three aspects of our humanity? The truth is, Paul never develops this idea in any detail. He doesn't provide hard-and-fast definitions of each word and a comprehensive tract on the biblical vision of human personhood. But we know enough from his writings to say the following: that the spirit (*pneuma*) is that part of us which is designed to relate to God, that the soul (*psyche*) is that part of us which is designed to relate to our own selves, and the body (*soma*) is that part of us which is designed to relate to the outside world and to others. The spirit is about the upward dimension, the soul the inward dimension and the body the outward dimension of human being.

The human spirit

When a person becomes a Christian something extremely powerful happens at the level of the spirit. The human spirit is dead in sin up until this moment. As a person experiences rebirth through repenting of sin and believing in Jesus, their spirit is quickened with life. The Holy Spirit brings life to their spirits and this life is not just physical life; it is abundant, eternal and resurrection life.

In the New Testament there are two Greek words translated "life". One is *bios* and refers to our biological life. It is the word from which we get "biography". The other is *zoe* and it refers to infinite, spiritual life – to the life of the Spirit, who raised Christ Jesus from the dead.

BIOS

• Finite, physical life

ZOE

• Infinite, spiritual life

C. S. Lewis also drew attention to the difference between these two words at the end of Chapter 23 of *Mere Christianity*. It is a passage that's worth quoting in full. He wrote:

The difference between Biological life and Spiritual life is so important that I am going to give them two distinct names. The Biological sort which comes to us through Nature, and which (like everything else in Nature) is always tending to run down and decay so that it can only be kept up by incessant subsidies from Nature in the form of air, water, food, etc., is Bios. *The Spiritual life which is in God from all eternity, and which made the whole natural universe, is* Zoe.

Bios *has, to be sure, a certain shadowy or symbolic resemblance to* Zoe: *but only the sort of resemblance there is between a photo and a place, or a statue and a man. A man who changed from having* Bios *to having* Zoe *would have gone through as big a change as a statue which changed from being a carved stone to being a real man. And that is precisely what Christianity is about. This world is a great sculptor's shop. We are the statues and there is a rumour going round the shop that some of us are some day going to come to life.*[5]

Readers here may remember the wonderful moment in C. S. Lewis' children's story *The Lion, the Witch and the Wardrobe* when Aslan the lion (symbolic of Jesus) breathes upon the statues in the witch's palace. The witch has literally petrified these creatures but now Aslan's breath brings them back to life so that they can fight and win the battle against the witch and bring an end to her rule in Narnia.[6] That is *zoe* life. It is supernatural life. It is resurrection life. It is carried by the breath of the Lion of Judah, Jesus of Nazareth. It turns hearts of stone into hearts of flesh and it brings the dead and the dying to life.

When a person is born again their human spirit is made alive in Christ. It was dead in sin but now it is given *zoe* life. Jesus said in John 10:10, "the thief comes only to steal and kill and destroy; I have come that they may have life, and have it to the full." Only Jesus can breathe this kind of spiritual life into human spirits. As the Apostle John put it in 1 John 5:12, "He who has the Son has life; he who does not have the Son of God does not have life." When I surrendered my life to Jesus on 17 January 1977, the Father's spiritual life entered my human spirit and brought something dead to life. That is why the next morning I woke up and felt truly alive for the first time in my life. My spirit was made alive to commune with the Living God and worship him.

C. S. Lewis points out in Chapter 26 of *Mere Christianity* that "in our natural state we are not sons of God, only (so to speak) statues. We have not got *Zoe* or spiritual life: only *Bios* or biological life which is presently going to run down and die."[7] It is only when we have been born again by the Holy Spirit that our spirits are made alive and we move from being statues to sons and daughters. People are not by nature sons and daughters of *Abba*, Father. Rather they are spiritual orphans living in a state of slavery. It is only by encountering Jesus and committing our lives to him that we can find ourselves moving from slavery to sonship, from being orphans to being the children of God.

The soul and the body

Many make the mistake of thinking that salvation is designed to change the human spirit alone. They think that it applies only to the spiritual part of our being and that it means only the transformation of the human spirit from death to life. In reality, salvation applies to more than just our spirits. It applies to the whole person.

Here we need to remember that the New Testament does from time to time distinguish between spirit and soul, between *pneuma* and *psyche*. We tend to treat spirit and soul as synonyms. But they do not seem to mean the same thing in the Bible. In 1 Thessalonians 5:23, Paul talks about the spirit, the soul and the body of every believer becoming "sanctified through and through". In other words, he speaks about a process in which the whole person – the spiritual, psychological and physical parts of us – is made more and more holy and whole during the journey of the Christian life. In another well-known passage the writer to the Hebrews talks about the power of the Word of God in relation to this process. In Hebrews 4:12 he says:

For the word of God is living and active. Sharper than any double-edged sword, it penetrates even to dividing

> *soul and spirit, joints and marrow; it judges the*
> *thoughts and attitudes of the heart.*

Here again "soul" is differentiated from "spirit". What then is the soul?

If the spirit is that part of our being that relates to God, the human soul is that part of our being that relates to ourselves. The *psyche* is the dimension of our lives in which we think, feel and choose. It is composed of what we would call the mind, the emotions and the will. When a person is born again, God's spiritual life impacts a person's human spirit, as we've just seen. This is such a seismic and dramatic event that the life of God radiates from the inside out, pouring out from the recesses of our spirits into the human soul. What this in turn means is that our thinking, our feelings, our decision-making all begin to be affected by this transformation. The soul begins to function differently. Instead of thinking selfishly, we start to think in alignment with the Word of God. Instead of giving in to negative emotions, we begin to experience brand-new affections or feelings like "love, joy and peace". Instead of making choices based on our own selfish values and goals, we start to make choices that please our Heavenly Father. The soul is therefore directly influenced by the life flowing out from the spirit at the moment of salvation. While this doesn't for a moment mean that a person is instantly perfect, it does mean that a person begins to change radically in the way they think, feel and act. Thus, when I experienced salvation in 1977, a journey started in which I began to think, feel and act more like Jesus. Over thirty years later this process is still going on.

Salvation is accordingly a journey. We have been saved; we are in the process of working out our salvation; and we will one day receive the fullness of our salvation. This journey begins at the moment of rebirth, in which the life of the Holy Spirit brings life to our human spirits. This life begins to penetrate the human soul – the place where all our thinking, our memories, our imagining, our reflection, our analyzing, our feeling, our experiences, and our decision-making happens. The journey of salvation therefore does not involve the human spirit alone. It embraces the human soul as well. Salvation commits a person to a process of having their thoughts, emotions and choices brought more and more into alignment with *Abba*, Father's design. That design means each of us, as the adopted children of God, becoming more and more conformed to the likeness of Jesus, who is the one and only Son of God. We are sons and daughters *by adoption*. He is the Son *by nature*. Salvation is a process in which the human soul is gradually transformed so that it takes on the family likeness and begins to resemble our perfect Older Brother, Jesus. In other words, salvation is a journey in which the spirit, soul and body become increasingly alive. As the early church father Irenaeus once said, "the glory of God is a human being fully alive".[8]

This journey also affects our body (*soma*), not just the soul and the spirit. *Abba*, Father is not just interested in the transformation of our spiritual and psychological life. He is passionate about the transformation of our physical bodies as well. When *zoe* life comes into our spirits, it not only radiates outwards through our souls, it also extends to our physical bodies so that other people actually see the difference in us physically when we are saved. Our faces in fact become radiant. Our eyes – which are the windows of the soul – lose their dark emptiness and are filled with light. I remember a few days after I had been born again in January 1977, I went to the pub with some of my soccer-playing mates to have a few drinks. I had been the school rebel, in many ways, and so my friends were somewhat colourful characters. As we spoke in the bar, I recall one of my friends saying, "There's something different about you. You've changed. I can see it in your eyes."

In 2 Corinthians 3:12–18 Paul speaks about how there is a veil over our faces until we turn to Jesus. It is a spiritual veil which keeps us blind to the truth of God's Word. But when we turn to the Lord in repentance and faith, the Holy Spirit removes the veil from our faces so that we can see who Jesus truly is. Paul says that the Holy Spirit can do that because the Holy Spirit is in the business of setting people free from all that binds and blinds them. He then goes on to add this extraordinary statement about the journey of transformation that every new believer in Christ begins. It is a journey in stages that not only affects the human spirit and soul. It also affects the physical body as well, so that our faces light up, just as the face of Moses used to whenever he met face to face with God in the Tent of Meeting:

> *And we, who with unveiled faces all reflect the Lord's glory, are being transformed into his likeness with ever-increasing glory, which comes from the Lord, who is the Spirit.*

Paul uses the Greek word *metamorphoo* when he speaks of us being transformed. This is the word from which we get "metamorphosis". A Christian is a person who experiences increasing metamorphosis over the course of his or her life. We begin by looking and behaving like sinners. We end by looking and behaving like the Saviour. In this journey, we gradually become more and more healed, more and more free. This applies to every part of our lives. Our spirits become more alive. Our souls become more alive. Our bodies become more alive. That is why old people who are wholly devoted to the Lord look far more alive than young people who are not. When we commit our lives to the Father we turn from the earth-bound restriction of the chrysalis to the unrestricted flight of the butterfly. We move from bland darkness to glorious colour. Everything is transformed – *pneuma*, *psyche* and *soma*. Our faces become shiny. Our eyes are ablaze. There is resurrection life in our mortal bodies.

William James once said,

When we commit our lives to the Father we turn from earth bound restriction of the chrysalis to the unrestricted flight of the butterfly. We move from bland darkness to glorious colour.

"Human beings, by changing the inner attitudes of their minds, can change the outer aspects of their lives."[9] That is so true. The salvation that Jesus won for us at Calvary doesn't just affect our spirits. It affects everything. As we change on the inside – at the level of spirit and soul – we change on the outside as well. Salvation should therefore not be understood in the simplistic Greek sense, as something applying to the soul but not the body. It should be understood in the far more glorious Hebraic sense, as something applying to the spirit, the soul and the body together. A fully orbed understanding of salvation is called for. We need to understand that the benefits of the Cross apply to us holistically. As we experience more and more of our salvation in Christ, we walk down a road of increasing freedom. We become more and more liberated from the old nature and we become more and more released into the new nature. We are set free from our old, false identities and wooed into our brand-new identities as the adopted sons and daughters of the High King of Heaven. As this happens we begin to think like Jesus, talk like Jesus, walk like Jesus, and behave like Jesus. In the end this means that we will be seen to look like Jesus when he returns on the clouds in great glory on the last day. As the Apostle John writes in 1 John 3:1–2:

> How great is the love the Father has lavished on us, that
> we should be called children of God! And that is what
> we are! The reason the world does not know us is that it
> did not know him. Dear friends, now we are children
> of God, and what we will be has not yet been made
> known. But we know that when he appears, we shall be
> like him, for we shall see him as he is.

The joy of liberation

To anyone who has experienced the loss of freedom, liberation is an indescribable and unparalleled experience. When slaves are emancipated, when POWs are set free, when unjustly imprisoned victims are released, the ecstatic feeling of freedom is almost beyond the capacity of the human mind to portray. Even my father, a scholar of English literature who was being mentored by C. S. Lewis – a brilliant communicator – found it hard to put it into words. In the epilogue of his book he wrote about how challenging he had found it to express himself:

> *Perhaps after all I was foolish to try to write this book so soon after the events described, and at a time when, not having put pen to paper for more than two years, the crudity of my style or lack of style was bound to be painfully obvious. I have left unsaid so much that could and should be said...* [10]

Philip Stibbe, the author's adoptive father.

The truth is, every Christian knows something of the exhilaration of liberation. The Bible teaches that we live in a world at war – a war between light and darkness. The crucial turning point in this spiritual conflict was the birth, life, death and resurrection of Jesus Christ. Through his self-sacrificial death on the Cross, Jesus has brought freedom to those who acknowledge their need to be delivered from slavery and imprisonment. As Jesus said in Luke 4:18–19:

> *The Spirit of the Lord is on me,*
> *because he has anointed me*
> *to preach good news to the poor.*
> *He has sent me to proclaim freedom for the prisoners*
> *and recovery of sight for the blind,*
> *to release the oppressed,*
> *to proclaim the year of the Lord's favour.*

In this chapter I have tried to suggest that the freedom that Jesus has won for us is a freedom that should affect us at every level of our lives. It should not be confined to the spiritual part of our human being. It should be applied to the totality of our personhood – spirit, soul and body. In light of this, far more attention should be given to

The freedom that Jesus has won for us is a freedom that should affect us at every level of our lives.

the healing of the soul than has been up until now. Our thinking needs to be liberated. Our emotions need to be healed. Our decisions need to be transformed. The whole of our lives needs to be impacted by the work of the Spirit, not just part. The Gospel applies to everything.

In the remainder of this book I want to look at how we can travel further down this road of glorious freedom. I especially want to look at how the human soul can be restored in the image of *Abba*, Father so that we are no longer bound by the tendencies of our old identities but set free to enjoy the thoughts, feelings and choices befitting our new identities. Before we look at the keys that unlock our chains, we need in the next chapter to look at the importance of the work of the Holy Spirit within the human soul. We need to look at how the Holy Spirit can help us to transform the way we think, the way we feel and the way we behave. My central claim will be that it is the Spirit of adoption that we need if we are to be free as well as forgiven. This will lead us to the subject of encountering *Abba*, Father's love in our hearts. Only a positive experience of our Heavenly Father's presence can displace the negative experience of an earthly father's absence. Only the positive experience of *Abba*, Father's love can displace the negative experience of an earthly father's hatred, and so on. We need to experience this divine affection in a direct and personal way, and the good news is that the Bible clearly teaches us that we can feel the flame of God's love – the love of all loves – and receive the hug of heaven. With that fire burning in our hearts, we will be able to live actually free, not just legally free.

Chapter 10

RECEIVING THE RING

I have an American friend called Ruth Graham. She is the daughter of Dr Billy Graham, the celebrated evangelist, and she runs a ministry for Christians with broken hearts.[11] I first had the privilege of meeting Ruth in Northern Ireland and then subsequently in Scotland. On both occasions we were the main speakers at a conference. Ruth heard me speak about the Father's love and subsequently told me how she had made many mistakes during her life. She shared about broken marriages and failed relationships with honesty and dignity. She then told me how she had decided that it was time to go home to her father and to put her life right. She had travelled a long distance to do that and she had been filled with some trepidation. How would her father respond to the return of his prodigal daughter? I will let Ruth tell the story in her own words:

I wound my way up my parents' steep, mountain driveway in North Carolina, unsure if I would be welcomed or rejected. I was broken by the choices I had made. Stubborn and wilful, I had followed my own path, and now I would have to face the consequences. I had caused pain for my children and loved ones. I feared I had embarrassed my parents. It seemed I had wrecked my world. The shame was almost unbearable.

I had driven sixteen hours from South Florida, stopping to pick up my youngest daughter at boarding school, and now I was tired and anxious. The familiarity of my childhood environs did little to subdue my fears. The February mountain air was crisp and clean. The bare trees — maple, poplar and oak — lining the drive up to my parents' house afforded a great view for the time of year, but I was too absorbed to notice.

What would my life be like now? I had gone against everyone's advice. My family warned me. They had tried to stop me. But I had not listened. I needed to do what was best for me, I had told them. And now my life was a shambles. I was a failure in my own eyes and certainly would be in the eyes of others who learned what "Billy Graham's daughter" had done. I feared I had humiliated those I held dearest. How would I be able to face them?

Driving up the mountain, my fears multiplied. Adrenaline kept my foot on the gas. I felt my hands grip the steering wheel. My mind was spinning. I tried to remember my mother's insistent tone from our phone conversation a few days earlier. "Come home," she had urged. I was desperate when I called her. I told her of my mistake and was trying to piece together a plan when she interjected with the voice of a loving, protective parent. But how would she and my father respond when they saw me? What would they say to me? Would they say "You've made your bed, now lie in it"? Would they condemn me? Would they reject me? Despise me? They had every right.

As I rounded the last bend in the driveway, Daddy came into view. He was standing in the paved area where visitors usually park. Rolling the car to a stop I took a deep breath and prepared to greet my father. I turned off the ignition, opened the car door, and stepped into the driveway. Then I looked up — Daddy was already at my side. Before I could say a word, he took me into his arms and said "Welcome home."[12]

Billy Graham may be known all over the world as the greatest evangelist of the twentieth century and one of the most influential men of his generation. But to Ruth he is known as a loving and accepting father. When his daughter eventually made her homecoming, he was there waiting for her with his arms opened wide. Billy will no doubt have talked about God's love a million times in his life, but I doubt whether he's ever illustrated it more memorably and vividly than in that one simple phrase uttered to his heartbroken daughter – "Welcome home." When Ruth whispered the story to me during a conference, I was moved. When I saw the full version of her testimony in this written form, I was moved again. There is nothing quite like a forgiving, loving, affectionate dad!

The homecoming

Ruth tells the story of a prodigal daughter. Nearly two thousand years ago, Jesus told the story of a prodigal son. I have already devoted a great deal of attention to this timeless story in my book, *The Father You've Been Waiting For*. We have already examined some aspects of this great parable in this book too. It is perhaps the greatest story ever told by the world's greatest storyteller, Jesus of Nazareth. Just a brief summary is therefore needed. The parable tells the tale of a younger son who goes to his father and asks for his share of the inheritance while his father is still alive. This is a big insult in that particular culture and it is a deep rejection. Amazingly, the father lets his son have what he asks for – just as our Heavenly Father sometimes gives us what we want in order to expose what we really need. The boy goes off into the far country and throws away his dad's hard-earned money on wild, reckless and hedonistic living. Eventually, having lost everything, the boy experiences an awakening. He realizes that the servants back home are better off than this son in a foreign land. So he hatches a cunning plan. He will return to his father and say sorry, adding that he is prepared to spend the rest of his life working as a slave to pay off all his debts.

The boy starts the journey home. As he draws closer, the camera – as it were – turns back on the father who has been waiting for his son's homecoming. As the silhouette of his emaciated boy appears on the horizon, the father does something extraordinary. We read about his response in Luke 15:20: "But while he was still a long way off, his father saw him and was filled with compassion for him; he ran to his son, threw his arms around him and kissed him." What an amazing reaction! Every one of Jesus' original listeners would have gasped in amazement. We should too. This father goes way beyond anything that would have been expected of a dad in the Middle East, or anywhere else for that matter. What love he shows!

There are five things the storyteller tells us about the father's reaction in this one great verse (Luke 15:20). First of all, he tells us that the dad saw his son. That means that the father was keeping a lonely vigil day and night, waiting for his boy to come home. No one else took on this responsibility. Indeed, as Jack Winter once remarked, it is a good job that the elder brother wasn't the one on the lookout that day. If he had been the one on duty, the younger son would probably have been sent packing!

The second thing the storyteller tells us is that the father had compassion on his son. This was no shallow sentimental feeling. In the Middle Eastern context it conveys the idea of the intestines being cut open. This father is moved deeply. He feels an intense sense of pity for his boy deep within his guts. He is not overwhelmed with anger at his son's rebellion. He is overcome with heartfelt sympathy at his son's long-awaited return.

The third thing Jesus tells us is that the father runs to his boy. The word "run" has the notion of "racing". The father ran like the wind to get to his boy. His motivation was no doubt to get to his son before the other villagers did. They would have known about the shame this boy had brought upon his father's house and would have insulted him or perhaps worse. The father races to get there first and in doing so he lifts up his robe to reveal his undergarments – something no man over the age of thirty would ever have done in that cultural context. This father doesn't care about his own honour. He just wants to protect his son's!

The fourth thing that this father does is he embraces his boy. The word literally means that he fell upon his boy's neck. Keep in mind that this son has been sleeping with the pigs in the far country. He has been on a journey from "affluent to effluent", to use Adrian Plass's great description. The father probably smelt his boy before he saw him! Covered as he is in porcine excrement, the boy is truly untouchable. Pigs are not kosher or clean animals in Jewish thought. Yet the father doesn't care. He doesn't worry about revealing his own undergarments and he doesn't care about the son's unclean state. He engages in a beautiful and spontaneous act of paternal affection. He hugs his son.

The fifth and final thing that the father does is he kisses his boy. The verb has the sense of a continuous and fervent action. It is as if he kisses his boy once, then kisses him again. He kisses him again and then keeps kissing him. This kissing is repeated, earnest and sincere. Truly, this is a very demonstrative father.

Five actions – he saw him, felt for him, ran to him, embraced him, and kissed him continuously. He produces five actions and no words. Actions truly speak louder than words! This father is displaying unusual and extravagant love. He is the perfect father. He is a picture in story form of the world's greatest Dad – *Abba*, Father.

How deep the Father's love

The younger son now embarks upon his carefully rehearsed speech. He says, "Father, I have sinned against heaven and against you! I am no longer worthy to be called your son." But this is as far as the boy gets. He never reaches the point of saying, "take me on as one of your hired servants." His father won't let him. This father has no intention of letting his son become a slave. Having said nothing so far, the father now speaks quickly to his servants. He tells them to go and fetch a special robe that used to hang in his house. This robe was a beautiful garment reserved for visiting dignitaries and especially honoured guests. We would call such people VIPs – very important people. The servants, no doubt with confused and surprised looks on their faces, run back to the house, fetch the robe, and bring it to their master. They obey his orders here. They have a servant–master relationship with him. The boy, on the other hand, enjoys a son–father relationship.

As if to emphasize this point, the father now places the robe over his weary, bedraggled and dirty son's body. Now all the unclean stains are covered by this festal garment. All the smells of his former life are blotted out by the fragrance of the ornately woven cloth. To the servants and the villagers who are watching, this gracious act can only mean one thing – that the boy has been totally, instantly, unconditionally forgiven. The boy is not going to be allowed to earn his father's love by embracing a life of servitude. This father has completely pardoned his son, no strings attached. At the party that follows, when the fatted calf is barbequed, this son would have continued to wear this special robe. It would have been an iconic, constant and public reminder to every partygoer of his father's forgiveness.

At this moment the boy must have been speechless. Certainly he says nothing. But then, as we saw in the last chapter, being forgiven can render you speechless. He is even more stunned into silence by what happens next. The father tells the servants to put "the ring" on the boy's finger. What is this ring? It is the family signet ring. No doubt the son had taken it off as he left home. The father had kept it and cherished it, hoping that one day his son would return because this ring was precious. It signified the son's position. It told everyone about his identity and his authority. To anyone who saw this ring, it said, "This boy is the father's son", and "This boy has the authority and the right to make decisions and to give orders around his father's estate." The father's act of returning the ring is just as special as the giving of the robe. If the robe said, "You're forgiven", the ring says, "You're family."

The boy is now fully reinstated. The robe has signified his pardon and the ring has signified his position. He is forgiven, and he is now free. As if to emphasize his son's freedom, the father gives his boy a new pair of shoes. These shoes are not "sandals", as the New International Version rather tamely and lamely puts it. They are luxury leather shoes. Sandals were worn by slaves. Leather shoes were worn by free men. The father sends a very clear signal through the gift of these shoes. His boy wanted to embrace the life of a slave or a servant, but the father wants him to embrace the life of a son, of a free man. Once again we have a very public, symbolic gesture within this particular cultural context. The robe says, "You're forgiven." The ring says, "You're family." The shoes say, "You're free."

Now, kitted out in an entirely new wardrobe, the boy goes into the party that his father holds. A calf is cooked, enough for about 200 people to eat. The whole of the father's family and indeed the entire village must be invited! The son is seen by everyone, walking around with this dazed look of relief on his face. He has truly been surprised by joy. He has been visited by the love of all loves. He has been beautified by amazing grace. And now everyone can see him, dressed in a special robe, wearing his ring, and looking with wonder at his feet, at his brand-new leather shoes.

The Prodigal Son parable in "F"

Feeling footloose and frisky, a feather-brained fellow forced his fond father to fork over the family finances. He flew far to foreign fields and frittered his fortune feasting fabulously with faithless friends.

Finally facing famine and fleeced by his fellows in folly, he found himself a feed-flinger in a filthy farmyard. Fairly famished, he fain would have filled his frame with the foraged foods of the fodder fragments left by the filthy farmyard creatures.

"Fooey," he said. "My father's flunkies fare far fancier," the frazzled fugitive found feverishly, frankly facing facts. Frustrated by failure and filled with foreboding, he forthwith fled to his family.

Falling at his father's feet, he floundered forlornly. "Father, I have flunked and fruitlessly forfeited family favour."

But the faithful father, forestalling further flinching, frantically flagged the flunkies. "Fetch forth the finest fatling and fix a feast."

But the fugitive's fault-finding frater frowned on the fickle forgiveness of the former folderol. His fury flashed. But fussing was futile, for the far-sighted father figured, such filial fidelity is fine, but what forbids fervent festivity?

The fugitive is found! "Unfurl the flags, with fanfares flaring! Let fun and frolic freely flow! Former failure is forgotten, folly is forsaken! And forgiveness forms the foundation for future fortitude."

Timothy E. Fulop
Assistant Dean of Faculty, Columbia Theological Seminary[13]

The robe and the ring

We need to remember at this point that Jesus is telling a parable, and that a parable is a down-to-earth fiction illustrating a heavenly and eternal truth. What is the truth that Jesus is transmitting through this masterful storytelling? He is telling his listeners that the father in the story is a picture of what God is really like. God is the perfect Father. He is one who welcomes those who come running home with tears of regret. He is the most affectionate of dads and his generosity knows no bounds. To those who were lost but now are found, he gives out gifts as if there was no tomorrow. Out of his infinite abundance he gives robes, rings and shoes and throws the most joyful of parties! This parable is accordingly a priceless treasure-chest of revelation concerning *Abba*'s love. It is truly a window onto the Fatherhood of God. It betrays the divine love at every point. And the best news of all is that this is fact, not fiction! God is not some mythical Santa Claus with a big sack and lots of presents. He is the Father who is alive forever and who loves us more dearly and more lavishly than we could ever possibly know. He is truly the Father we have all been waiting for.

> **God is the perfect Father. He is one who welcomes those who come running home with tears of regret.**

While it is always a temptation to press every detail of a parable too far, I personally believe there is something immensely significant about the robe and the ring given by the father. If we look at the robe first of all, this speaks of total forgiveness, as we have just seen. In that respect the robe is a picture of what Christian theologians call "justification".[14] Justification is one of the great doctrines of the church and it is absolutely foundational to the Gospel. Justification teaches that God is the most perfect judge, we are all law-breakers, we are under a sentence of death, but that Jesus has come into the world to take the punishment that was legally ours. Jesus was the only man in history who was perfectly "in the right" in God's eyes. His righteousness was perfect. On the Cross, Jesus took the consequences of all our unrighteousness. He took the heat for every one of us. He willingly embraced the penalty for our sins so that we, who were in the wrong, could now be in the right. Thanks to the blood that Jesus shed, those who choose to put their trust in the Cross can be totally forgiven, just like the prodigal son. They too can receive a robe of righteousness and be justified – "just-as-if-I'd" never sinned (as Dr Billy Graham has been fond of putting it). They can truly know that Dad's not mad with them any more.

But the robe isn't the only gift the father gives. The father also gives a ring, and this sends the signal that the boy has been given the position of a son. In this respect the ring is a picture of what Christian theologians call "adoption". If justification is a legal picture, adoption is a relational picture. In this framework, God is the most perfect, loving Father, we are spiritual orphans, we are destined to be forever separated from the Father, but God's Son has come into the world to demonstrate God's love at Calvary and to bring us home into the Father's arms.

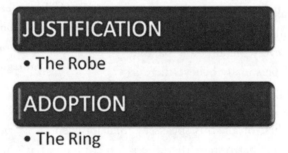

JUSTIFICATION
- The Robe

ADOPTION
- The Ring

When a person comes home in repentance to the Father, they receive two things. First of all, they receive the robe of righteousness. This is the gift of justification and that gift is given simply by believing in the finished work of the Cross. We are justified through Christ alone and by faith alone. When that happens, in God's law court we are regarded as not guilty and in the right. Secondly, they receive the ring of adoption. The Father not only gives them the gift of total forgiveness. He also gives them the gift of sonship and daughterhood. As adopted children of the King of Kings, they have a brand-new identity and an extraordinary authority. Their identity is in the fact that they are sons and daughters, princes and princesses, in the royal family of heaven. Their authority derives from this new position. The ring is therefore vital too. It is as vital as the robe. Indeed, while wearing the robe is a great thing, wearing the ring is a greater thing still.

Rediscovering adoption

One of my favourite verses in the Bible is right at the beginning of Paul's letter to the Ephesians. He begins his letter by giving praise to *Abba*, Father. In a breathless passage of praise he lists many things that he wants to thank God for, and he begins with these majestic and sublime thoughts:

> *Praise be to the God and Father of our Lord Jesus Christ, who has blessed us in the heavenly realms with every spiritual blessing in Christ. For he chose us in him before the creation of the world to be holy and blameless in his sight. In love he predestined us to be adopted as his sons through Jesus Christ, in accordance with his pleasure and will.*

Paul is saying many things here but perhaps the greatest thing of all is his declaration that *Abba*, Father chose those who are in Christ before the universe was formed and the earth was created. It has truly been said that while there are many unplanned pregnancies, there are no unplanned adoptions. How true that is of those who are said to be "in Christ". *Abba*, Father planned to adopt us into his family before he formed the galaxies!

The word that Paul uses for "adoption" in Ephesians 1 is a word he uses five times in his letters. As I have shown in my book *From Orphans to Heirs*, the subject of adoption is far more important to Paul and indeed to the New Testament than has ever really been acknowledged.[15] Paul mentions adoption much more than being "born again", yet you would never think this from the emphasis that is given to rebirth and the inattention that has been given to adoption in the history of the church. People are much more likely to ask, "Are you born again?" than "Are you an adopted child of the Father?" That said, Paul emphasizes adoption and when he talks about it he uses the Greek word *huiothesia*, which literally means "making someone a son". In Paul's time it referred to a specific series of legal acts in the Roman world by which a boy was given the position of a son in another person's family. This process was referred to by the Latin word *adoptio*.

Paul was not only a Jewish Pharisee and a Christian missionary. He was also a Roman citizen by birth. So he uses the Roman legal rite of adoption as a stunning picture of what *Abba*, Father has done for us through his Son and in the power of the Holy Spirit. The normal practice in the Roman world that Paul knew was for a childless couple to adopt the son of a family of slaves within their own estate. This was something that benefited both parties. The son of the slave would be set free from a life of servitude – a life that was often extremely precarious and consistently blighted by poverty. The couple would be set free from the stigma of not having a son to pass on the family name – the *pater familias*, as it was called in Latin.

It has truly been said that while there are many unplanned pregnancies, there are no unplanned adoptions. *Abba*, Father planned to adopt us into his family before he formed the galaxies!

How did a Roman man go about adopting the son of a slave into his or another man's household? There were two main stages to the process of adoption. The first involved the selling of the slave's son to the adopting father. This sale was done three times. At the end of the third sale the child was deemed to be no longer under his biological father's authority (*patria potestas*, as it was known) but under his adopting father's authority. In the second stage this sale was ratified before a Roman magistrate and the adoption finalized. The great New Testament scholar William Barclay elaborates:

> *There were two steps. The first was known as* mancipatio, *and was carried out by a symbolic sale, in which copper and scales were symbolically used. Three times the symbolism of sale was carried out. Twice the father symbolically sold his son, and twice he bought him back; but the third time he did not buy him back and thus the* patria potestas *was held to be broken. There followed a ceremony called* vindicatio. *The adopting father went to the praetor, one of the Roman magistrates, and presented a legal case for the transference of the person to be adopted into his patria potestas. When all this was completed, the adoption was complete. Clearly this was a serious and an impressive step.*[16]

Paul has this picture in mind when he talks about our salvation, which of course applies to women, not just men. Until Jesus came, we were under the authority of the orphaned slave-driver whom the Bible calls Satan. But *Abba*, Father decided that this tragedy should not continue, so at the perfect moment in history he sent his one and only Son into the world to die for us on the Cross. On the Cross, Jesus paid the full price for our redemption, not in gold or silver but in his precious blood. As a result of this, anyone who chooses to turn from their old way of life and put their trust in Jesus will be brought out from underneath the toxic authority of the father of lies (Satan) and brought under the life-giving authority of *Abba*, Father. When that happens, the consequences for the newly adopted believer are immense. The inheritance is indescribable.

To understand the full implications of what our adoption in Christ entails we need to go back for a moment to the Roman practice of adoption. What did the adopted boy receive from his new-found status and identity? What were the major consequences and benefits? Here is William Barclay again:

> *There were four main ones. (i) The adopted person lost all rights in his old family and gained all the rights of a legitimate son in his new family. In the most binding legal way, he got a new father. (ii) It followed that he became heir to his new father's estate. Even if other sons were afterwards born, it did not affect his rights. He was inalienably co-heir with them. (iii) In law, the old life of the adopted person was completely wiped out; for instance, all debts were cancelled. He was regarded as a new person entering into a new life with which the past had nothing to do. (iv) In the eyes of the law he was absolutely the son of his new father.*[17]

The benefits for an adopted child in Paul's day were huge. The boy received a new father, a new family, a new fortune and a new freedom. And in the process he was set up for a new future! He stood to inherit everything that a natural son would inherit!

The ramifications for our spiritual adoption are clear. When a person chooses to turn to the Lord, they are not just sold out of slavery, they are also declared to be legally the adopted son or daughter of *Abba*, Father. We benefit considerably from all of this. We find that we have a new Father – *Abba*, Father, the one who loves us like no earthly father ever could. We find that we have a new family – *Abba*, Father's family on the earth, in which we have nearly 2 billion adopted sisters and brothers! We find that we have a new fortune – all our previous debts are cancelled and we now have a Father who owns the cattle on a thousand hills! Finally, we find that we have a new freedom – the chains of the past no longer have a hold on us and we now enjoy the glorious liberty of the children of God. What an astonishing example of the extravagance of the Father's love! What a picture of amazing grace!

The witness of the Spirit

When I describe spiritual adoption in these terms, it seems astonishing that this has not been shouted from the rooftops over the last two thousand years. I can only assume that the enemy has been seeking to keep this treasure buried for as long as possible. But his work is now being undermined. The church's best-kept secret is about to be divulged to a fatherless world! Many spiritual orphans are about to encounter *Abba*, Father's love and receive the adoption won for them at Calvary through the blood of Jesus. The Holy Spirit is beginning to work throughout the earth to put the glorious truth of spiritual adoption right back into the foreground of the church's thinking. As William Paul Young, the author of the best-selling novel *The Shack*, said recently to a friend of mine:

> When a person chooses to turn to the Lord, they are not just sold out of slavery, they are also declared to be legally the adopted son or daughter of *Abba*, Father.

Everywhere I go things are happening, and there is this sense of the wind changing. People are talking about the father heart of God. So many of us have been hurt either by the abusive presence of a father, or simply by the absence of a father; and so many of us have painted the face of God with the face of our father. And suddenly, that's beginning to change. We're beginning to realize we don't know the Father. We can't just take our own dad and mask the face of God with his. So that's a big change, and there's a sense that we, as individuals, are growing up with an understanding now that maybe we can actually, in this relationship, sense the presence of the Father and hear his voice...[18]

The Holy Spirit is truly moving. And it really is the Holy Spirit that we need if we are to enter into the full experience of our adoption. Everything necessary for our adoption has been achieved at the Cross *objectively*. But we who are in Christ now need the work of the Spirit in our hearts if we are to experience *Abba's* love *subjectively*. We need the witness of the Holy Spirit if we are to enter into the fullness of what it means to be an adopted son or daughter of the High King of Heaven. We need the flame of the Father's love in our hearts. It is not enough to have light in our heads. We need heat in our hearts. Light and heat together make fire. We will only ever be people on fire if we know the truth of our adoption not just in our heads but also in our hearts.

Paul speaks about the importance of the Spirit of adoption in several passages, such as Galatians 4:4–6 and Romans 8:15–17. It is worth just noting that both of these letters were written to congregations in Roman contexts, so it should come as no surprise that Paul uses a Roman picture (that of *adoptio*) when writing to these specific churches. In Romans 8:15–17 Paul describes the work and the witness of the Spirit in our adoption. I am using the New King James Version in what follows because the New International Version, for some reason, has chosen not to use the word "adoption":

> *For you did not receive the spirit of bondage again to fear, but you received the Spirit of adoption by whom we cry out, "Abba, Father." The Spirit Himself bears witness with our spirit that we are children of God, and if children, then heirs – heirs of God and joint heirs with Christ, if indeed we suffer with Him, that we may also be glorified together.*

We cannot miss the important role given to the work of the Holy Spirit in these three verses in Romans chapter 8. Paul specifically describes the Holy Spirit as "the Spirit of adoption". We might say that the Holy Spirit is the one who makes our spiritual adoption a reality in our hearts. It is the Holy Spirit who witnesses to our human spirits (the deepest parts of our being, the part that is designed to relate to *Abba*, Father, our Creator) and his testimony is that we are the adopted sons and daughters of the Living God. We are no longer slaves; we are sons and daughters. We are no longer bound by fear; we are liberated into a life of security. We are no longer consigned to despair; we are co-heirs with Jesus and have a glorious future! All this we can actually know in a direct, personal, experiential way because the Father's love has been poured out in our hearts by the Holy Spirit (Romans 5:5).

The work and witness of the Holy Spirit is accordingly critical in the realization of our new identity and status as adopted sons and daughters. Paul specifically mentions the witness of the Spirit here in Romans 8:16. The role of witnesses was vital in the ancient Roman rite of adoption as well. Indeed, Paul is thinking of this part of the adoption process in his description of the work of the Holy Spirit in our hearts. William Barclay once again explains how this all ties together:

> *Paul uses still another picture from Roman adoption. He says that God's spirit witnesses with our spirit that we really are his children. The adoption ceremony was carried out in the presence of seven witnesses. Now, suppose the adopting father died and there was some dispute about the right of the adopted son to inherit, one or more of the seven witnesses stepped forward and swore that the adoption was genuine. Thus the right of the adopted person was guaranteed and he entered into his inheritance. So, Paul is saying, it is the Holy Spirit himself who is the witness to our adoption into the family of God.*[19]

We need the Holy Spirit if we are to experience the reality of *Abba*, Father's love in our hearts. We need the Holy Spirit if we are to know with complete assurance that we are the children of God. We need the Holy Spirit if we are to know the glorious inheritance that lies ahead of us as co-heirs with God's Son. We need the Holy Spirit! And we need him not as a theological proposition but as a personal experience. The greatest ministry of the Spirit is the work of adoption. How on earth can we do without him in the church today?

It's time to wear the ring

One of the main burdens of my heart over the last few years has been to take this message of the Father's love, spiritual adoption and the healing of orphan hearts all over the world in order to help people to experience the freedom that we truly have in Christ. As an adopted child in the natural, *Abba*, Father has given me a very personal understanding and appreciation of what it means to be adopted in the spiritual. Wherever I go, I emphasize the need for believers not only to receive their pardon but also to understand their position, not only to hear "you're forgiven" but also to hear "you're family". I am utterly convinced that believers need to wear the ring, not just the robe. They need to experience the full blessings of adoption, not just the full blessings of justification. Salvation isn't just being saved from something – our sins and their consequences. Salvation is being saved to something – a new identity as sons and daughters and a wonderful intimacy with the world's greatest Dad. It's time for Christians to possess their possessions. It's time for us all to put on and wear the ring.

I remember an occasion not long ago when I was preaching in a city in a beautiful part of Norway. I shared my message from Luke 15 about the father who gave a robe and a ring to his returning son. I call this message "The Robe and the Ring" and it is available from our website. I explained that the robe and the ring are symbols of justification and adoption. I told my listeners that justification means "just-as-if-I'd never sinned", and being adopted means "Dad-opted for me". As I was speaking, a tall man in his thirties left his seat at the back of the hall and started to walk towards where I was speaking. He came down the central aisle of the church building and walked straight past me. He then lay face down on the floor and began to weep. At this stage I hadn't invited people to come forward for ministry. That was to happen later! So this man's behaviour came as a bit of a surprise, but I continued to speak until the end of my message.

Later I found out about this man. He had been brought up by Christian parents. He'd reached the age of thirteen, when he became extremely rebellious. The parents decided they couldn't cope any more so they threw him out of the house. He spent a year in an orphanage and then two years on the streets. During that time his parents took in a young girl and gave her his bedroom. So while they abandoned him they adopted her. Later he became a Christian and decided that he wanted to preach the Gospel to teenagers. He got married and started his ministry as an evangelist. But his marriage soon hit problems and, to make matters worse, his relationship with his son deteriorated. By the time I came to his city to preach, his wife was hanging on by her fingernails and his son, now twelve years old, was showing the same signs of rebellion that he himself had shown at the same age. His life was literally falling apart and his family was suffering immensely.

We subsequently learned what happened to the man as I was preaching that night in Norway. Sobbing on the stage at the front of the church, he was simply saying over and over, "I've got the ring." He had always known he was forgiven but he wasn't free. He had always heard about the robe but never the ring. That night in Norway, this man recognized that he had the ring of adoption and he put it on. As he did so, the wounds of abandonment in his heart began to heal up. He went straight home and apologized to his wife, then went upstairs to his son's bedroom and apologized to him for not showing him any affection over the years. He hugged and wept over his boy and as he did so, the heart of the father was turned towards the son, and the heart of the son was turned towards the father.

Isn't it time we put on the ring, not just the robe?

The heart of revival

What I have been talking about in this chapter is not just vital for our personal freedom. I believe that it is also crucial for revival as well. In other words, the revelation of the Father's love doesn't just have the capacity to transform our lives. It has the power to change our families, our communities and even nations. Indeed the revelation of the Father's love could result in Reformation, not just revival. As I have often said over the years, the Reformation in the sixteenth century brought the truth of justification back into the light. Europe was transformed by this rediscovery. I believe another Reformation is coming, one in which adoption is going to be put on the map. Only the revelation of the Father's love will heal this fatherless continent and world. Only a move of the Spirit of adoption will bring healing to orphan hearts and release freedom to a broken, bound-up world.

For all this to happen, there needs to be a transformation of the church first. A fatherless church cannot bring liberation to a fatherless world. The church needs a revival in the Father's love. Christian leaders in particular need to come before *Abba*, Father and ask for a personal experience of his embrace. If leaders are to lead people into a fatherless world as agents of *Abba*, Father's love, then they too must have put on the ring, not just the robe. They too need to have the Spirit of adoption poured out upon their hearts.

> If leaders are to lead people into a fatherless world as agents of *Abba*, Father's love then they too must have put on the ring, not just the robe.

A Christian leader from a previous era who illustrates my point is the Welsh revivalist Howell Harris. Harris was a great influence on John Wesley and in many ways achieved as much in Wales as Wesley did in England and beyond. Howell Harris was converted in an extraordinary way, after the Vicar in his local church at Talgarth was giving the notices or announcements. The year was 1735 and the Vicar mentioned that there was a Holy

Communion service the following Sunday. He said that he knew some would not come because they felt unworthy of partaking of it. So he added these words:

If you are not fit to take Communion you are not fit to pray, if you are not fit to pray you are not fit to live, and if you are not fit to live you are not fit to die.

These words really hit home with Harris and the following Sunday he came to the Communion service in a very serious frame of mind. He began to experience a deep sense of conviction about his self-centred life. He continued to try to find peace until Pentecost Sunday on 25 May, when he returned to Talgarth parish church to take Communion once again. He had a tremendous battle raging in his soul during this service until at last he found forgiveness at the Cross. This is what he was later to recall:

At the table, Christ bleeding on the Cross was kept before my eyes constantly; and strength was given to me to believe that I was receiving pardon on account of that blood. I lost my burden; I went home leaping for joy, and I said to my neighbour who was sad, Why are you sad? I know my sins have been forgiven... Oh blessed day! Would that I might remember it gratefully ever more!

You would think that, after such a dramatic conversion, Harris would have felt satisfied. But he did not. He had found peace with God and knew that he was forgiven. But he had not found full assurance with God and he didn't yet know he was family. He had received the robe but he hadn't put on the ring. That happened three weeks later when he was reading the Bible and praying in the tower of Llangasty church on 18 June. He later described it thus:

*Suddenly I felt my heart melting within me like wax
before a fire, and love to God for my Saviour. I felt
also not only love and peace, but a longing to die and
to be with Christ. Then there came a cry into my soul
within that I had never known before – Abba, Father!
I could do nothing but call God my Father. I knew that
I was His child, and He loved me and was listening
to me. My mind was satisfied and I cried out, Now I
am satisfied! Give me strength and I will follow Thee
through water and fire.*

What an amazing description of an encounter with *Abba*, Father's
love! Three weeks after receiving the robe, Harris put on the ring.
Three weeks after being justified, Harris now knew that he was
adopted. Wearing this ring, Howell Harris now lived as a free man.
He no longer lived like a slave. He lived like a son. Empowered
by grace, not law, he went about his country preaching the Good
News about Jesus. He did this not from a place of striving but from
a place of rest. He did this not for approval but from approval. It
is precisely because he knew that he was so deeply loved and liked
by *Abba*, Father that Harris witnessed to the lost. Years later, he
wrote about this encounter on 18 June as the turning point in his
ministry:

*This day 28 years ago I was (when I did not seek it as I
had never heard of it) sealed by the Spirit of adoption
and feeling that I loved God with all my heart, that I
was in God and He in me. I longed to be dissolved and
to be with my own dear Father.*[20]

Harris put on the ring and the robe and then he went on to put
on the shoes. As a man with a new-found freedom, he put on the
shoes of the Gospel of peace and went about preaching the Gospel
to the lost, and the hallmark of his preaching was compassion.
Having been overwhelmed by the Father's love, Harris found

that his heart was now breaking for those who neither knew their pardon nor their position. Revival broke out in Wales as thousands came to know Jesus through Harris' ministry. He was a man on fire and there was no stopping him. Having been captivated by divine love, there was no mountain too high for Harris to climb. He would do anything for *Abba*, Father. The whole of Wales felt the impact of that complete devotion.

The antidote to fatherlessness

In our orphan generation today we need church leaders and Christian communities that have welcomed the Spirit of adoption in their lives and who have received true freedom in the Father's love. No doubt there are political and economic strategies for dealing with the prevailing problem of fatherlessness. But the distinctive contribution which the church alone can make is the revelation of the Father that the world is waiting for. While others may address the pandemic of fatherlessness at a human level, we are equipped to deal with it at a spiritual level and to offer an alternative way of looking at the issue.

To bring the life-changing revelation of *Abba*'s love to the lost, Christians first need to receive it themselves. When we ourselves have entered the Father's embrace – as the prodigal son did – then we can lead others into the same place. We cannot take people to places where we haven't been ourselves. The destination is *Abba*'s love. There is nothing more lasting or more life-transforming than that. As Brennan Manning has said, "In the end, only one thing remains… *Abba*'s love."[21]

For this to happen, the church needs to stop fighting and squabbling about peripheral issues and focus on the main thing. The main thing is that we have come to the Father's arms in repentance and received the robe of our pardon and the ring of our position so that we can put on our shoes and go and share the Gospel with the lost. Majoring on minor issues – even issues like whether you get the ring at conversion or later – is just going to delay what is now an urgent mandate. That mandate is to bring the Father's love to the fatherless and to bring an end to the global pandemic of fatherlessness. So it's truly time for the church not just to be forgiven but also to be free. In the next chapter I will provide seven essential keys for our freedom in Christ. I hope that we'll all be able to pray that the chains that hold us down will fall off so we can be freedom fighters for a fatherless world.

Chapter 11

UNLOCKING OUR CHAINS

We come now to the issue of how we can find healing for the wounds inflicted by our fathers. How are we to be liberated not only from the signs and the symptoms that flow from this wound, but from the orphan heart condition itself? In this chapter I am going to suggest from both Scripture and my own experience that there are seven keys that we need to use to unlock our chains. I am not claiming that this is a complete and exhaustive list of what a believer needs if they are to be free. Nor am I claiming that this is the final word on the healing process. But I have found that these keys are the ones that people most frequently need for their breakthrough.

Before I deal with these seven keys individually, I want to stress three things. First of all, the keys that follow are not a seven-step programme. In other words, I am not proposing that a person must take and use these keys in the order in which I am presenting them. *Abba*, Father is sovereign and he moves in our lives in the way that he thinks fit. In addition, we are all unique individuals with very different histories. For both of these reasons it is important to understand that the keys I'm about to describe may be employed in different sequences. Some people may use these keys in the order that I describe them – 1, 2, 3, 4, 5, 6, 7. Others, however, may find that they use the keys in a different sequence – say, 7, 1, 4, 2, 3, 5, 6! Some may need to use all the keys. Others may need to use some or even just one. There is a glorious variety about the way people find healing and freedom in *Abba*, Father's love. We should not restrict or limit the ways of God.

The second thing I want to say is about timing. Some people are healed and set free very quickly. Others have to take a slower journey. It is not for us to ascribe a time limit to the healing process. Some people would be utterly overwhelmed by a sudden healing. Others would be well able to cope with such an instant release. Again, *Abba*, Father knows best. He shapes us according to his will and our individual capacity for change. We need simply to be available and position ourselves to receive the Father's healing touch in our lives.

The third and final thing I want to say is about individual responsibility. Even though the Father is absolutely sovereign to do whatever he wills, whenever he wills, to whomsoever he wills, I also believe that we are called to exercise our own freedom to choose. Human free will is a gift from *Abba*, Father. It is something he completely respects. We can accordingly choose to co-operate with his Holy Spirit by being active rather than passive in the healing journey. Rather than sitting back and waiting for our healing to come by osmosis, I want to encourage us to pursue our healing by taking these keys in our hands and choosing to use them. Here, then, are the seven keys.

Key no. 1: Revise your understanding of God

What is your God-image – your picture of God? As you come to him in worship, who is it that you speak to? How do you approach him? What name or title do you use as you pray? How do you know him? These are critical questions and they reveal a great deal about the condition of our hearts in relation to the father wound.

If we are to be set free from the hurts that bind us, we must learn to see God as he really is – as *Abba*, Father. In the Bible,

God is of course known by many names. If we begin with the Old Testament, the names and titles for God are in the Hebrew language. *Elohim* is one of these names; it is translated simply as "God" and is used 2,570 times. There is also *Yahweh* which is used 6,823 times and means something like "Always", though is translated in English Bibles as "the LORD" (with capital letters). There are in addition the *Yahweh* names like *Yahweh Shalom* (the LORD our Peace), *Yahweh Jireh* (the LORD our Provider), *Yahweh Nissi* (the LORD our Banner) and *Yahweh Rophe* (the LORD our Healer). Then there are the names of God beginning with the Hebrew word *El* (meaning "strong" or "mighty"). *El Elyon* means "God Most High". *El Shaddai* is often translated as "God Almighty". *El Olam* means the "Everlasting God". In addition, the name *Adonai* is used 300 times in the Hebrew Scriptures and is translated "Lord". These are just some of the regular names for God in the Old Testament.

The New Testament reveals that the premier name for God is *Abba*, Father. Indeed, every other title and name for God is explained by this one pre-eminent name. For example, we know that God is Creator and Redeemer. But he is only the Creator and Redeemer because he is first the Father. He creates and redeems us because he is *Abba*, Father. As our perfect Heavenly Father, God is love. He created us not only out of love, but in love and for love. Everything he does reflects a fatherly love. He redeems and rescues us because he is a loving Father. He protects, provides, heals, sustains and fights for us because he is our *Abba*, Father. Everything that can be said about God in the Bible derives from the supreme fact of his Fatherhood. He is *Abba* – Daddy, Papa, Father, Dad. If the Son hadn't come to tell us this, we would never have known it. We owe it all to Jesus!

When we come to God and call him *Abba*, Father we are honouring everything that Jesus did for us. If we simply call him "God", "Creator", or "Lord", we really are no different from those who follow other religions. But when we call him *Abba*, Father we are clearly demonstrating that we have understood what Jesus came to do and what Christianity is really all about. We are giving God the name that Jesus came to give us. We are relating to God in a way that only the death of Jesus has made possible. *Abba*, Father is the Christian's unique name for God.

What distinguishes the Christian view of God from all others is this intimate title and name – *Abba*, Father. The degree to which a Christian uses this name and delights in this name is the degree to which they are truly living in the revelation of God uniquely given by Jesus. The fact that many Christians don't relate to God as *Abba*, Father and simply call him "God", "Lord", "Creator", or some such title is sad. It is not just the result of poor teaching. It is the result of the enemy's master plan to make the name "Father" as negative and meaningless as possible in our human experience. All too easily we transfer the face of a human father onto the face of our Heavenly Father. If we have had good dads, this may work for us for a while. But many have not had good fathers. They have had abandoning and abusive fathers. As long as we see God's Fatherhood through the lens of our earthly fathers, we will always have a distorted God-image. Even the best earthly fathers cannot compare with *Abba*, Father. He invented fatherhood.

> **Instead of projecting our experience of fatherhood onto God, we should reverse the process and let God project his experience of fatherhood onto us.**

All this means that if we are to engage in any kind of projection at all, then it had better be "reverse projection". In other words, instead of projecting our experience of fatherhood onto God, we should reverse the process and let God project his experience of fatherhood onto us. Look at what Paul says in his prayer in Ephesians 3, which begins with these magnificent words in verses 14–15:

For this reason I kneel before the Father, from whom his whole family in heaven and on earth derives its name.

The word translated "family" is a word that can equally well be translated "fatherhood". If fatherhood is the right translation then Paul is saying that he kneels before *Abba*, Father from whom all fatherhood derives its character. If that is the case, then Paul is saying God is the source of fatherhood. He determines its character because he is the true Father.

How then shall we picture this Father? The best answer is "through Jesus". Jesus said to Philip, "he who has seen me has seen the Father" (John 14:8). Everything Jesus ever did or said is a window onto the Fatherly heart of God. Every word, every action, is a reflection of *Abba*, Father's love. In particular, the picture that Jesus paints of the father in the parable of the returning son in Luke 15 should form the foundation of how we see the divine Father. This dad waits for his boy to come and watches out for him. He feels compassion for his returning son, not anger. He runs to his boy and demonstratively shows his undying affection, through a warm hug and tender kisses. He dresses his dirty and unkempt child in a special robe. He restores the ring to his son's finger and puts the finest shoes on his feet. He throws the biggest and best party in celebration of this much-longed-for homecoming and goes round all the guests expressing his unbridled joy. What a dad! This is truly a picture of what *Abba*, Father is like. Nothing less will do.

However negative the word "father" may be in our hearts, we can retrain our hearts and minds to think differently by understanding that God is the perfect *Abba*. We can realign our God-image to what Jesus shows us rather than to what our earthly fathers may or may not have shown us. If you are only used to calling God "God", "Creator", "Lord", "Almighty", or a similar title, start using the greatest name of all – *Abba*, Father. It is not that he isn't all these things – God, Creator, Lord and Almighty – it's just that he is so much more. As long as we refer to him in titles and names like these, God will always be remote rather than relational. If, however, we start to have our minds renewed by the God-image that Jesus reveals, then God can become *Abba*, Father to us as well. Instead of being distant and unapproachable, he becomes immanent and intimate. We can begin to agree with Pope Benedict XVI's words: "God is not a relentless sovereign who condemns the guilty but a loving father whom we must love, not for fear of punishment, but for his kindness, his quickness to forgive."[22]

It is important then to reject our false, distorted images of God. In particular, we need to come before *Abba*, Father and ask for forgiveness for creating him in the image of our own fathers. Saint Augustine put it beautifully when he honestly confessed the following:

> *God our Father, we find it difficult to come to you,*
> *because our knowledge of you is imperfect. In our*
> *ignorance we have imagined you to be our enemy;*
> *we have wrongly thought that you take pleasure*
> *in punishing us for our sins; and we have foolishly*
> *conceived you to be a tyrant over human life. But since*
> *Jesus came among us, he has shown that you are loving*
> *and that our fear of you was groundless.*[23]

That is a good prayer. In addition, we can do what Hailey did in the following testimony. We can take responsibility and start choosing to call God our *Abba* when we pray to him:

> *I don't remember calling anyone, dad, ever. When*
> *I was little, my parents got divorced. Not too long*
> *afterwards my mum remarried and I gradually stopped*
> *seeing my biological father. Even though my mum*
> *and stepdad married when I was four, in the eleven*
> *years that they were together I never called him dad.*
> *After they divorced I felt like I had lost my chance to*
> *use the word; to call someone, dad. I felt that no one*
> *deserved the name because I was so hurt by the men*
> *I wanted so badly to call my father. There were times*

when I wanted to. Times when I wished so badly to be able to say, "Hi, Dad" or "I love you, Dad" or say, "That's my father." But I never could. I remember being jealous when I saw my friends with their dads or when I heard them use the word. So obviously it was difficult for me to address God with such an intimate name as "Father". I had built a wall around my heart. But in my alone time with Him I kept saying "Abba" and piece by piece the wall began to fall. I know that He is my Father, my Dad. And I can now say with confidence, "Abba, I belong to You."

Hailey took the key. She chose to revise her understanding of God. She changed her God-image and began to rise up out of the victim state by worshipping *Abba*, Father. We can all do this. We can take the key. We can take responsibility.

> Loving *Abba*, Father, I pray in Jesus' name that you would help me to see you as you really are. I ask that you forgive me where I have embraced wrong beliefs and seen you through the spectacles of my pain, or other people's errors. Help me to know you as your Son revealed you – as my *Abba*, Father, my Papa, Daddy God. I repent of transferring my experience of my earthly father onto you. Help me to see your face, not the face of my earthly dad. Give me a correct image of who you are. Heal me of every wound of separation and release to me the truth that you're the Dad who will never abandon me. I ask in Jesus' name. Amen.

Key no. 2: Make a choice to face your pain

Someone once said that we all have to face the music even when we don't like the tune! That is so true. One of our mottos at the Father's House is this: "If we won't get real, we won't get healed." Reality is absolutely critical in the healing process. As Jesus said, "you will know the truth and the truth shall set you free" (John 8:31). The word "truth" can equally well be translated "reality". It's reality that sets us free. It's the reality of who Jesus is. It's the reality of who we are. No one is ever really helped by constructing their own reality. The chances are we will indulge in selectivity and fantasy if we do that, and those are both symptoms of the condition from which we need to be liberated! No, we are only ever really set free by facing our reality, by facing the facts about our past, by acknowledging that we were wounded by our earthly fathers and naming the wound specifically. Burying our pain rather than choosing to confront our pain is not the answer.

I know of a Pentecostal Bishop from Zimbabwe who buried his pain and didn't face it for forty years. When he was five years old, his mother and father drove him to his uncle and aunt's house. His parents had to leave him there for four or five months because they needed to be away a great deal on business. They didn't want to leave their son behind, but they felt that they had no choice. If they were to get their business off the ground, their son would have to live with his relatives. And so the day came when they drove away from the house, leaving the little boy behind, confused and desperately anxious. All he remembered of that scene, besides the agony of watching his parents drive away, was a song by the Beatles playing on the radio.

Months, years and even decades passed. The boy became a man and forgot the incident from his childhood. Then he went as a Bishop to preach in the USA. He was forty-five years old. During the conference he had some time off so he decided to visit a shopping mall. As he walked down the mall, he heard a song playing over the loudspeaker system. It sounded familiar. Suddenly he realized that it was the same Beatles song that had been playing forty years before when his mum and dad left him behind. He was so overcome with emotion that he had to sit down. All the buried pain surfaced from deep within his soul and he sat down and sobbed his heart out. As he did so, he faced his pain and forgave his parents and was set free from a wound of abandonment that had been lodged in his soul for four decades.

Later, the Bishop would share his testimony and in it he would speak about what he called "split soul syndrome" – the tendency of human beings to split their souls into two halves. The deeper level is the level in which are located the kinds of hurt he eventually had to face. The surface level is the level at which most people choose to live – the level of not facing our pain but passing it off as unimportant or masking it with addictive behaviour. But then come those moments in our lives when we have to face reality, where living in the fantasy land of the surface level cannot sustain us any more. These are critical moments when we must confront the truth about ourselves.

The second key to our liberation is to make a choice to face our pain. Instead of opting for pain-avoidance strategies, like denial or addiction, confront the facts about what happened to you. Talk to someone you trust, like a counsellor, or a friend, or a pastor. I know that it is perfectly understandable to be fearful of experiencing pain. But the Bible promises that even though there may be tears in the night there will be joy in the morning. Let me encourage you gently: you can take the reality key. You can take responsibility.

Loving Father, I covenant with you right now that I will face whatever I need to face in my heart. I forbid denial in Jesus' name. I permit reality and truth. Help me to see who you really are. But help me also to see who I really am. Let your light shine so that my shadow may be fully disclosed. Let those hidden things in my shadow – secret sins, secret wounds – be addressed right now, by your tender Holy Spirit. Help the real me to come into the light and help me to walk in the light. I give you permission to reintegrate my split soul – to bring the deeper and the surface levels of my being together into a transparent unity in Christ Jesus. Help me to get connected with what lies beneath the surface of my life. Heal my spirit, my soul and my body. I ask this in Jesus' name, Amen.

Key no. 3: Repent of your orphan tendencies

In Part 2 we identified the ten symptoms of the orphan heart. These are internal, negative feelings experienced by someone with an orphan heart condition. They are abandonment, rejection, loneliness, hopelessness, worthlessness, sadness, insecurity, hypersensitivity, fear and poverty. Then there are the ten signs of the orphan heart. These are outwardly observable behaviour patterns. We identified the following: mistrust, hiding, superficiality, attachments, manipulation, anger, selectivity,

In Hebrew the word for repentance is *teshuvah* and in its highest form is understood as the action of a child choosing to turn around and come home to their father.

fantasy, misinterpretation, and independence. The final tendency we noticed is both a symptom and a sign, and that's striving. Having discussed these twenty-one symptoms and signs in Part 2, I now want to ask some soul-searching questions. How many have you experienced in your life? How many are a part of your life right now?

One of the most important keys in the healing and liberation process is the key of repentance. Now repentance is an unpopular word in our contemporary, orphan generation. We live at a time when the prevailing mood is that there are no longer any moral absolutes, that you shouldn't judge anyone for doing anything and that everyone and everything should be treated with tolerance. But such an attitude is totally unbiblical and is in reality a reflection of the orphan-hearted nature of the culture we live in. It is an indication of the deep-seated independence and rebellion that many have embraced as the new normal today. In such a world, words like "repentance" are greeted either by howls of scornful mockery or by squeals of pain. Orphans don't like to be accountable.

Followers of Jesus cannot and must not take this view today. I know it is all too easy to give in and compromise. But that is a defeatist option and it is behaviour befitting a slave and an orphan, not a son or a daughter. The courageous option is to confront the reality of who we are and to resolve to change and be an agent of change. Transformation is what we're after and transformation not only means becoming more whole, it also means becoming more holy. In fact, we should remember that *Abba*, Father wants two things from us. He first of all wants intimacy; in other words, he wants us to enter into an affectionate life of sonship and daughterhood. But he also wants purity; he wants us to live holy lives, and to be holy means to be set apart from, to be different from, the wayward norms of the world. It is no good stressing just intimacy. Intimacy without purity leads to sin. It is no good just stressing purity. Purity without intimacy leads to striving. We need intimacy and purity together. Indeed, we should remember that *Abba*, Father chose and adopted us for a purpose, and this purpose is clearly indicated in Ephesians 1:4: "He chose us in him before the creation of the world to be holy and blameless in his sight." Why have we been adopted by the world's greatest Dad? The answer is, "to be holy and blameless in his sight." We are to be part of a counter-cultural family.

Repentance is therefore a vital part of the healing process. Repentance means changing the way we think, the way we feel and the way we behave. It means coming home to the Father's house and living by the Father's norms rather than staying in the far country and living by the norms of the pigpen. This is the true Jewish understanding of repentance. In Hebrew the word for repentance is *teshuvah* and in its highest form is understood as the action of a child choosing to turn around and come home to their father.

We must accordingly repent of all our orphan tendencies. If we need to repent of anger, we must repent of anger. If we need to repent of attachments or addictions, we must repent of these too. If we have manipulated and controlled other people, we must repent of this as well. Repentance means turning from the orphan state and coming home into the Father's arms. It means leaving the life of the slave behind and choosing to live like a royal prince, a royal princess. It means living out of our brand-new identities as adopted sons and daughters rather than our old, toxic identities as orphans and slaves. It means putting off the old self and putting on the new self. As Paul put it in Colossians 3:5–11:

> *Put to death, therefore, whatever belongs to your earthly nature: sexual immorality, impurity, lust, evil desires and greed, which is idolatry. Because of these, the wrath of God is coming. You used to walk in these ways, in the life you once lived. But now you must rid yourselves of all such things as these: anger, rage, malice, slander, and filthy language from your lips. Do not lie to each other, since you have taken off your old self with its practices and have put on the new self, which is being renewed in knowledge in the image of its Creator.*

We can take the repentance key. We can take responsibility.

Abba, Father, I repent of every trace of the orphan heart condition in my life. I turn away from the orphan state and I choose to come home into your arms of love. I repent of my feelings of abandonment, rejection, loneliness, hopelessness, worthlessness, sadness, insecurity, hypersensitivity, fear and poverty. I also repent of every destructive behaviour pattern, especially mistrust, hiding, superficiality, attachments, manipulation, anger, selectivity, fantasy, misinterpretation, and independence. Most of all, I repent of striving to earn your love (and the love of others) through performance and I choose to rest in the revelation that you love me for who I am in Christ. Help me now to live like an adopted, royal child of God. I realign my feelings and my behaviour to those that are worthy of sonship. Thank you for your forgiveness and your amazing grace. I choose life in Jesus' name. Amen.

Key no. 4: Forgive those who have hurt you

If there is one key that everyone needs to use in the healing process, it's the key of forgiveness. Forgiveness is in many ways the determining factor in whether we are healed or not. If we fail to forgive our fathers, then this causes a blockage in the flow of love between *Abba*, Father and ourselves. Nothing seems to obstruct the Father's love more effectively than our own inability to forgive our earthly dads. It is almost as if *Abba*, Father is saying, "I cannot pour out the fullness of my fatherly love upon your life until you have released your own fathers from the pain they caused you." So long as the word "father" has a negative resonance to it, we will not enter into the complete inheritance that *Abba*, Father has for us as his adopted children. Unforgiveness is the primary obstacle to the freedom that is ours in Christ. We must learn to forgive our fathers, and we must learn to forgive them from our hearts.

In Mark 11 Jesus teaches on the power of forgiveness. The context is this: the disciples have witnessed him speak words of judgment to a fig tree. Jesus was hungry and had expected there to be *paggim*, the springtime early yield of figs, within the lush foliage of the tree. But there were none. So he cursed the tree for its unproductive nature. It had the appearance of life but no fruit. The

Nothing seems to obstruct the Father's love more effectively than our own inability to forgive our earthly dads.

next day the disciples and Jesus walk past the same tree. They see that it has withered from the roots and died. The disciples are amazed and ask Jesus how on earth he managed to destroy the tree through the power of his words. This is his reply in Mark 11:22–25:

> *"Have faith in God," Jesus answered. "I tell you the truth, if anyone says to this mountain, 'Go, throw yourself into the sea,' and does not doubt in his heart but believes that what he says will happen, it will be done for him. Therefore I tell you, whatever you ask*

for in prayer, believe that you have received it, and it will be yours. And when you stand praying, if you hold anything against anyone, forgive him, so that your Father in heaven may forgive you your sins."

There are two things that Jesus points to here in answer to the disciples' query. The first is faith. If we want to do what Jesus did, then we must have faith in God. As adopted sons and daughters, we are people of faith. We do not see God, but we choose to believe in him and put our trust in him. When we are confronted with the mountains of life – those things that obstruct our path and our vision – we can exercise our sonship and speak with faith to the mountain. This does not mean telling God how big the mountain is. It means telling the mountain how big our God is! Adopted sons and daughters know that their Father is greater than the mountain, however intimidating it may be. That's faith, and faith means believing God even when you cannot see him.

But then there is a second thing that Jesus points to. Almost in a "by the way", a postscript, at the end of this teaching, Jesus adds, "but before you do anything else, forgive anyone you have a grudge against." Not only do we need faith if we are to have the breakthrough in our lives. We also need forgiveness. Faith operates at the vertical level, in the relationship between ourselves and the Father. Forgiveness operates at the horizontal level, in our relationships with others. In exercising faith we look up to the Father and we put our trust in his invisible greatness. In exercising forgiveness we look to those who have hurt us and we freely give them a gift they don't deserve – the gift of our total, unconditional forgiveness.

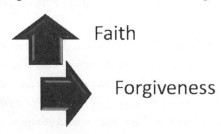

Faith

Forgiveness

Many of us have unproductive things in our lives. The orphan heart condition would probably be top of many people's lists. There is something utterly destructive about this kind of life. Like the fig tree, we may masquerade as healthy when in reality we are fruitless, sad and barren. This orphan heart condition needs to be terminated by love so that we can live as sons and daughters, not as slaves. To do that we need two things: first of all we need to forgive our earthly fathers for the wounds they have caused us. Whichever of the seven negative father types in Part 1 applies to us, we need to name the wound and release forgiveness to our father. Secondly, we need to exercise our faith as a son or a daughter. We need to believe that our Heavenly Father is far more powerful than those things that have been looming large in front of our field of vision and obstructing our view of the future. We need to exercise our authority as a royal child and cast that mountain into the sea. When we do these two things our breakthrough will come, because forgiveness + faith = freedom!

How then do I forgive my father? The process of forgiveness involves the following. I need to first of all renounce the right to retaliate against my father. Forgiving him means I will no longer seek revenge or fantasize about getting my own back. I will simply give up the desire I have to harm him. This is vital, for as my friend Tiffany Vale puts it, "If you hold onto the grudge, the mountain won't budge!"

Secondly, forgiveness means tearing up the IOUs. It means declaring that my father owes me nothing. Every debt has been cancelled. Every obligation is now null and void.

Thirdly, it means ending or cancelling my judgments. I may have every right to criticize my father for the way he treated me (and others), but forgiving him means that I cease to make any negative statements about him.

Fourthly, it means giving my father a gift he doesn't deserve, the gift of my unconditional forgiveness. Our Heavenly Father has given us a gift we don't deserve – the gift of unconditional forgiveness. Freely we have received, so freely we give. We pass it on. We pay it forward rather than paying it back (Colossians 3:13).

And finally, it means choosing to bless my dad, even though he may have cursed me. Jesus commanded us to bless those who curse us. In obedience to that, we do the really subversive thing and we bless the one who wounded us. In making that one radical step alone, we rise up out of the state of the victim and we enter into the state of the victor.

My own story is this. For thirty-five years I had an unforgiving, bitter attitude towards my biological father who abandoned my twin sister and me. I wasn't aware of how deep this bitterness went because I was suffering from split soul syndrome. I had buried the pain of not knowing my dad for over three decades. But then

I began an extraordinary journey of forgiveness and everything changed.

It all began in April 1996. I was speaking at a conference and a lady had a prophecy for me. She saw me while I was on the platform with a ball and chain around one of my feet and a golden key in one of my outstretched hands. She told me she didn't know what the vision meant but that I would know by the end of the year.

In October of that year I travelled to Toronto for the Catch the Fire '96 conference. I was desperate for a breakthrough in my relationship with my Heavenly Father. I didn't feel he was close to me at the time. I felt he was far away. The night before I left for Toronto I told my wife Alie about my spiritual condition and she said that she thought it was to do with my abandonment by my earthly father. She added that she felt the Lord was going to heal me in Toronto!

The next evening I was in the Catch the Fire conference, standing at the front in the ministry time, waiting to receive prayer. I was desperate for a touch of God. As I stood there a lady came up to me. She didn't know anything about me but she put her finger on my heart and prayed, "Father, minister to the sense of abandonment in this man's life." Then she looked me in the eye and asked, "Does that mean anything to you?"

At that moment I did something very un-British. I grimaced in pain as a loud cry began to emerge from the deepest recesses of my soul. All the anger and grief at being abandoned by my dad surfaced for the first and the last time and I sobbed and sobbed. The lady continued to pray for me briefly as I lay upon the carpet, doubled up in pain. "Fill up the love deficit", she kept praying. Then she left me to pray for the hundreds of others receiving ministry.

The next thing I knew, I could hear this voice at the front of the stage speaking over a microphone. "I have just had a vision. I see many of you. It's like you have a ball and chain around one of your feet and a golden key in one of your outstretched hands. Forgiveness is the golden key. If you can forgive those who have hurt you, you will be free."

At that moment I suddenly understood what I had to do. I chose to forgive my natural father for walking out on me. I chose to bless him in spite of the pain he had caused. I chose to honour him as my dad. As I did so, the power of the Father's love absolutely overwhelmed me and I was fully immersed in his joy and peace.

That was the most amazing experience of the Father's embrace, the most intense encounter with the Love of all Loves. It completely and utterly transformed me. It transformed my relationship with God, with my wife, my children and my church. Something massive happened in my soul and I can safely say that it was forgiveness that unlocked my freedom that night on a hotel floor in far-away Canada.

Forgiveness is the golden key! Forgive your earthly father or father figures. And don't forget in all of this to forgive yourself as well. Many of us far too readily believe the "bad dad, good child" myth. The truth is, we may well have to release ourselves from a grudge. We may need to renounce the right to retaliate against ourselves and cease rejecting, judging, hating and even harming ourselves. We may need to release to ourselves the undeserved gift of unconditional forgiveness and we may need to learn to bless rather than curse our own selves.

We can all do this. All our Heavenly Father is waiting for is for us to choose – to choose life instead of death, blessings instead of curses, mercy instead of justice. When we make the decision, his power gets behind our choice and we find ourselves free.

So take the forgiveness key – the golden key! And exercise your responsibility.

Loving Father, I thank you that you gave me a gift I didn't deserve, the gift of your forgiveness. I thank you that because of the Cross, every negative judgment against me was cancelled and I am no longer under condemnation.

I pray right now that you will help and empower me to choose mercy over justice, love over law, just as you have done with me.

Especially, right now, I choose to forgive my father. I renounce the right to retaliate against him. I wish him no ill from now on. I tear up every IOU and I declare that from this moment he owes me nothing. I cancel every negative judgment about him. I release to my father a gift he doesn't deserve – the gift of my unconditional forgiveness, and I bless my father and I honour him too.

I choose to use the golden key and as I do so, I cast the mountain of my pain into the sea, by faith in Jesus' mighty name. Set me free of all that's unproductive in my life. Heal my wounds. And make me fruitful in you.

Thank you, Dad. I receive all this right now by faith. In the name of Jesus, Amen.

Key no. 5: Go to the Cross for your healing

We must never forget: the freedom that has been won for us by Jesus has been won at a great cost. It was purchased for us by the blood that he shed on the Cross at Calvary. Our freedom is free, but it wasn't cheap. If we are to enter into the fullness of our inheritance, then we must go to the Cross for our healing. Orphan hearts are set free at the foot of the Cross, nowhere else. The Cross is the only place where we can find lasting breakthrough. Sooner or later we have to return there to find our true liberation.

Why is the Cross so important for the healing of the orphan heart condition? Let's go back to Part 2 again and remember the core components of the orphan heart condition. If you recall, I proposed that the primal wound known as the orphan heart is made up of two things, separation and shame. There is first of all separation – the experience of being separated from a father's love. The scenarios for this are multiple, as we saw, but they all share this one common theme of being separated, of losing one's moorings in the most stabilizing of loves – the love of a good father. There is secondly shame. The person with the orphan heart starts to play the blame game and the person they end up blaming more than anyone else is themselves. They start believing the lie that if they had been more beautiful and valuable then their father would have loved them, stayed with them, been kind to them and cherished them. As I said in Part 2, when a father leaves by the front door, shame creeps in at the back door. In the absence of a loving father, there is a profound honour deficit and people start to believe that they're ugly, worthless, pointless and a mistake. Separation and shame are accordingly the core components of the orphan heart condition.

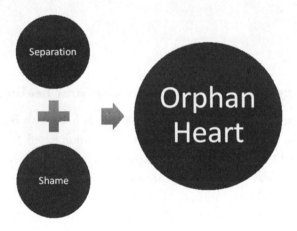

Why is the Cross so important for the healing of the orphan heart? The answer is because Jesus' death is the source and the location for our freedom from the spiritual slavery that we call the orphan state. On the Cross, Jesus embraced the core components of the orphan heart condition. He first of all embraced the experience of being separated from a father's love. On the Cross, Jesus felt that his Father was no longer there, no longer close to him. All the sins of the world had been placed upon his shoulders and he could no longer sense his Father's intimate presence. We know that sin separates human beings from God. On the Cross, our sin separated Jesus from his Father's love. That is why he cried out, "My God, my God, why have you abandoned me?" In his humanity, Jesus sensed the Father's absence, which can only mean that he took into his dying, crucified body the excruciating experience of paternal abandonment. This does not mean that the holy and undivided Trinity was fractured at Calvary. What it does mean is that *in his humanity Jesus felt as though he had been forsaken and abandoned by his* Abba. What a great source of comfort and healing this is for all those who have experienced separation from a father's love. Jesus has walked where we walk. He has felt what we feel. He truly understands and that makes me want to worship him!

Secondly, on the Cross Jesus embraced the experience of shame. The Letter to the Hebrews says that on the Cross Jesus in fact scorned the shame (Hebrews 12:2). We must remember that crucifixion was the most shameful form of execution in the ancient world. It involved the utter degradation of the whole person. It was a form of torture and execution reserved for the lowest of the low – for criminals and slaves. In fact it was known as "the slave's punishment" and it was often accompanied by the mockery of many spectators. Jesus embraced shame at Calvary. He took the experience of being shamed into his body on the Cross. This is important. In the Western world, our understanding of the Cross tends to be focused on guilt. In other words, we are more inclined to see the Cross as the place where we are forgiven for what we've done. In the East, the picture shifts. Christians in the Eastern part of the world tend to understand the Cross in relation to shame. They are more inclined to see the Cross as the place where we are set free from who we are. In truth it is, of course, "both-and", not

273

"either-or". At Calvary, Jesus dealt with our guilt and our shame. The good news for those afflicted by the orphan heart condition is that the Cross heals our shame. That is something we have tended to forget in the West.

All this indicates why the Cross is so vital for our healing. It is because Jesus experienced the primal wound of the orphan heart at Calvary. Not only did he experience separation, he also experienced shame. He absorbed the full torment of the orphan heart condition. Indeed, we could put it this way: *The Son became an orphan so that we who are spiritual orphans might become sons.*

The Cross is accordingly vital in the healing and liberation of spiritual orphans. I myself have experienced this first hand. In Part 2 I wrote about the nightmares that I had for ten months when I was in my twenties, training for the ordained ministry at a theological college in the UK. These all revolved around the same theme – being separated from my wife. They were horribly realistic and it took a great deal the next day to shake off their debilitating after-effects. In the end I went to my pastoral tutor for some counselling and he identified that I was suffering from an acute separation anxiety. Having been separated from my earthly father before I was born and my birth mother after I was born, I was terrified of being separated from a loved one again, especially from my wife. My tutor advised at the end of four counselling sessions that I should go forward for prayer at the next healing service. I did just that at a college chapel Communion service about a month later and was prayed for by some trusted friends who had walked with me and knew my story. As they prayed for me in the context of the Lord's Supper (an act remembering Christ's death), I had a powerful vision of Jesus on the Cross and I saw a shadow – like a thin black shawl – leaving my body and entering his. I heard him cry, "My God, my God, why have you abandoned me?" At that moment, I knew that I was free. I knew that something had left me. I was 100 per cent delivered of my separation anxiety. I have never had another nightmare since.

The Cross is indeed the place where our freedom was won. Not only is it the place where we were forgiven. It is the place where we are truly and lastingly set free. We must go to Calvary if we are to receive our full inheritance and walk in the glorious freedom of the children of God. At the Cross a great exchange takes place. Jesus gets our separation. We get his reconciliation. Jesus gets our shame. We get his honour. At the Cross, his wounds heal our wounds. These wounds

> The son became an orphan so that we who are spiritual orphans might become sons.

are very often wounds that affect the whole of our personhood, not just a part of it. In other words, they are wounds that impact our souls, our bodies and our spirits. This means that our journey may well have to take us into inner, emotional healing, physical healing and even deliverance (as above).

In addition, there may even be a need for us to be healed and released from *generational* hurts – especially the generational wound of fatherlessness. Often our fathers abandon us because they were abandoned by their own dads, who may also have been abandoned by their dads. Father wounds can pass down the generations, especially in the case of addicted (particularly alcoholic) fathers and abusive fathers. Somewhere, someone needs to make a stand and say, "This far and no further!" This is so important because, as Beth Erickson says, "Unless the blueprint is changed, the legacy of unresolved father loss becomes part of the estate handed down from one generation to the next."[24] We cannot therefore bypass the Cross. We need to go to the Cross and take the key, take our responsibility and ask for healing at every level.

Loving Father, I come to the Cross and I pray for my emotional healing. Heal me of my father wounds, especially the deep-down wounds of separation and shame. Satisfy my father hunger with your abundant love. Replace all my shame with your honour. Overwhelm me with the love of all loves and heal me of my hurts.

I come to the Cross and I ask that you would heal my body too. Where my wounded soul has led to disease or disability, I pray for your divine healing, in Jesus' name. Let every ache and pain in my life leave right now. I command the spirit of infirmity to go in Jesus' name. Heal me physically as well as emotionally, I pray.

I come to the Cross and ask that you would also heal me spiritually. I pray that you would release me from any unclean spirits that have been afflicting my life because of my orphan heart. I close the door to every single one of them right now, in Jesus' name. As a child of the King of Kings, I take my God-given authority and I bind every spirit contrary to the Holy Spirit and forbid it from having any more influence in my life or my relationships. I cast out every spirit, especially the spirit of fear. Go to the place that Almighty God has reserved for you, hurting no other, and never come back. I loose and permit the Holy Spirit to come now and fill up the cavity left by any unwelcome spirits. And from this day on, I forbid any demonic spirit from coming anywhere near my heart, in Jesus' name.

And finally I come to the Cross and I pray that any generational curse of fatherlessness in my family tree would be broken right now, in Jesus' name. I exchange the curse of fatherlessness for the blessing of the Father's love, from this day on. And I resolve to turn what was once a generational curse into a generational blessing – the blessing of the Father's love to my children, grandchildren, great-grandchildren and so forth. I resolve to leave a legacy of the Father's love to those who will come after me, until Jesus returns. Amen.

Key no. 6: Experience the Father's embrace

One of the claims I have made in this book is that we need a positive experience to displace a negative one. In other words, if we have experienced the trauma of being separated from a father's love, we need that to be displaced by the positive experience of a father's love. Most people look for this positive experience in the wrong places – in sexual relationships, romantic attachments, addictive substances and so on – but these never ultimately satisfy. What we all need is a personal, direct revelation of *Abba*, Father's love. We need to experience the healing and comforting power of his divine embrace.

Hildegarde of Bingen once said this: "God hugs you. You are encircled by the arms of the mystery of God."[25] I love that! So far in this book I have included a number of stories of Christians who have found healing in the Father's arms. Like the story of the Prodigal Son, these testimonies demonstrate the liberating and life-giving power of the Father's embrace. In all of this I have made my position very clear. God is *Abba*, Father; he is the world's greatest Dad. He is not a fiction or a myth. He is the living, loving God. Moreover, the experience of his divine embrace is not the sentimental fantasy of a deeply deluded and troubled mind. It is the most real and releasing force in the universe. It is the power of the Father's love. It is the Spirit of adoption working in our spirits, souls and bodies. It is the flame of love within our hearts – a supernatural flame that burns deep within our being and releases the *Abba* cry from our hearts.

So Hildegarde was right. God hugs us. But she was also right when she said that we are encircled by the arms of the *mystery* of God. There is a mystery about the ways in which the Father embraces us. He doesn't come to everyone in the same way. His visitations are varied. His affection for us is expressed in unique ways. Let us explore a few thoughts about this for a moment.

First of all, to some people the Father comes suddenly; to others he comes gradually. We must understand that the wind blows where it wills (John 3:8). The Holy Spirit does not work in the same way in every person. Some people receive the revelation of the Father's love like a sudden flash-flood. Other people receive the revelation of the Father's love like a gradual, rising tide. Is one better than the other? No! *Abba*, Father will come and hug us in the way that he knows is best for us. That may be an instant and spontaneous encounter or it may be a progressive wooing. Father God is sovereign.

Secondly, to some the Father comes even though they haven't sought him; to others he comes in response to their seeking. This, incidentally, applies to unbelievers as well as believers. Just recently I received an email at Father's House from a non-Christian who had been watching television one night. He was surfing the channels and found me speaking about the Father's love on Christian television. He was not a religious man at all, to use his own words, but he felt drawn to pause and listen. At the end of my talk I invited people to stand to receive a touch of the Father's love. He did that in his front room and felt embraced by God! The truth is, the Father comes to those who haven't even sought him, whether they are Christians or not. To others he comes because he has been pursued. Is one better than the other? No! They are just different because the ways of the Spirit are diverse. To put it in Hildegarde's language, we are encircled by the Father's arms but these arms are the arms of the mystery of God.

Thirdly, I have also discovered this. To some the Father ministers his love through a human intermediary; to others he ministers his love directly, without any human intermediary. I remember one time a man was listening to a talk I was giving. He was in his sixties. He was sitting all on his own at the back of a large auditorium. When he closed his eyes during my talk he experienced big, strong, loving arms around him. No one was anywhere near him. Later he realized that he had been hugged by his Heavenly Father. This was especially significant because his dad had died when he was only five years old and for sixty years he had never felt a father's embrace. That night he did. He experienced the Father's hug and went back to his church with the news that "God is relational, not remote." Some people receive the Father's love like that. Others receive it when people pray for them with the laying on of hands. Is one better than the other? No! Everyone is different. God hugs us, but his ways are indeed mysterious.

We truly are encircled by arms of mystery. There is such a great variety about the way the Father embraces his children. I have four children. They are wonderfully unique even though they all have the same dad. Do I hug them in exactly the same way? No. Do I hug them all at exactly the same time? No. They are all different, so I express my affection for them differently. I hug them in different ways at different times, whether they have asked me or not!

Encountering the love of *Abba*, Father is a vital part of the healing process. We all of us need to experience the Father's embrace, or "God's hug", as Hildegard called it. As for how that comes to each individual believer, that is the Father's decision. All I can say is this, that when we receive the positive experience of our Heavenly Father's presence, it completely displaces the negative experience of an earthly father's absence. When we receive the positive experience of a loving Father's tender touch, it completely displaces the negative experience of an earthly father's abuses. Such a positive experience of *Abba*'s love breaks the chains that have bound us into our past and banishes the drive to earn love through striving and performance. Experiencing Dad's hug puts us in a place of rest that the world – with all its medication and counselling – simply cannot give. It frees us from our hurtful history. It secures us in our true identity. And it transports us towards our unique destiny. There is simply no experience on earth like the hug of heaven.

Perhaps no one has described this divine embrace more eloquently or simply than the great Dr Martin Lloyd Jones, formerly senior pastor of Westminster Chapel in London. He writes movingly about what he called "this extra outpouring of love" that I am talking about here, and he used the analogy of a father's intimate relationship with his child in order to illustrate the way *Abba*, Father embraces us:

> *A man and his little child are walking down the road and they are walking hand in hand, and the child knows that he is the child of his father, and he knows that his father loves him, and he rejoices in that, and he is happy in it. There is no uncertainty about it all, but suddenly the father, moved by some impulse, takes hold of the child and picks him up, kisses him, embraces him, showers his love upon him, and then he puts him down again and they go on walking together.*
>
> *That is it! The child knew before that his father loved him, and he knew that he was his child. But oh, the loving embrace, this extra outpouring of love, this unusual manifestation of it – that is the kind of thing. The Spirit bearing witness with our spirit that we are the children of God.[26]*

What a great description! Make it your aim to ask for the Father's loving embrace. Take the key. Take responsibility.

Abba, Father, I thank you that you have given me the loving Spirit of adoption. I pray that through the power of your Holy Spirit you will bring me into an encounter with the love of all loves. I want to run into your arms, just like the Prodigal Son. I want to feel your embrace and feel the hug of heaven. I know that in your arms I will find rest, healing and freedom. So I submit to the process of receiving the flame of love in my heart. Let it burn within me. I pray for an extra outpouring of your love and an unusual manifestation of your grace. Would you seize my heart with the greatest affection in the universe. I make myself available to receive your loving embrace, in Jesus' name. Amen.

Key no. 7: Build a strong identity in Christ

We began this chapter by seeing more clearly who God is – the one whom Jesus revealed as *Abba*, Father. We end this chapter by seeing more clearly who we are, the adopted and beloved children of the world's greatest Dad. This is really important. The devil is into identity theft. He wants to rob us of our brand-new identities in Christ. He wants us to live as slaves not as sons, as orphans not as heirs. He wants to steal our identity and our inheritance. We need to make a stand against this thief and protect the great truth about who we are in Christ.

The Bible teaches that a new believer in Christ is a brand-new creation. As Paul says in 2 Corinthians 5:17, "if anyone is in Christ, he is a new creation; the old has gone, the new has come!" When we turn to Christ, our old life is crucified and buried with him and we rise to a brand-new life in Christ. This is the symbolism of baptism. A new Christian is immersed in the waters of baptism as a public and outward sign that their old life is now washed away. Their old identity is now dead and buried. They are then lifted from the waters as a sign that they have been raised to a new identity. As Paul reminded his readers in Ephesians 4:22–24:

> *You were taught, with regard to your former way of life,*
> *to put off your old self, which is being corrupted by its*
> *deceitful desires; to be made new in the attitude of your*
> *minds; and to put on the new self, created to be like*
> *God in true righteousness and holiness.*

Once we have repented of our sins, trusted in Christ, received the Holy Spirit and been baptized in water, we have a new identity. No longer are we orphans and slaves; we are sons and daughters of the King of Kings. No longer is our identity tied up with what we do; it is now tied up inextricably with who we are. In Christ, we are the beloved, adopted sons and daughters of the High King of Heaven.

Part of the healing journey involves building a strong and joyful sense of our new identity. In this endeavour we must understand that we have an enemy who specializes in stealing blessings from believers. He is Satan, the original orphan. He hates the very idea of a new believer entering into mature sonship. He wants us to drift back into the orphan state where our identity is derived from our performance, not from our position. In short, he wants us to become slaves again. Jesus warned us about this when he said that the devil had come to rob, steal and destroy (John 10:10). In building our robust new identity in Christ, we have an enemy who seeks to rob us of our new self. He is constantly at work, engaging in a spiritual version of identity theft. We must resolutely resist his attempts to steal and destroy our new identity as sons and daughters. We must cultivate and protect our new self and celebrate the gift of honour that *Abba*, Father has given us in proclaiming over us what he declared over his Son: "You are my beloved child, my chosen one, with you I am well pleased!"

I mentioned in Part 2 that I owe a debt to a Ugandan called Paul for identifying the symptoms and signs of the orphan heart condition. As I wrote then, Paul was an orphan who was put in a Christian orphanage. He subsequently became a Christian himself. After a period of struggle, Paul came to rejoice in his status as an adopted son of God. When that happened he realized he had a brand-new identity, so he decided to change his name. His name was Paul Nyabenda but his new name is Paul Kusuubira. Kusuubira means "hope". What a great name to give yourself – Paul Hope! To celebrate this new identity, Paul composed a worship song in praise of *Abba*, Father's love:

> *Thank you, Lord, my God, for your love for me*
> *Yes, your love for me has brought me from far away!*
> *Look at that wondrous love! Look at that wondrous love!*
>
> *Once I was fatherless, but now I've got a family*
> *A beautiful family, with God as my Father*

*Look at that wondrous love! Look at that wondrous
love!*

*Once I had no hope, but now I've got new hope
The only hope that I have comes from my Lord!
Look at that wondrous love! Look at that wondrous
love!*

*Once I was lonely but now I've got my friend
The sweetest friend that I have is Jesus Christ!
Look at that wondrous love! Look at that wondrous
love!*

*When trials come, Lord, I pray, make me stand
When trials come, Lord, I pray, make me stand
And make me a witness for your love!*

So take hold of this last key, the identity key. Build a strong sense of your new identity as an adopted child of God. Take responsibility and celebrate!

A Love Letter from God

Dear Child,

I want you to know how much I love you. This is your new identity: you are my child, my heir and in you I take great delight.

I am your Heavenly Father and I love you even as I love my Son. I'm so proud of you and can see much of myself in you.

I have known you before you were born. I knit you together in your mother's womb. I have had a plan for you from before the beginning of time. My plans are good.

My love is unconditional. I will always love you. Nothing you can do will make me love you less; nothing you can do will make me love you more. Nothing will ever separate you from my love.

I want you to know my love for you, to feel it deep in your heart. As you do, my joy will bubble up inside of you. I will comfort you when you are in trouble. I will rejoice with you when you rejoice.

I am your provider. You need never worry or be anxious about having enough. I will provide. I know you intimately. I know every detail about you, and your days are numbered before me. I have determined the exact place where you will live and my timing for your life is perfect. Trust me.

You are my treasured possession, my own darling child. And I love you.

I AM

Your loving Father.

And finally

Once we have used these keys (however many, and in whatever order), we need to be open to the possibility of a great miracle, the miracle of reconciliation with our earthly fathers. Now in some cases this may be impossible. If your father is dead, then this scenario sadly does not apply. If your father is dangerous, then it would be unwise for you to try to be reconciled. Unless he has opened his heart to change as well, it would be dangerous to seek to rebuild a relationship with him, especially if he is an abusive father.

Having said all that, it is also true that the Father is moving by his Spirit in many situations to turn the hearts of the fathers towards their children and the hearts of the children towards their fathers (Malachi 4:6). We are entering a season in which there are an increasing number of people giving testimony to extraordinary miracles of reconciliation with their fathers. Having had their own hearts transformed, they are finding that their fathers' hearts are being transformed as well. This further goes to prove that the best prayer we can all pray is "change me" rather than "change him". When we get changed, he gets changed!

To encourage you to believe for such a miracle (if it applies in your situation), I will finish this chapter with the powerful testimony of a good friend, Greg Haslam. Greg is the senior pastor of Westminster Chapel in London, UK and a few years ago he experienced a remarkable healing in his relationship with an estranged father. Greg draws attention to the significance of Malachi 4:6 in the unfolding of this dramatic episode in his life. I believe we are entering a Malachi 4:6 season of supernatural reconciliation between fathers and their children – even grown-up children. So read this and be encouraged!

> *See, I will send you the prophet Elijah before that great and dreadful day of the Lord comes. He will turn the hearts of the fathers to their children, and the hearts of the children to their fathers; or else I will come and strike the land with a curse.*
>
> MALACHI 4:6

I grew up in a rough area of Liverpool during the 1950s, along with my twin sister Jenny and my older brother Raymond. My mother was a lapsed Anglican but had a respect for God. My father was a complete secularist, with no faith or felt need for one, and he had a deep and marked opposition to religion or any talk about God. He sought to ensure in every way he could that our access to Sunday School or church was limited, or non-existent. Our home was an unhappy one, marked by many noisy parental rows and angry outbursts, that as a very young child I never understood, but which left many emotional scars and fears in my life.

It was probably inevitable that my parents were divorced when I was just six, and Dad went out of our lives completely except for a couple of brief but very difficult contacts with him when I was aged eleven and subsequently when I was newly married at twenty-seven years of age. He was completely absent during all of that time, with no warm contact at all. I'm sure he missed us, but the distance grew and it became a major emotional hurdle for the children to bridge such a wide gap, though we tried, and he probably felt the same. But in his last ten years — partly through the impact of Malachi 4:6 on my mind and heart — I sought a real and growing contact and relationship with him, believing God for good things to happen between us, even though Dad was still a strong and outspoken atheist.

A decade later, he had just passed his eighty-fourth birthday in late January 2005, when he was admitted to the Liverpool Royal Hospital with abdominal pains. After waiting two weeks for test results, it was confirmed that this was due to extensive cancers in his left lung that had also spread to his liver. He was declared untreatable. Thankfully, he was not in a great deal of pain and was even quite comfortable right up to his death, one week later. Furthermore, some amazing developments were to unfold during this very special period of his final few days.

I travelled north as soon as I could, and got to spend the whole day with him in hospital on Monday 7th February. I felt it was quite an amazing time. We talked of the past and of our mutual losses and pains, stemming from the break-up of the family when I was so young. There was no doubt that my father had mellowed significantly, and had come to terms with many painful regrets. I assured him of my forgiveness and of my love for him, and also of the honour I felt for him as my father. This was what I so wanted to be able say to him again before he died.

I was moved beyond words to hear him say that he also loved me, and I was to pass on the same words to my sister (my elder brother had died some years beforehand), and he even had kind words for my mother which was not usual. I saw all of this as a fulfilment of Malachi 4:6 in our lives, a text I have spoken on many times, and which I've sought to act upon myself, in terms of my determined response to love my Dad. I also felt an urgency to talk simply and meaningfully with him for as long as he would listen, about the Lord Jesus and his need of God's grace to rescue from all that death could and would do to him. It was not too late for him to awaken to the fact he was going into eternity without any faith in Christ, whilst clinging to the sinking raft of his stubborn atheism and its denial of the reality of God's love and grace. Thankfully, he had been befriended by two wonderful and caring believers in Liverpool, who genuinely loved him and had sown the seeds of Gospel truth into his mind whenever the opportunity arose to do so. None of this was wasted on him, though it looked as though it had been right to the very end. Little did we know!

It became obvious to me as we spoke that he had begun to let go of the strong and virulent atheism that he had vehemently adhered to for so long, and he'd clearly realized it was not going to support him in any way during this last and greatest trial of his life. I lovingly assured him of God's reality and of his love and mercy towards him, and of my desire to see him again, and the fact that this could certainly happen in the new heavens and earth. I then went on to share the Gospel with him very simply. I spoke of Christ's willingness to accept him, basing this on Jesus' strong care from John 10 – the Good Shepherd – and then the story of the dying thief on the Cross. He seemed so humbled before the God he had ignored and denied for all of his life. He was in deep concern about his past, though not in great distress, more a genuine humbling and ready admission that he had been wrong. He was then open and willing to seek God's mercy, and he prayed to ask God for forgiveness and to trust in Christ as his Saviour and Lord, much as the dying thief had done at the end.

His subsequent words to me and our family were proof positive that his heart was already completely changed. I was stunned at God's grace to him, and to me! I prayed God's peace, comfort and protection over him as I said goodbye, and then I privately asked that the Lord would spare him from a long drawn-out death, with all the agonies that brings to the suffering victim and also to his relatives. He died peacefully in bed a short 48 hours later.

Amazingly, the last words he spoke just before he died, were all about a vision he was receiving of an incredibly beautiful, vast and sunlit garden spread out before him over a great distance, and bathed in golden sunlight. This garden was filled with luscious trees and gorgeous colourful flowers spreading out in every direction. He could see vast crowds of people fading off into the long distance, and said he even recognized some of them! I took this to be a glimpse of the very same paradise that Jesus assured the penitent thief about on the cross, dying as he was beside Jesus at Golgotha. The thief asked the Lord, "Remember me Lord, when you come into your kingdom." Jesus replied, "Truly, truly I say to you, today you will be with me in paradise" – a death-bed conversion if ever there was one! My father's surprise vision may have been more for my reassurance than for his, as I knew its significance in terms of my last conversation with Dad.

I feel this was the best possible ending to years of estrangement from and rejection by my father. My contact with him in recent years had become increasingly more positive, and I am now eternally grateful for the chance I had to see him alive before he finally went from my life permanently. To have been able to talk heart to heart with him as I did, on that and other significant occasions in that last decade, especially just before he died – was amazing! I am overwhelmed by the mercy of God both to him, and to me.

As a postscript, it was wonderful to see another surpising outcome unfold just days later from that last visit to Dad, when I returned to the pulpit at Westminster Chapel, London, the church I lead as their Senior Pastor. That morning, I spoke from Paul's testimony to God's grace in his own life that he recounts in 1 Timothy 1:12–17, highlighting God's mercy to the most unlikely candidates. I told the full story of Dad's conversion that morning to a church that had covered my tracks with fervent prayer during my visit to Dad earlier that week. I preached on "God's Amazing Grace". Four people came to faith in Christ that morning — and I realized with joy, that because of his amazing story, my father had already been instrumental in winning his first converts to his newly found Saviour.

God is a God of great surprises and unforeseen happy endings, even in the most battered and bruised relationships we sometimes have with our estranged fathers.

Truly, with God, it is always possible that "all shall be well. All shall be well. And all manner of things shall be well!" (Dame Julian of Norwich).

Chapter 12

HEALED FOR THE HARVEST

I want to finish *I Am Your Father* by asking a question: "What is all this healing for?" Let's assume that you have come to this book with a wounded heart and that *Abba*, Father has done a deep work of healing in you as you have read it. What do you do with this healing? Does the journey end here? Or is there something you're supposed to do with your new-found freedom?

To answer that question I want to look at a story in the Gospels. It is one of the passages of the New Testament that I find myself coming back to time and time again, and so often I have found new things there. The episode involves Jesus and a meeting that he had with a woman from the country of Samaria. This took place outside the town of Sychar and it's narrated in John 4:4–42.

The story begins with Jesus walking through Samaria. Pious Jews avoided Samaria like the plague. But not Jesus! As he travels, he is tired and thirsty, so he sits down beside a Samaritan well to have a drink. He is all alone; his disciples have gone off into the town to buy some lunch.

It is noon and the sun is high and its powerful rays are beating down upon his head. Beads of sweat are beginning to appear on his forehead. He pulls his robe over his head to protect himself from the intense heat. As he does so a woman with a large water jar appears out of the haze of heat that hangs like a shimmering veil between the well and the town. She draws near and then arrives at the lip of the well where she rests her jar, sighing with relief as she does so. She ignores Jesus and wipes the moisture from her forehead and her face. She picks up the jar again and is about to draw water when the mysterious man in the dusty robe stirs and asks her for a drink.

For a moment the woman looks at him. Suddenly it hits her. This man is not from her town or her country. He is a Jew. She shudders. Jewish men hate Samaritan women. Every woman in her nation knows the proverb that Jewish men frequently utter: "The daughters of the Samaritans are dirty from the cradle." She knows that Jewish men despise people like her. She knows that a Jewish Rabbi was not supposed to speak to a woman he didn't know in public and that he should have withdrawn to a distance of twenty feet. So she goes on the defensive and asks him why he's talking to her, a Samaritan woman.

The man slowly withdraws the robe from his head and looks up into her eyes. She sees the piercing nature of his gaze under his dark long hair. There is truly something different about this man. She can't put her finger on it. But she knows. She knows instinctively that these eyes are looking right into her heart and that he is no ordinary man.

And then he speaks. He tells her that if she knew who it was that was speaking to her, and what a great gift he was offering, then she would have asked him and he would have given her "living water".

This phrase "living water" sounds strange to her ears. She thinks he means "running water", which of course is nonsense when you're at a well full of still water. She points this out with feisty sarcasm, saying that he hasn't even brought a leather bucket to fetch some water. Jesus ignores her comment and presses on with his offer of living water, stressing that the person who receives it will never go thirsty again. The woman looks at Jesus. This sounds like good news. There is something different about this Jewish man who is ignoring social prejudices and cultural protocols and who is offering her a gift from God himself. So she says, "Give me some of this living water, so that I won't have to keep coming back to this well over and over. It's hot work and I'm exhausted."

The man smiles and says, "Go fetch your husband. What I have for you I have for him as well." With this the woman is momentarily caught off guard. She hasn't expected him to address the issue of her marital status, nor does she want him to. She has had a very wounded past on the marriage front. Time and again she has sought for love in a man's arms. She has gone from one relationship to another looking for affection in all the wrong places and all the wrong people. She has been married many times and she is now in another relationship; the destructive cycle has begun all over again. So without thinking, the woman replies, "I have no husband."

What happens next takes her breath away. Instantly the man stands up and looks straight into her eyes. With great tenderness he speaks to her. "You're telling the truth. You've been married to five men and the man you're living with is not your husband."

Suddenly the woman feels as if the ground is no longer strong and steady beneath her feet. Her world has been rocked. How does this man know her so intimately? She has never met him before and there is no chance that anyone in her town would ever have told him her life story. There can only be one possible solution. He must be a prophet. After all, only the prophets can read the secrets of people's hearts.

As the two unlikely companions stand together, the conversation turns to religion. The woman, trying to change the subject, starts speaking about the central site for Samaritan worship on Mount Gerazim. The man doesn't question this but he chooses instead to tell her that she can worship God as Father anywhere, not just in great temples. Time and again he uses this word "Father" as he speaks to her. On his lips, it is the

Aramaic word *Abba*, meaning "Daddy". Every time he says it, something reverberates deep within the woman's soul.

Her heart is now racing. She knows that one day the Messiah will come and explain all these things to her people. The Samaritans, like the Jews, expect the coming of the Messiah, the Anointed One. She tells the man that there'll come a time when this kind of worship will become clear and real to them.

He replies, "I, I am."

The woman drops the water jar she's been holding onto throughout the conversation. "I am." "I am." Where has she heard this phrase before? She thinks for a moment. And then, back in the distant recesses of her history – a history that the Samaritans share with the Jews – she hears a voice coming from a burning bush in the desert of Midian. It is the voice of God himself as he speaks to Moses and tells Moses his name, "I am who I am." Could it be? Could it be that this Jewish man, who has seen right into the secret places of her heart, is the I Am in person?

She runs back into town. She chases everyone she can find in the busy marketplace of Sychar, where scores of people are selling fish, meat, fruit, vegetables, clothes and trinkets. She pulls on the sleeves of all the people she speaks to. "Come to the well! Come to the well! There's a Jewish man there who just told me everything about my life. I've never met him before, yet he knew absolutely all my secrets. Could this be the Anointed One – the One we've been waiting for? Come and see! Come on, come and see!"

And with that the people leave their haggling and their market stalls and follow the woman. She is so well known, not least because of all the disastrous relationships she's had, that many think cynically that this could be quite entertaining. But when they reach the well and they meet the man, all that changes. There is the Rabbi, with his disciples now sitting at his feet, drinking the water that he'd never managed to get from the woman. They discover that his name is Jesus, *Yeshua* in Aramaic, a name that means literally "salvation".

The crowd of Samaritan men and women gathers around the stranger from Judea. The woman is earnestly repeating her testimony, that this man told her everything about her life. Many of her people believe that she is right, that he truly is the Anointed One. As they all sit at the Rabbi's feet and listen to him, many others come to believe as well. Even though he's a Jewish man, they are drawn to the life-giving power of his words and it's not long before they acknowledge him for who he is. They call him "Saviour of the World" – a title reserved in their day for the Roman Emperor. They defy political protocols and choose to call him "the World's Saviour" instead. Not just Israel's Saviour but the *world's* Saviour – their Saviour too. With this a spiritual harvest begins in Sychar. A great awakening begins in a Samaritan town.

The "In" Stage

The reason I have retold this story is not only because it is one of the most moving encounters in the Gospels, but also because it helps us to answer the question, "What do I do with my healing?" If we look at what happens to this Samaritan woman we can see that she goes through discernible stages in her meeting with Jesus. For many of us today, these three stages take a long time. But in the presence of the incarnate Son of God, this woman experiences acceleration. She is fast-tracked through seasons of the heart that take people like you and me a long time. She experiences in ten minutes what can sometimes take as much as ten months or even ten years.

The first stage that she experiences I will call the "In" Stage. By that I mean a stage in which the emphasis is on her needs. The "In" Stage is a season of the heart in which *my* wounds are exposed and *my* needs are brought to the light. We all of us have shadows and when we come into the light our shadows

> The "In" stage is a season of the heart in which my wounds are exposed and my needs are brought into the light.

are revealed. This woman is in the presence of the Light of the World. Her hurts are uncovered in the presence of Jesus. Her dark side is exposed.

Every single one of us has this shadowy side to our personalities. We have parts of our soul where the deepest hurts are hidden and where our secret sins are concealed. The "In" Stage is really a *me* stage; it is a phase in which the Holy Spirit places a spotlight on the wounds that need healing and the sins that need forgiving. This stage is characterized by words like "I" and "me".

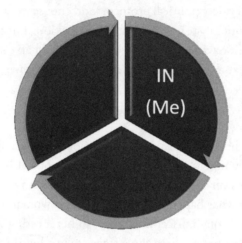

If we look at the first part of the encounter between the woman and Jesus in John 4:4–42 we see that these words surface in the woman's comments. Here are a few examples:

The Samaritan woman said to him, "You are a Jew and I am a Samaritan woman. How can you ask me for a drink?"

(VERSE 9)

The woman said to him, "Sir, give me this water so that I won't get thirsty and have to keep coming here to draw water."

(VERSE 15)

"I have no husband," she replied.

(VERSE 19)

Notice how the woman is focused on her own issues here.

In the first part of the woman's encounter there are some tell-tale clues about the primary need in her life. In Part 2 of this book I spoke about the symptoms and signs of the orphan heart – of the heart that has been wounded as a result of the experience of being separated from a father's love, the heart blighted by a deep sense of shame. If we look closely at the woman's actions and words we can see a number of these symptoms and signs.

1. Hiding

The storyteller tells us in verse 6 that "it was about the sixth hour". That means noon, the hottest time of the day. This is the one time of the day when anyone in their right mind does not fetch water from a well. The preferred and sensible times are early in the morning or early in the evening, when it is much cooler. This woman's behaviour is telling. She comes to the well when she thinks no one else will be there. Clearly she is hiding from human company. She wants to be alone.

2. Loneliness

In coming to the well when no one else will be there, she reveals the profound loneliness in her life. A sense of shame and worthlessness has resulted in her shunning human company. This loneliness is accentuated later on in the story when it is revealed that she has been married five times and is now living with a sixth man. Clearly she is desperately looking for intimacy – for someone that she can truly share her heart with.

3. Mistrust

When Jesus asks the woman for a drink she asks him why he is talking to her (verse 9). At the very least she is mistrustful of him because of the social conventions of the day. He is Jewish; she is a

Samaritan. He is a man; she is a woman. However, her defensive reaction to Jesus after these opening words suggests that she is mistrustful of men in general. She lives in the paradox of needing men but not feeling safe with them, all at the same time.

4. Misinterpretation

When Jesus talks about offering her "living water" she misinterprets what he is saying. The phrase "living water" can mean "running water" or "living water". She interprets Jesus literally when he is speaking spiritually and figuratively.

5. Striving

When Jesus says that the woman will never be thirsty again if she drinks living water, she jumps at the offer, saying in verse 15 that she really doesn't want to have to keep coming back to this well every day to draw water. Clearly her life is one of exhausted servitude. She is a slave, trapped in a life of keeping going and staying alive rather than living in a place of rest and hope.

6. Selectivity

When Jesus tells the woman to go fetch her husband, she replies very tersely in verse 17 that she doesn't have a husband. While this may reflect in part her perception of her situation, I think we could call this "being economical with the truth"! Or, to use the language of our orphan heart symptoms and signs, we would call this "selectivity".

7. Attachments

Jesus reveals that he knows the real truth. He tells the woman that she has been married five times and is now living with a sixth man. This suggests that she has an attachment to men. It points to what today we would call "relationship addiction". She has been desperately trying to anaesthetize the pain in her soul through marrying men. These marriages haven't lasted, probably because the men concerned have – in most of the cases – divorced her. She is now about to embark on the same destructive cycle with a sixth man. All this underlines the fact that there are attachments in her life. In the arms of men, she is looking for what she can only find in *Abba*, Father. She is suffering from acute love hunger, or more accurately, "father hunger".

Within the space of just sixteen verses, this woman exhibits seven out of twenty-one of the classic symptoms and signs of the orphan heart condition. The good news is that Jesus is her Saviour, and salvation includes not just the forgiveness of sins but also the healing of the soul. She is in the "In" Stage, to be sure; at this point, the focus is on "I" and "me". But she is in the company of the Anointed One. Indeed, if you count the numbers here – married to five men, living with a sixth man – Jesus is the seventh man! Seven is the perfect number in Judaism; it is a number that symbolizes perfection, wholeness, completeness. She is with the Perfect Man, the most perfect man who's ever lived, and she is about to enter into a spiritual (as opposed to a physical) relationship with him. In his presence, her life is about to be turned upside down. The wounds of separation from her earthly father are about to be healed. She is about to be set free from the deep pain of her shame by *Yeshua*, by the one whose name means "salvation".

The "Up" Stage

It is fascinating to watch how the encounter with Jesus proceeds from this point. The woman acknowledges that Jesus is a prophet and then immediately starts talking about their respective religious traditions, and specifically the two religious sites where they worship – Jerusalem and Mount Gerazim. Jesus doesn't ignore this topic but continues it. He is happy to talk about worship. He says in verses 21–24:

> *Believe me, woman, a time is coming when you will worship the Father neither on this mountain nor in Jerusalem. You Samaritans worship what you do not know; we worship what we do know, for salvation is from the Jews. Yet a time is coming and has now come when the true worshipers will worship the Father in spirit and truth, for they are the kind of worshipers the Father seeks. God is spirit, and his worshippers must worship in spirit and in truth.*

Notice the prophecy that Jesus utters here. He declares, "you will worship the Father". Jesus is intentionally redirecting the woman's attention to the Father. Her wound looks like it's a father wound. Certainly she has many of the symptoms and signs of the orphan heart condition. For this reason Jesus introduces this woman to *Abba*, Father. In talking so much about *Abba* Jesus now redirects the worship drive in her life away from men and onto the Father, away from the created and onto the Creator. Relationships with men cannot fill the hole in her soul. Only an intimate relationship with the perfect Father can meet her need. So Jesus helps this

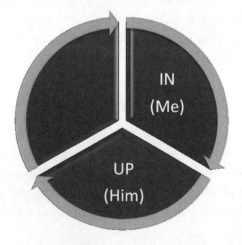

woman to embrace a transition in this part of the encounter. He takes her from the "In" Stage to the "Up" Stage. She takes her focus away from herself and places it firmly on the Father. He moves her, in short, from "me" to "him".

In talking about worship Jesus uses the Greek word *proskuneo*. This verb is made up of two words, *pros* (meaning "towards") and *kuneo* (meaning "I kiss"). The verb *proskuneo* accordingly has the idea of approaching someone in order to embrace them. Whatever else Jesus means by this word, he certainly at the very least means this: that the worship of God that he is making possible is all about intimacy. He is prophesying to the woman that she will no longer be self-absorbed and focused on her own needs. She is going to have a life of approaching and embracing the world's greatest Dad. She is going to worship her Father in spirit (in the Holy Spirit) and in truth (in Jesus, who is "the Truth"). She is going to draw near to *Abba*, Father and find that he draws near to her. She is going to cease looking for intimacy in the arms of one man after another and find true intimacy in the arms of the world's greatest Dad.

In speaking this way, Jesus helps the woman to move from "In" to "Up". This is absolutely vital. Instead of becoming stuck in a lifestyle of desperate attachments and toxic self-absorption, the woman is encouraged to fall in love with the Father. Instead of looking *in* all the time, she is encouraged to look *up* and see the Father she's been looking for, for all of her life. This is important; it is a truly desperate thing when people become locked in the "In" Stage. Their whole focus is themselves. They go time and time again for counselling and they come time and time again to the front of church at every call for ministry. Their whole life is one of narcissism – of looking at themselves. But this is not where Christians are meant to live. To be sure, it is completely permissible to focus on yourself when the Father leads you into that season of the heart that we call the "In" Stage. But to remain there indefinitely is harmful and it is not *Abba*, Father's will for you. There comes a moment when you need to choose to look *up* and focus on him – on the Father you've been waiting for. This is where true freedom is found.

Right now I'm thinking of a woman called Doreen who sent me a testimony after I spoke at a conference at her church in Swansea in Wales. She wanted me to know her story of the Father's healing in her life. This is what she wrote:

My childhood was one of verbal and sometimes physical abuse; if I was frightened and cried then I would be "given something to cry for". There was always a lot of anger and quarrelling between my parents. Often threats were made to leave each other and part of the fear in my childhood was that one day I would come home from school and one or both of my parents would be missing.

I was born again and baptized in the Spirit in the 1970s. The years passed and I was comfortable with knowing Jesus but the word "Father" had connotations that I could not and did not relate to.

Then recently our pastor put on a three-day event called "The Father Heart Conference". One of the seminars was about the Prodigal Son and one of the speakers asked those who would like to experience the Father's embrace to come forward. My pastor started to whisper words of the Father's love towards me and as he did something changed. The arms around me were no longer his. I felt another pair of arms around me and another voice. The voice said, "This is what my love feels like. There is no need to be afraid; I am not going to hurt you."

Months later I went to a School of Prophecy. On the first Sunday before the school commenced I arrived early at the church and walked into the auditorium. As I walked in I was suddenly engulfed by this "Being". I

*felt as if I had stepped into the inside of a very warm
personality and I heard a voice quietly saying, "I have
been waiting for you." I was not afraid because total
unconditional love and acceptance flowed into me
and around me. I was completely stunned and unable
to move or speak. It took a few minutes to get to a
chair where I just sat in a state of shock. This Presence
stayed with me, surrounding me and filling me for the
next ten days. I felt quiet and totally complete. The
"Presence" was my Dad.*

*When I came home I was sad because I thought
His Presence would become less real. In a sense it* **is**
*different but I know His Presence is always with me
even though I do not feel it always in the same way.
Sometimes in the early hours of the morning I sing to
Him and tell Him He is a good Dad and I love Him to
bits! Sometimes in my room I am covered in gold dust
or rain. Since I am in my bedroom it can only come
from Him. My Pastor and friends have told me I have
changed. It is impossible not to change when I now
have the security and love of my Dad. I will never be
the same again. I love Him more than anyone else and
He loves me. Nothing else matters. I no longer worry
about what people think of me, He loves me, so who
cares when people think I am slightly potty because of
my beliefs or anything else.*

*I have written this poem which expresses just a
little of what is going on in my life:*

In My Father's Presence
So close – I can hear Your every heartbeat
So close – I can hear the whisper of my name
So close – Your arms embrace, enfold me.
Your love is always the same.

And when this world crowds in around me
When sin and evil seem to reign
I draw aside into the stillness of Your Presence
And my spirit is made whole again
So close – Your perfect love surrounds me
So close – my every need You meet
So close – nothing else is needed
And I rest in adoration at Your feet.

It's hard for me to imagine a better testimony to illustrate the point I'm making here. Doreen went from the "In" Stage to the "Up" Stage. Through a direct, personal encounter with the Love of all loves, she went from a *me*-focus to a *him*-focus. Doreen now lives in the reality of her healing. She has been set free from the wounds from her earthly father and has found wholeness in the arms of her Heavenly Father. A negative experience of being fathered has been displaced by a positive one – only this time it is her Heavenly Father who is present to her. She is now a radical worshipper who draws near to *Abba*, Father to embrace him. Her poem is a heartfelt testimony to the hug of heaven, to the encounter she has had in the Father's love. Doreen shows us that we can all move on from the "In" Stage to the "Up" Stage. We can learn to worship *Abba*, Father in spirit and in truth.

The "Out" Stage

The woman of Samaria is helped on her way from in to up in her meeting at the well with the Rabbi from Nazareth. But even this isn't the end point. She doesn't stay at the well. She drops her water-jar and goes running into her town to share her testimony. Her heart has been captivated by the Father's love. To use Brennan Manning's famous phrase, her heart has been seized by the power of a great affection.[27] Now she goes to her community to tell others.

It is at this point in the story in John 4 that the disciples return. They have had lunch in Sychar and they now come back to the well and feel guilty that they have filled their stomachs while their Rabbi has eaten nothing. But Jesus tells them he has another kind of food. He is nourished by doing his Father's will and completing the work that the Father has given him to do. The disciples scratch their heads but Jesus elaborates. He starts speaking to them in verses 35–38 about the harvest.

> Do you not say, "Four months more and then the
> harvest"? I tell you, open your eyes and look at the fields!
> They are ripe for harvest. Even now the reaper draws
> his wages, even now he harvests the crop for eternal life,
> so that the sower and the reaper may be glad together.
> Thus the saying "One sows and another reaps" is true. I
> sent you to reap what you have not worked for. Others
> have done the hard work, and you have reaped the
> benefits of their labour.

If we are to understand what Jesus is saying here, we must remember what is happening in the background as he says these words. The woman he has been ministering to is now bringing almost her whole community to Jesus! Her heart has been captivated by the Love of all loves and now she cannot stop speaking about what she has found. She is now utterly contagious; she spreads the fire of the Father's love all over her town until there is a tipping point in which nearly everyone follows her on the way to the well to meet Jesus. As that happens, Jesus teaches his disciples that the harvest is right now. Even as the Samaritans are approaching the well, Jesus decrees that it's time for the harvest. The time for gathering in many souls is right now. They don't have to wait four months. He has just sown the Father's love into this woman's heart. Now is the hour for the disciples to reap what they haven't sown. It's time for them to bring a whole community of Samaritans into the kingdom. It's harvest time. It's time for rejoicing.

There is a simple point here and it's quite startling. The disciples do not bring anyone to Jesus. But the woman brings many to him. In her world, not only has she moved from *in* to *up*, she has now moved from *up* to *out*. Having fallen in love with *Abba*, Father, she now seeks to give that love away to all the lost people in her town. She doesn't stay in the *up* phase. In other words, she doesn't stay at the well with Jesus and have an endless worship meeting. No, her experience of worship propels her into active and dynamic witnessing. Indeed, she cannot stop herself! Having fallen in love with the Father through the revelatory ministry of the Son, she now seeks to give away freely what she has freely received. She goes into town and starts sowing the Father's love into the lives of the many lost people who have known her for years. In doing this she becomes the unlikely catalyst for a town-wide awakening. This is a powerful moment of transition in the story. In short, she moves into the "Out" Stage, where the focus is on *them*.

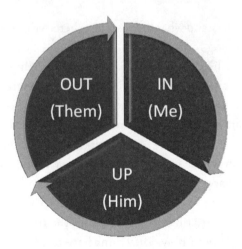

Just as it's a desperate thing when Christians become marooned in the "In" Stage – endlessly focusing on their wounds – so it's a desperate thing when Christians become stuck in the

"Up" Stage – thinking life is a matter of perpetual praise meetings. The fact is, there's work to be done. There's a world to be won. There's a harvest to be gathered in. And harvest-time is hard work. It involves effort and commitment. It means sowing the seeds of *Abba*'s love into the hearts of lost people. Truly, we are healed for the harvest.

Free people set people free

The old saying is true: "Hurting people just end up hurting people." We need to help believers to confront their father wounds. For far too long we have failed to provide healing programmes in the local church that are specifically designed to address the wounds from our past, particularly the wounds from our fathers. The consequences have been serious. Either this has resulted in people becoming permanently stuck in the "In" Stage, unable to break out of their sense of self-absorption and therefore never entering into the "Up" Stage, let alone the "Out" Stage. Or it has resulted in people reaching out to lost people with unhealed hearts and with wrong motives. The second scenario is disastrous because it really is true that hurting people end up hurting people. Believers who are bound by their past histories can often end up projecting their hurts onto the very people who need saving and healing. The opposite is however also true, that free people can set people free. In other words, believers who have received healing for their orphan heart condition and who are working from approval, not for approval, can be extraordinarily effective in outreach. Indeed, those who have encountered *Abba*, Father's affectionate love are the most dynamic evangelists of all!

As I write this I am thinking of a woman called Nycolette

> Believers who have received healing for their orphan heart condition and are working from approval, not for approval, can be extraordinarily effective in outreach.

whom I first met when taking a team from the Father's House Trust to her church to conduct a day workshop on "Experiencing the Father's Love". Nycolette's story proceeds through the three stages of "In", "Up" and "Out".

1. The "In" Stage

Nycolette first writes about the father wound from her past and how it adversely affected her life as a Christian many years later:

> *I was left very bereft from an early age when my parents' marriage broke down. I missed having a dad. I really began to miss him in my late teens and twenties. I worked in a vibrant buzzing office with girls whose dads would just pull up at lunchtimes to take their daughters to lunch – how I envied them. A tinge of sadness filled me on my wedding day when he was not there to walk me down the aisle. Although my two brothers stepped in on the day, the aisle was not wide enough for all three of us so I ended up going solo with them a pace behind. I carried the pain for many years and I found it difficult to understand and relate to our heavenly Father's love, as I could not equate having a father to anything good. Then a Fathers House team came to our church and shared about the Father's heart and it changed my life. I now understand how much God loves me and that I truly am his child – his daughter – and that he cares about everything I do. Even though my earthly father was absent, my Heavenly Father was there at every parents' evening, every school play and every recital. I saw that he had brought gifts of friendship and love into my life that helped and did not harm me.*

2. The "Up" Stage

Having gone through a phase where her father wounds were exposed and healed, Nycolette now began to see God as *Abba*, Father. Notice the intimacy of the language that Nycolette uses. This really is proskuneo worship of the Father:

> *For years I lived with rejection but now I truly was able to make peace with my past. I was able to speak to my own father for the first time in thirty-seven years and I realised that I didn't need him anymore – my heavenly Father is more than enough. When I get sad, disappointed and bruised by the world I know that I can crawl up into his lap and have him wrap me in his blanket of love. I picture myself holding a warm mug of hot chocolate whilst gently resting in the security of his loving arms, feeling safe. The teaching helped me to understand that my Father is all sufficient and supports and soothes me in a way that an earthly father cannot. I feel that I am his daughter and I finally belong to someone who truly loves me.*

That truly is intimate worship of the Father.

3. The "Out" Stage

What is encouraging about Nycolette is that her journey to true freedom doesn't end with worshipping the Father on her own in the secret place. Her response to her healing was to give the Father's love to those who have never known it. Having learned to walk in *Abba*, Father's love, she has now started to give it away, especially to the lost and the broken-hearted.

I saw this very vividly when we revisited her church and shared her testimony on a DVD as part of my teaching in the main services. Nycolette was there that morning, as were many hundreds of other people. She wrote to us at Father's House the week afterwards to explain what had happened in the immediate aftermath of the service.

> *Just a quick update: following the viewing of my testimony I was approached by several people wanting to share how it had touched their lives. I was told that two people had decided to commit their lives to Christ once they started talking about it in the lounge after the service. Later that day, I went to visit a friend who is also a member of our church and she had guests staying who had also been at the second service on Sunday. A young girl (seventeen) and her mum began to share with me how they had cried through the whole service and found the whole experience moving. During our conversation it was clear that God was still at work and their tears began to flow. At some point as others left to make refreshments the conversation became more drawn to where this young lady was going in her life. As I shared and encouraged her it was evident that God had begun an amazing work in her heart and during the conversation she accepted Jesus. I was able to lead her in a prayer of salvation and she came to faith and began a relationship with Christ.*

This is a wonderful illustration of how free people set people free. In Nycolette's story, "In" leads to "Up" and "Up" leads to "Out". Wholeness leads to Worship and Worship leads to Witness. Nycolette has truly been healed for the harvest.

The world is waiting for our freedom

The Apostle Paul said that the whole of creation is groaning in travail like a mother in the last stages of childbirth, waiting for the revelation of the sons of God (Romans 8). The whole planet is waiting for Christian believers to rise up as the adopted sons and daughters of *Abba*, Father. The whole of creation is eagerly longing for you and me to enter into the fullness of what it means to be *Abba*'s children. The birds in the air, the fish in the sea, the trees in the fields, are all pining for the church to become what it was always called to be – a family of forgiven and freed-up sons and daughters who are passionate about taking the Father's love to the fatherless, whatever the cost.

So all this healing is for a reason. We are not embraced by *Abba*, Father so that we can live an isolated life, nor even so that we can

The whole planet is waiting for Christian believers to rise up as the adopted sons and daughters of *Abba*, Father.

attend endless praise meetings to worship him in spirit and in truth. Ultimately we are healed for the harvest. We are set free to go out and set others free. Everyone and everything is poised, waiting for this moment in history when the flame of the Father's love is burning within the hearts of men, women and children, making them an unstoppable force of holy love on the earth. Only then will the curse of fatherlessness begin to be reversed. Only then will communities and cities begin to change. Only then will the planet start to breathe a sigh of relief, knowing that the endless cycle of decay is nearly over and the glorious freedom of the children of God is here.

In the meantime, the unwashed orphan wiping her desperate eyes is waiting for your freedom.

The young woman trafficked for sex and weeping in her dirty bedsit is waiting for your freedom.

The widow sitting all alone in her armchair with a photo of her husband on her lap is waiting for your freedom.

The prisoner smashing his head against his prison wall is waiting for your freedom.

The young girl with the sad and vacant stare who is dying of HIV/AIDs is waiting for your freedom.

The teenage daughter who is harming and starving herself to

death is waiting for your freedom.

The lost son who has run away from home is waiting for your freedom.

We are set free to go out and set others free.

The schoolboy furtively stealing money and sniffing cocaine is waiting for your freedom.

The friends you mingle with every day are waiting for your freedom.

Even the members of your own family that you share your house with are waiting for your freedom.

Everyone, everything, is waiting, sighing, weeping, crying for your freedom.

So receive the Father's freedom.

Then go set the captives free.

Prayer

Dear Loving Heavenly Father, I thank you so much for all that you've done in my life.

Thank you for taking me through a season in which my own heart has been healed. I give you praise for every new freedom that I enjoy as a result. I thank you that this has been like sitting at a well with Jesus and having my wounds exposed and then healed. Thank you for taking me through the "In" Stage and healing my orphan heart condition.

Thank you *Abba*, Father for showing me more and more about who you are – that you are the Father who loves me like no earthly father ever could, the Perfect Dad, the Father I've been waiting for. I am deeper in love with you than ever before and I give you praise that I can now call you Daddy, Papa, Dear Father. Thank you so much for tenderly teaching me what you're really like and taking me through the "Up" Stage. I want to be lost in wonder, love and praise from now on. I want to approach you every day to embrace you. Help me to experience the hug of heaven as I do. Teach me more and more how to worship you in spirit and in truth.

And thank you, Dad, that you have called me to walk in

your love and give it away. Thank you that you have made me a part of your family, the church. I commit myself to giving your love away to my adopted brothers and sisters in Christ, through service and the expression of my God-given gifts. I covenant to be in community. Thank you also that you have given me an assignment, to take your love to those outside the church – those who are still spiritual orphans and who so desperately need your love. Thank you for leading me into an "Out" Stage. I pledge myself to being more intentional than I have ever been to the process of bringing people into your arms of love.

I pray in Jesus' name that you will help me to know in what ways I can now reach lost people with your love. Help me to be so in touch with your heart that I know how to act and what to say when I'm with people who don't yet know you. Help me to do this out of Grace not Law, and to have the great joy of seeing many come into your house.

In your name, and for your glory. Amen.

NOTES

Part 1: The Wound

1. Obama, Barack, *Dreams from my Father*, Three Rivers Press, 2004.
2. You can watch the whole speech on YouTube: http://www.youtube.com/watch?v=Hj1hCDjwG6M. President Obama has spoken out against fatherlessness, specifically in the black community. In an interview after this well-known Father's Day speech, Obama said: "The government – and society as a whole – has an obligation to deal with poverty, particularly poverty that is deep-rooted. Not just in the inner cities but in rural communities all across America. But we also have to recognize there's a particular problem when more than half of African American children are growing up without a father in the house, and oftentimes not even knowing their father." He added: "That's a problem, and I won't back up one bit in asserting that is a problem that we have to be honest about." Read the rest of the story in the Washington Post online: http://voices.washingtonpost.com/the-trail/2008/07/13/obama_vows_to_keep_talking_abo.html
3. See the comments made by Pastor Troy Goode in his endorsement to *I Am Your Father*. For more on fatherlessness in the African American community, see the interesting article at http://www.boston.com/news/local/massachusetts/articles/2006/07/09/the_black_rebellion_against_fatherlessness/
4. This is from Blankenhorn, David, *Fatherless America: Confronting our Most Urgent Social Problem*, Harper Perennial, 1996.
5. For the full details of the background for these statistics go to: http://www.massey.ac.nz/~kbirks/gender/econ/nodad.htm
6. See "Families, Poverty and Social Justice – the UK Perspective" by the Rt Hon. Iain Duncan Smith MP, speech to the Institute of Marriage and Family in Ottawa, Canada: http://www.centreforsocialjustice.org.uk/default.asp?pageRef=266
7. For this UK research see "Every Family Matters", a speech by the Rt Hon. Iain Duncan Smith MP, Parliament, 13 July 2009: http://www.centreforsocialjustice.org.uk/default.asp?pageRef=266
8. Prison statistics from a speech by Iain Duncan Smith at the Prison Ministry Conference on 20 November 2009 at Holy Trinity Brompton, South Kensington. The UNICEF statistic is from "Child Poverty in Perspective: An overview of child wellbeing in rich countries", Innocenti Report Card 7, 2007, UNICEF Innocenti Research Centre, Florence, p. 4.
9. "Every Family Matters", Rt Hon Iain Duncan Smith MP.
10. Michael Jackson's 1993 interview with Oprah Winfrey, The Oprah Winfrey Show, 10 February 1993. For Joe Jackson's comments about whipping his son with a belt, see Louis Theroux interview, "Louis, Martin and Michael", BBC, 16 November 2003.
11. Michael Jackson, chair of "Heal the Kids Foundation", speech to Oxford Union, 6 March 2001.

12. George A. Rekers, PhD, distinguished Professor of Neuropsychiatry and Behavioural Science Emeritus, University of South Carolina School of Medicine.
13. Anonymous quote from our Father's House Trust booklet (self-published), *The World's Greatest Dad*. Available from www.fathershousetrust.com
14. Attributed to Elisabeth Elliot and quoted in our booklet cited in note 13.
15. McGee, Robert, *Father Hunger*, Ann Arbor, 1993, p. 55.
16. Myers Drew, Dr Jane, *Where Were You When I Needed You Dad? A guide to healing your father wound*, Tiger Lily Publishing, 1993, pp. 13–21.
17. Poulter, Dr Stephan B., *The Father Factor: How Your Father's Legacy Impacts your Career*, New York: Prometheus Books, 2006. See Section II.
18. McGee, Robert, *Father Hunger*, pp. 55–65.
19. McGee, Robert, *Father Hunger*, p. 49.
20. "US department of Health and Human Services Alcohol and Drug Information", Prevention Alert, Vol. 6, No. 5, 18 April 2003: http://ncadi.samhsa.gov/govpubs/prevalert/v6/5.aspx. For the effects of a drug-addicted father on his children, see the study by University of Buffalo, Research Institute on Addictions (RIA), published in Journal of Family Psychology, June 2004. And see: http://www.hopenetworks.org/addiction/Children%20of%20Addicts.htm
21. For this poignant testimony, see http://www.helium.com/items/1420126-drug-addicted-fathers-and-their-daughters. This adult daughter concludes, "As childish as it may seem, I'm going to say it: 'I WANT MY DADDY BACK!'"
22. Poulter, Dr Stephan B., *The Father Factor*, pp. 83ff.
23. Quoted in our Father's House booklet, *The World's Greatest Dad*.
24. Myers Drew, Dr Jane, *Where Were You When I Needed You Dad?*, p. 21.
25. McGee, Robert, *Father Hunger*, pp. 58–59.
26. McGee, Robert, *Father Hunger*, chapter 17.
27. Blankenhorn, David, *Fatherless America*, p. 1.
28. See Fullerton, William Young, T*homas Spurgeon: A Biography*, General Books, first published by Hodder, 1919.
29. For the full script of this classic sermon, see: http://www.toll-booth.net/ccel/s/spurgeon/till_he_/notorphn.htm
30. Buechner, Frederick, *The Sacred Journey: A Memoir of Early Days*, Harper One, 1991.
31. Quoted in the paper on "Honour and Shame" at http://www.ivpress.com/title/exc/1572-1.pdf
32. For our teaching on the nurturing heart of God and the healing of the wounds from our mothers, go to the shop section of our website, www.fathershousetrust.com
33. Martin Luther quote at http://www.answers.com/topic/quote-4?author=King%20Jr.%20Martin%20Luther&s2=King%20Jr.%20Martin%20Luther
34. Conservative Spring Conference, Manchester, UK, 8 October 2009. For highlights from this speech go to: http://www.youtube.com/watch?v=hwUlDR9LmFA
35. Katrina Clark, "My Father was an Anonymous Sperm Donor", Washington Post, 17 December 2006. For the full article see: http://

www.washingtonpost.com/wp-dyn/content/article/2006/12/15/
AR2006121501820.html

36. Blankenhorn, David, *Fatherless America*, p. 76. The original quote is from Vanity Fair magazine, September 1993, p. 164.
37. Blankenhorn, David, *Fatherless America*, p. 84. The original quote is from Frank Pittman's *Man Enough: Fathers, Sons, and the Search for Masculinity*, Putnam's, 1993.
38. Reviews of *Fatherless America* have been mostly positive, to the extent that the book is now seen as the Bible for the movement addressing fatherlessness in the USA. A lot of sociological research went into the making of this book, research that is backed up in many other contexts as well. See for example: http://www.paternita.info/america/fatherless-america.pdf. My one comment is that Blankenhorn is strong on diagnosis but not so strong on prognosis, or what in Part 3 of *I Am Your Father* I call "The Cure". This is, after all, not just a sociological issue; it is a spiritual problem. And spiritual problems call for spiritual solutions.
39. Sullivan, Robert, *Life with Fathers*, Life Books, 2009.
40. Quoted in Sullivan, Robert, *Life with Fathers*.
41. Cantalamessa, Raniero, *Life in Christ*, Collegeville, 1990, p. 97.
42. Quoted in Sullivan, Robert, *Life with Fathers*.
43. Quoted in our Father's House booklet, *The World's Greatest Dad*.
44. Quoted in our Father's House booklet, *The World's Greatest Dad*.
45. Quoted in our Father's House booklet, *The World's Greatest Dad*.
46. Quoted in Sullivan, Robert, *Life with Fathers*.
47. Quoted in Sullivan, Robert, *Life with Fathers*.
48. Strong, Sidney, *What I Owe To My Father*, Delany Press, 2007 (first published 1931).
49. Interview with Ingrid Sischy, February 2004. Quoted in Sullivan, Robert, *Life with Fathers*.
50. Quoted in Sullivan, Robert, *Life with Fathers*.
51. Quoted at http://www.wow4u.com/father/index.html
52. "Geldof on Fathers", Channel 4, 2004. To watch this extraordinarily powerful documentary in its entirety, go to http://angelmind.net/index.php?option=com_content&task=view&id=46&Itemid=37 and http://www.dadsontheair.net/geldofonfathers/
53. "The Real Love that Dares not Speak its Name: A Sometimes Coherent Rant", by Bob Geldof, in Bainham, A., Lindley, B., Richards, M. (eds.), *Children and Their Families: Contact, Rights and Welfare*, Hart Publishing, 2003.

Part 2: The Scars

1. O'Connor, M., *Fathers 4 Justice, The Inside Story*, Weidenfeld & Nicolson, 2007, p. xvii.
2. O'Connor, M., *Fathers 4 Justice*, p. 4.
3. Eldredge, John, *Fathered by God*, Thomas Nelson, 2009, pp. 57–58.
4. Quote from interview in the *Telegraph*, 29 January 2002.
5. "The Last Word", interview in the *Washington Post*, 19 February 2001.

6. *Darkness Visible*. Interview with Kerry Fried on amazon.com.

7. See the poignant 2008 article in the *Independent* where Pullman states, "He was a father I never really knew. He was never at home. He was always off flying. My father, to me, was a figure of glamour and mystery and absence; his presence was more a matter of the smell of beer and cigarettes than anything else." http://www.independent.co.uk/news/people/profiles/philip-pullman-his-dark-materials-834043.html

8. Pullman, P., *The Amber Spyglass* (*His Dark Materials*), Scholastic, 2007.

9. See Chapter 7 of this book.

10. Vitz, Paul, *Faith of the Fatherless: The Psychology of Atheism*, Spence Publishing Co., 2000.

11. Vitz, Paul, *Faith of the Fatherless*, p. 15.

12. Vitz, Paul, *Faith of the Fatherless*, p. 21. Original quotation from Nietzsche's *Ecce Homo*, trans. R. Hollingdale, Penguin, 1979, p. 51.

13. Vitz, Paul, *Faith of the Fatherless*, p. 22. Hayman, Ronald, *Nietzsche: A Critical Life*, Oxford University Press, 1980, p. 17.

14. Cantalamessa, Raniero, *Life in Christ*, Collegeville, MN, 1990, p. 85.

15. Bailey, Kenneth, *The Cross and the Prodigal*, InterVarsity Press, 2005. This has to be the most insightful book on the parable of the lost boy in Luke 15. My friend Ken Bailey spent four decades in the Middle East researching Jesus in his original context. I was very reliant on Bailey's research when I wrote my book *The Father You've Been Waiting For*, as was Henri Nouwen when he wrote *The Return of the Prodigal Son*.

16. Bailey, Kenneth, *Jesus Through Middle Eastern Eyes*, InterVarsity Press, 2008. See pp. 94–100 for an excellent and up-to-date explanation of the word *Abba* on the lips of Jesus.

17. Barclay, William, *The Plain Man Looks at the Lord's Prayer*, Fontana, 1964, p. 31. Barclay, studying the word *Abba* in the original Aramaic in which Jesus spoke, writes: "There is only one possible English translation of this word in any ordinary use of it, and that is 'Daddy'" (p. 41). He adds, "The plain fact is that no one in all the world had ever thought of God like that before, and to this day, apart from Jesus Christ, no one can think of God like this."

18. Quoted in Barclay, William, *The Plain Man Looks at the Lord's Prayer*, pp. 47–48.

19. Slack, Kenneth, *Praying the Lord's Prayer Today*, SCM Press, 1973, p. 26. Slack also cites John Huxtable on the same page: "No man is ever less alone than when he prays in secret." Slack also rightly points out: "The tragedy of not a little of the worshipping tradition of the church has been that it has not taken seriously enough that single word 'Father' as controlling all our prayer. Wonderful as the heritage of the English-speaking world is in the Book of Common Prayer, at times in some of those matchlessly-phrased collects you catch more the vision of a Tudor despot who has to be wheedled than one of a caring Father" (p. 24).

20. Hybels, Bill, *New Identity: Discovering Who You Are in Christ*, Zondervan, 2005.

21. Quoted in our Father's House booklet, *The World's Greatest Dad*.

22. Dickens, Charles, *A Christmas Carol*, online version at http://www.literature.org/authors/dickens-charles/christmas-carol/index.html, chapter

2, "The First of the Three Spirits".

23. Dickens, Charles, *A Christmas Carol*, chapter 2.

24. Dickens, Charles, *A Christmas Carol*, chapter 2.

25. Dickens, Charles, *A Christmas Carol*, chapter 5, "The End of it".

26. Harris, T. A., *I'm OK, You're OK*, Arrow Books, 1995 edn.

27. See Frost, Jack, *Spiritual Slavery to Spiritual Sonship: Your Destiny Awaits You*, Destiny Image, 2006. See also the article "Slavery to Sonship (2)" at http://www.shilohplace.org/resources

28. John Powell, cited at http://thinkexist.com/quotation/human_beings-like_plants-grow_in_the_soil_of/194439.html

29. *The American Experience: The Orphan Trains*, PBS, Edward Gray Films, 1995. For the quotation see http://www.pbs.org/wgbh/amex/orphan/orphants.html.

30. *Thoughts of a Free Thinker*, commencement address, Hobart and William Smith Colleges, 26 May 1974.

31. Peale, N. V., *The Power of the Plus Factor*, Orient Paperbacks, 2006.

32. Cited (along with a number of other revealing quotes) at http://www.brainyquote.com/quotes/authors/p/peter_sellers.html. See also the fascinating article about Peter Sellers at http://drnorth.wordpress.com/2008/09/26/there-used-to-be-a-me-peter-sellers-on-the-muppet-show/

33. Quoted at http://www.shadyoldlady.com/location.php?loc=455

34. Reagan, Michael, *Twice Adopted*, Nashville: Broadman and Holman Publishers, 2004, p. 11.

35. Fuse, T. Brill, *Modernization and Stress in Japan*, International Studies in Sociology & Social Anthropology, 2006. For the quotation go to the article on this topic at http://books.google.co.uk/books?id=wLIfAAAAIAAJ&pg=PA70&lpg=PA70&dq=koji+konjo+orphan+mentality&source=bl&ots=nSCxTPteAS&sig=4zJv_89rNkUvumKSP8fkXBbE7k0&hl=en&ei=q3XJS_XCJ5mWsQbBg6X5Ag&sa=X&oi=book_result&ct=result&resnum=1&ved=0CAgQ6AEwAA#v=onepage&q=koji%20konjo%20orphan%20mentality&f=false

36. McKay, Hugh, "A Seasonal Promise of Renewal", *The Age*, 25 March 2005.

37. Homer, *The Iliad*, Bk. IX, l. 386.

38. Nietzsche, F., *Beyond Good and Evil*, Penguin Classics, 2003.

39. Emerson, R. W., *Worship from The Conduct of Life*, 1860.

40. Source unknown. http://www.quotationspage.com/quote/302.html

41. Foster, Richard, *Celebration of Discipline: The Path to Spiritual Growth*, Hodder & Stoughton, 2008.

42. Covey, Stephen, *The 7 Habits of Highly Effective People: Powerful Lessons in Personal Change*, Free Press, 2004.

43. Stibbe, Mark, *O Brave New Church*, Darton, Longman & Todd, 1995, chapter 3.

44. Jung, Carl, *Memories, Dreams, Reflections*, Fontana Press, 1995 (originally published 1962).

45. "Toxic family life of Edlington Brothers", *The Guardian*, 22 January 2010.

46. Colton, Charles Caleb. Origin unknown.

47. Jung, Carl, *Psychological Types or The Psychology of Individuation*, Rascher Verlag, 1921.

48. Eliot, T. S., *The Four Quartets*, "Burnt Norton" 1, Faber, 1936.
49. Reagan, Michael, *Twice Adopted*, p. 4.
50. See http://www.diggerhistory.info/pages-leaders/ww2/churchill.htm
51. Emerson, R. W., *Behaviour; The Conduct of Life*, 1860, cited at http://www.quotegarden.com/honesty.html
52. Agassi, A., *Open: An Autobiography*, HarperCollins, 2010, chapter 1.
53. Agassi, A., *Open: An Autobiography*, chapter 1.
54. Agassi, A., *Open: An Autobiography*, chapter 1.
55. Agassi, A., *Open: An Autobiography*, chapter 1.
56. Agassi, A., *Open: An Autobiography*, chapter 1.
57. Tournier, Paul, *Creative Suffering*, HarperCollins, 1983, p. 2. For a fascinating website dedicated to famous orphans, see http://www.thelizlibrary.org/fatherless/effects-of-fatherlessness.html. Tournier was himself an orphan.
58. Tournier, Paul, *Creative Suffering*, p. 4.
59. Tournier, Paul, *Creative Suffering*, p. 10.
60. From Michael W. Smith's DVD, *A New Hallelujah*, Sony Music, 2008.

Part 3: The Healing

1. Stibbe, Philip, *Return via Rangoon*, C. Tinling & Co., 1947. All quotations from Part IV ("Deliverance"), pp. 199–221. Second edition produced by Pen and Sword, 1995.
2. *Bono: in Conversation with Michka Assayas*, Hodder & Stoughton, 2005, p. 204.
3. *Bono: in Conversation with Michka Assayas*, p. 322.
4. William Cowper, *Table Talk*, l. 260.
5. Lewis, C. S., *Mere Christianity*, HarperCollins, 1997.
6. Lewis, C. S., *The Lion, the Witch and the Wardrobe* (The Chronicles of Narnia), Geoffrey Bles. Originally published 1950.
7. Lewis, C. S., *The Lion, the Witch and the Wardrobe*.
8. Irenaeus, *Against Heresies* (IV,20,7). The full quotation reads: "the glory of God is man fully alive, and the life of man is the vision of God. If the revelation of God through creation already brings life to all living beings on the earth, how much more will the manifestation of the Father by the Word bring life to those who see God."
9. William James, American pragmatist, philosopher and psychologist (1842–1910). Quoted at http://en.wikipedia.org/wiki/William_James
10. Stibbe, Philip, *Return via Rangoon*, p. 222.
11. For Ruth's ministry go to www.ruthgrahamandfriends.org
12. Graham, Ruth, *In Every Pew Sits a Broken Heart: Hope for the Hurting*, Zondervan, 2008, pp. 11–12.
13. For Timothy Fulop's excellent rendition of this parable, go to http://across.co.nz/ProdigalSon-inF.htm
14. For a revisionist understanding of justification, see N. T. Wright, *Justification: God's Plan and Paul's Vision*, SPCK, 2009; for a robust, traditional defence of the doctrine, see Piper, John, *The Future of Justification: A Response to N. T. Wright*, InterVarsity Press, 2008.

15. Stibbe, Mark, *From Orphans to Heirs: Celebrating our Spiritual Adoption*, Bible Reading Fellowship, 1st edn 1999. This was the first book, to my knowledge, to explore the glorious truth of our adoption by *Abba*, Father. Trevor Burke has followed suit, writing a similar study, *Adopted into God's Family: Exploring a Pauline Metaphor*, InterVarsity Press, 2006.

16. Barclay, William, *The Letter to the Romans*, New Daily Bible Study, John Knox Press, 2002, p. 125.

17. Barclay, William, *The Letter to the Romans*, p. 126.

18. Unpublished part of a *Church Times* interview with author and broadcaster Brian Draper, used with Brian's kind permission.

19. Barclay, William, *The Letter to the Romans*, p. 126.

20. All the Howell Harris quotes in this section of my book come from Dr Martin Lloyd Jones' seminal lecture entitled "Howell Harris and Revival", delivered in 1973. You can find it at http://bsrich.tripod.com/calvinistic/rev.htm.

21. From Manning, B., *Patched Together: A Story of My Story*, David C. Cook, 2010.

22. Address at Wednesday General Audience, 19 October 2005. See: http://www.corpuschristiparish.com/church/inspirational_quotes/255.pdf.

23. Quoted at http://www.corpuschristiparish.com/church/inspirational_quotes/255.pdf.

24. Erickson, Beth, *Looking for Dad: Father Loss and its Impact*, Health Communications Inc., 1998, p. 104.

25. Hildegarde of Bingen, quoted at http://www.corpuschristiparish.com/church/inspirational_quotes/255.pdf.

26. Lloyd-Jones, Dr M., *Joy Unspeakable: Power and Renewal in the Holy Spirit*, Kingsway, 2008, p. 105.

27. This great phrase, originating in the Deep South of the USA over a hundred years ago, is frequently used by Brennan Manning in his writings. See, for example, his book *The Signature of Jesus*, Multnomah, 1996, pp. 166–67.